THE

MUSNUD OF MURSHIDABAD

(1704-1904)

THE

MUSNUD OF MURSHIDABAD

(1704—1904.)

BEING

A SYNOPSIS OF THE HISTORY OF MURSHIDABAD
FOR THE LAST TWO CENTURIES
TO WHICH ARE APPENDED
NOTES OF PLACES AND OBJECTS OF INTEREST

AT

MURSHIDABAD.

COMPILED BY

PURNA CH. MAJUMDAR.

(*COPIOUSLY ILLUSTRATED.*)

MURSHIDABAD:

SARODA RAY,

Omraoganj.

1905.

PREFACE.

The want of a compendium, descriptive of the places and objects of interest at Murshidabad, the birth place and cradle of British rule in India, was keenly felt in the early part of 1902, on the occasion of the first viceregal visit to the old capital of Bengal. Since that event, which aroused a great deal of interest, many eminent tourists and sight-seers have visited this grave-yard of buried greatness. With the opening of the new railway, Lord Curzon's gift to Murshidabad, access to the city will be made easy and the number of visitors is likely to increase every year. The neighbouring civil station of Berhampore, which may any moment resume its military character, being brought nearer to Calcutta by faster means of communication, with its improved race course, its proposed skating rink, its beautiful square and other numerous charms, is likely to prove a holiday resort and a handbook of descriptive notes would probably be welcome and remove a long-felt desideratum.

The Notes on the Palace are necessarily more elaborate and comprehensive. Although some specimens of great rarity and historical value have been sent from its innumerable treasures for the Victoria Memorial at Calcutta, yet the visitor will find—and I say this from the unanimous verdict of connoisiers—a magnificent collection of books, manuscripts, paintings, arms and other historical relics and trophies, such as are not to be met with in any one single place in India. For examining these, I trust, the Notes will be found useful: no less interesting will be a mere perusal of them to those who cannot spare time to visit the Palace.

In the preparation of this hand-book, many valuable materials have been furnished to me by that inexhaustible store-house of useful information, Khondkar Fazl Rubbee, Khan Bahadur, the Dewan of Murshidabad, who spent with me, in and outside the Killah, several hours snatched away from the little leisures of an over-burdened official life, in discovering from internal evidence or otherwise the history of many interesting relics hitherto unknown. My sincere thanks are due to him, whose co-operation enabled me to amass useful information of a variety of descriptions.

For the photographs of the Nawabs (with the exception of that of Meer Kasem, which I owe to the courtesy of the authorities of the Bankipur Oriental Library) and the facsimiles of the treaties, from which the illustrations have been prepared, my respectful acknowledgements are and shall always be due to His Highness the Nawab Bahadur of Murshidabad, Amir-ul-Omrah, G. C. I. E., for the history of whose instructive life and the table of whose unique genealogy I claim a comprehensiveness, consistent with the scope of this compilation, which has not been attempted before. Those who know him intimately will find that His Highness deserves more than my feeble pen has been able to depict.

It has been possible to give, with one exception, facsimiles of the concluding portions only of the treaties, bearing the signatures of Clive, Warren Hastings, Vansittart, Watts, Meer Jaffer, Najmuddowla, Mobarukuddowla &c. These facsimiles as also the great genealogical table shewing the descent of His Highness of Murshidabad from Adam and the complete series of the portraits of the Nazims have never, like many more things in the compilation, been published before.

Of the numerous illustrations from blocks prepared by Mr. U. Rai by his half tone process, a few have been printed by the Kuntaline Press and the rest have been done elsewhere, as the blocks of these latter had been entrusted before the MSS were sent to the Kuntaline Press.

I shall not deem my labours lost, if this record, penned—'*lest we forget*'—will, in the least, help to keep alive memories, flickering round the Musnud of Murshidabad, which should never be allowed to fade.

I hope the indulgent public will accord to this compilation, imperfect as it is, a generous reception.

Murshidabad.
February 5, 1905.

P. C. M.

CONTENTS.

CONTENTS.

	Page.
PREFACE	i—vi
INTRODUCTION	1
PART I.—*Synopsis of the History of Murshidabad.*	
A List of the Nawabs with their titles, &c.	3
Murshed Kuli Khan	21
Shuja Khan	22
Serferaz Khan	24
Ali Verdi Khan	25
Serajuddowla	28
Meer Jaffer	32
Meer Kasem	33
Meer Jaffer re-instated)	36
Najmuddowla	37
Syefuddowla	40
Mobarukuddowla	42
Babar Jang	45
Ali Jah	47
Walah Jah	49
Humayun Jah	50
Feredun Jah	52
Ali Kadr	55
PART II.—*Places and Objects of Interest at Murshidabad.*	
Killah Nizamut	73
The Palace	74
Madina	118
Bachawali Tope	119
Imambarah	120

	Page.
Armenian Church	233
Farashdanga	233
The Temple of Doyamoi at Saidabad	233
Madapur	234
Berhampore Cemetry	234
Grant Hall	235
Berhampore Cantonments	236
Krishna Nath College	238
Choa	238
Faridpur	240
Dadpur	240
Mankar	240
Plassey	240
Saktipur	251
Rangamati	251
Fattehsingh	252
Jamo and Bagdanga	254
Kandi	258
Sonarundi	262
Talibpur	263
Salar	265
Sherpur Atai	268
Sagar Dighi	268
Mahipal	269
Ek Ana Chandpara	262
Sheik Dighi	270
Giria	270
Uduanala	271
Bhogwangola	271
Lalgola	272
Gysabad	272
Sadeqbagh	272
Barnagar	274

Page.

Azimganj 276
Lalkothi 276
Kriteswari 277
Morcha 280
The Neoara House 281
Conclusion 283

APPENDIX—

Holwell's Account of his Liberation by Serajud-dowla 287
Why there was so little bloodshed at Plassey . 288
Clive's Entry into Murshidabad . . . 288
Clive entertains Meer Jaffer with a Review . 289
The Deposition of Meer Jaffer . . . 289
Why the Musnud did not go to Miran's Family . 295
Meer Jaffer's Presents to Admiral Watson . . 295
Lord Clive's Justification of the acceptance of Presents from Meer Jaffer 296
Sums distributed from 1757 to 1766 . . . 298
Abwabs on Khalsa and Jaigire Lands in Bengal, 1722—1763 300
The Tumar or Standard Assessment of Bengal at the close of Meer Kasem's Rule, 1763 . . 301
The Grant of the Dewani 301
Lord Clive's Bill for an Entertainment in honor of the Grant of the Dewani 303
Statement of the Collections and Balances of the Land Assessment of Bengal covered by the Grant of the Dewani 304
The Four Dewans or Ministers . . . 304
List of Dewans Suba Bangala and Naib-Dewans . 306
List of Dewans Khalsa or Collectors of Revenue . 307
List of Dewans Nizamut 308

	Page.
What a Gubernotorial Tour to Murshidabab cost in 1763	309
From Murshidabad to Calcutta in two days in 1764	310
The Installation of Reza Khan	3'0
The East India Company's Presents and Entertainments to the Nawabs	311
Treaty and Agreement between the East India Company and Nawab Mobarakuddowla . .	316
The Nawab Nazim as the Fountain of Honor .	318
Nizamut Deposit Fund	319
Chhattis Karkhana	32:

LIST OF ILLUSTRATIONS.

	Page.
Nawab Murshed Kuli Khan (to face) . .	21
,, Shuja Khan	22
,, Serferaz Khan.	24
,, Ali Verdi Khan	26
,, Serajuddowla	28
,, Meer Jaffer and Miran . . .	32
,, Meer Kasem	34
,, Najmuddowla	38
,, Syefuddowla	40
,, Mobarukuddowla	42
,, Babar Ali	45
,, Ali Jah	47
,, Wala Jah	49
,, Humayun Jah	50
,, Feredun Jah	52
,, Ali Kadr Bahadur	55
The Hon'ble Prince Wasif Ali Meerza Bahadur .	64
The South Gate of the Killah . . .	73

Page.

The Palacer 74
A Niche in the Round Room of the Palace . . 78
The Drawing Room of the Palace . . . 80
The Banqueting Hall of the Palace . . . 82
Akber's Nowratn Durbar 86
The State Chair. 92
The Palace Armoury 92
Some Palace Jewels 98
An Elephant with the Umbari . . . 103
The Treaty of 1763 bearing the signatures of Meer Jaffer, Vansittart, Warren Hastings, &c. . 105
The Treaty of 1765 bearing the signatures of Najmuddowla and the Members of the Calcutta Council 106
The Agreement of 1765 bearing the signatures of Najmuddowla, Clive, Carnac, Sykes &c. . 108
The Treaty of 1770 bearing the signatures of Mobarukuddowla and the Members of the Calcutta Council 110
Lord Auckland's Letter of 1873 . . . 112
The Durbar of His Highness the Nawab Nazim of Bengal 116
The Old Madina and the Bachawali Tope . . 119
The Nizamut Imambarah 120
The Chowk Musjed of Mani Begum . . . 130
The Eed Procession 132
The Jaffraganj Cemetry . . . 141
The Nashipur Rajbari 145
Rajah Ranajit Sinha Bahadur . . . 150
Rani Bhowani's House 154
Jagat Sett's Thakurbari 154
The Place of Nawab Serajuddowla's Murder . 160
Nawab Murshed Kuli Khan's Tomb . . . 160

	Page.
Nawab Shuja Khan's Tomb	160
Nawab Serferaz Khan's Tomb	160
The Nizamut Stables	169
The Tripaulia Gate	169
The Great Gun at Topekhana	173
Plates on the Great Gun	175
Mobarak Monzel with the Stone Throne	179
Mobarak Monzel Garden House	180
The Grant of the Dewani	187
Lord Clive and Warren Hastings	189
Shahamat Jung's Mosque at Moti Jheel	190
Nawab Serajuddowla's Tomb at Khoshbagh	198
The Palace from Roshnibagh	200
Moti Jheel	206
Heera Jheel	206
Maharajah Manindra Chandra Nandi	220
Old English Residency at Cossimbazar	222
Rajah Ashutosh Nath Rai	224
After Rajah A. N. Rai's Installation	227
Site of the Old English Residency at Cossimbazar	236
Lady Hasting's Tomb at Cossimbazar	236
The Dutch Cemetry at Kalkapur	236
The Armenian Church at Saidabad	236
The English Cemetry at Berhampore	236
The Cantonments at Berhampore	236
Dewan Fazl Rubbee, Khan Bahadur	266
Rangamati	268
The temple of Neminath at Cossimbazar	268
Sagoredighi	268
The Durga at Gysabad	268
Rani Bhowani's Temple	275
Bhubaneswar Temple	275
The Temple of Kriteswari	278

	Page.
The Image of Bhoirab at Kriteswari	278
Gouranga	278
Stone Image at Rangamati	278
Some Boats of the Neoara	281
The Killah from Farrabag	283

LIST OF MAPS AND PLANS.

The Island of Cossimbazar with the Plan of Udhuanala and the Monument at Plassey	Frontispeice
The Nawab Nazims' Tombs at Jaffraganj	142
The Tombs at Moti Jheel	192
The Tombs at Khoshbag	199
The Battle of Plassey (to face)	244

LIST OF GENEALOGICAL TABLES.

Nawab Nazims' Family (to face)	13
Dulhin Begum	137
Nawab Shams Jehan Begum	138
Jaffraganj Family	144
Nashipur Raj Family	156
Jagat Setts' Family	156
Rajabazar Family	160
Bangadhicari Family	204
Mozaffer Jang's Family	212
Cossimbazar Raj Family	221
Jamo Baghdanga Raj Family	257
Kandi Raj Family	261

ERRATA AND CORRIGENDA.

Page xv, line 1, *from top for* Palacer *read* Palace.

„ *xv, line* 20, *from top for* 1873 *read* 1813.

„ *8, line 8, from bottom for* hadly *read* hardly.

„ 25, *line* 1, *for* son-in-law *read* sons-in-law.

„ 29, *line* 13, *from bottom for* to *after the word night, read* of.

„ 30, *line* 3, *from bottom for* 24th *read* 23rd.

„ 30, *last line for* 25th *read* 24th.

„ 39, *line* 3, *from top, for* rabbe *read* rabble.

„ 59, *line* 2, *from bottom for* deligence *read* diligence.

„ 60, *line* 15, *from top for* won *read* win.

„ 78, *lines* 13-14, *from top for* surpasing *read* surpassing.

„ 93, *line* 9, *from top for* damase *read* damasc.

„ 102, *line* 4, *from bottom for* by *read* for.

„ 117, *line* 8, *from bottom for* variety *read* rarity.

„ 126, *line* 5, *from top for* representations *read* representatives.

„ 127, *line* 11, *from top after* drawn *read* forth.

„ 127, *line* 7, *from bottom for* surmounded *read* surmounted.

Page 143, *line* 6, *from top for* exists *read* exist.

" 144, *line* 6, *from top for* interest *read* interment.

" 144, *line* 6, *from bottom for* comprises *read* comprise.

" 168, *line* 2, *from top for* unparelled *read* unparalled.

" 174, *line* 2, *from bottom for* 10,5000 *read* 10,500.

" 184, *line* 10, *from top for* form *read* forms.

" 188, *line* 12, *after* of *read* the.

" 189, *line* 6, *from bottom after* in *read* the.

" 217, *line* 3, *for* up *read* upon.

" 220, *line* 13, *from top for* heir-at-law *read* heiress-at-law.

" 232, *line* 15, *from top for* his marriage with *read* the marriage of.

" 283, *line* 7, *from bottom for* rivetted *read* riveted.

" 310, *line* 15, *from bottom for* supees *read* rupees.

" 318, *line* 18, *from top for* to *read* upon.

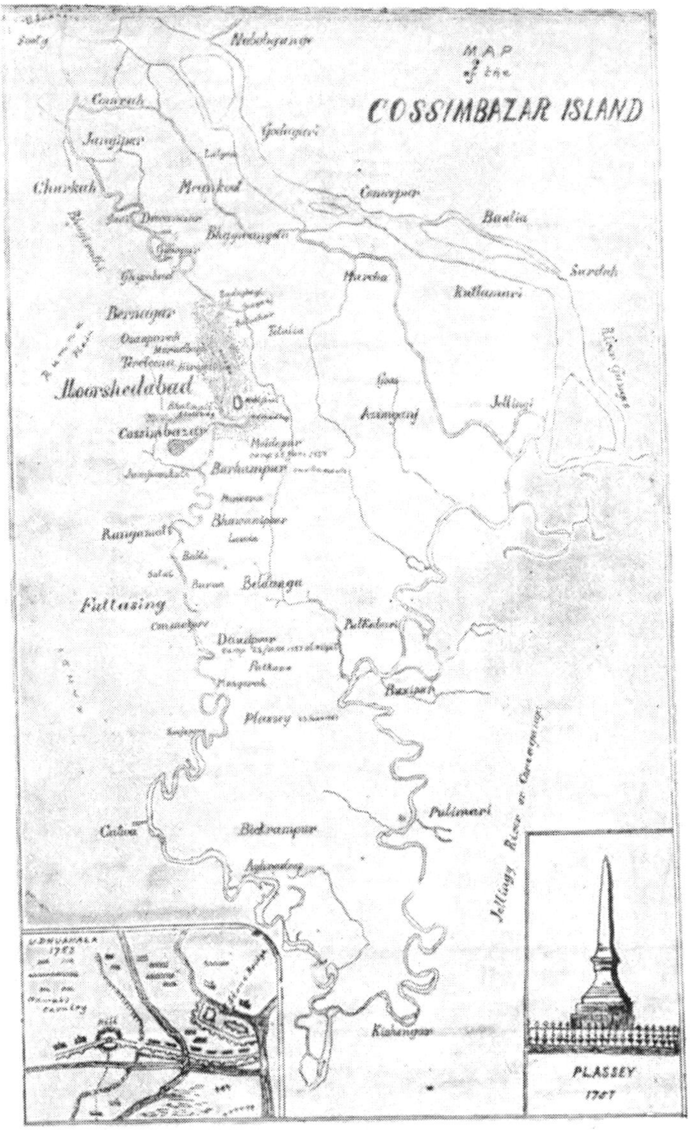

THE ISLAND OF COSSIMBAZAR.

MAJUMDAR'S MURSHIDABAD. FANCY PRESS.

INTRODUCTION.

Mahomedan sovereignty in Bengal, of which Murshidabad had not yet become the capital, was established about the year 1203, when Luknowti or Lakshanavati, known as Gour, a large city on the left bank of the Ganges, twenty-five miles south of Maldah, was the seat of Government. Lakshman Sen, the Hindu King of Bengal, whose capital was at Navadwip, had been told by his Court astrologers, that the kingdom would be subjucated by the Turks. The *ajanulambitabahu* (arms reaching the knees) of Bukhtiar Khiliji, the grandee of Ghor, who under the mandate of Kuttubuddeen, appeared before the gates of the Hindu capital with but seventeen horsemen, answered the description given by the Brahmins of the Mussulman Conquerer of Bengal. Through the back door of the palace, the king, whose panic-striken courtiers had already abandoned him, fled unmolested and undetected to Bikrampore, in the eastern parts of the kingdom and his capital fell into Moslem hands without a struggle. The banner of Islam then waved from the citadel of Navadwip. It was subsequently hoisted at Gour. During five long centuries, from the Mahomedan conquest of Bengal by Bukhtiar Khiliji in 1203, to the time of the imperial prince, Azeem Oshan, when the seat of Mahomedan Government was removed from Dacca to Murshidabad, in 1704, sixty-eight rulers sat on the throne of Bengal. One of these was Raja Kansa, a Hindu, who wrested the reins of Government from the hands of his Mussulman predecessor, Sultan Shumsuddeen. The reigning emperor then at Delhi was Feroze Sha. Raja Kansa held the throne from 1385 to 1392, when he was succeeded by his son, who became a convert to Islam, and assumed the name of Sultan Jelaluddeen. Only once more in the history of the Mussulman Government of Bengal, a Hindu convert to Mahomedanism became the ruler of the country. That was in 1704, when Aurengzebe yielded the imperial sceptre at Delhi and the Mahrattas all over the empire were exhausting the resources of the Great Mogul; and when Queen Anne reigned in England and Marlborough marched up the Rhine, destroying the Bavarian forces near Donauwerth and advanced against Tallard. This convert was Mahomed Hadi, in whose veins ran Brahmin blood, but whose Hindu nomencleture is sunk in oblivion and lost to posterity. The history of Murshidabad opens with Hadi as its first actor.

For the first half of the eighteenth century, the history of Murshidabad is the history of the progress of the Mahomedan Government of Bengal, while the latter half represents the history of the decline of the Mahomedan and the rise of the British power in that province. After the grant of the Dewani to the East

India Company in 1765, Murshidabad still continued to be the capital of independent Bengal. In 1793, the semblance of native power was gone, and the Nawab Nazim of Bengal lost the last shadow of authority when he was disrobed of the purple he wore. The impenetrable character of his killah was done away with and his sovereign rights, recognized by treaties, began to wane. The office of Nawab Nazim, however, continued as a position of rank and dignity akin to that of a ruler. Though devoid of royal power, he was surrounded by all the external emblems of royalty. He had attached to his court a British Resident and his public movements were proclaimed by salvoes of artillery. In 1880, however, with Feredoon Jah's abdication and retirement from the responsibilities of his office, the Nawab Nazimship became dead. The future representatives of the house of Meer Jaffer, the greatest ally of Great Britain, were accorded the statutary position, rank, dignity, rights and priveleges of the Premier Noble of the three provinces of Bengal, Behar and Orissa. With the reinstatement of Meer Jaffer, there have been sixteen ascensions on the throne of Murshidabad since its foundation in 1704; and in 1904, the Masnad of his ancestors is worthily occupied by the Nawab Bahadur of Murshidabad and Amir-ul-Omrah, than whom there has never been a greater Nawab and the history of whose predecessors, commencing with Murshed Kuli Khan, is succintly told in the following pages.

Troublous times of uncertainty and unrest have given place to an era of peace and security which have followed the trail of Pax Brittanica. England alone is destined to hold the orb of the Indian Empire, and the crown of India befits none more than England. To-day the flag of the Emperor of India waves where the banner of the Emperor of Delhi was never unfurled. The first Nawab Nazim of Bengal, who sat on the throne of Murshidabad, sat with his badge of authority from the Great Mogul. Two centuries later, the first Nawab Bahadur of Murshidabad sits on his ancestral masnad, imbued with dignity by a Greater Mogul, whose unrivalled, unprecedented and ever-expanding Empire is the admiration of the world and upon which, it has been truly said, the sun never sets.

The seat of this masnad is the city of Murshidabad, standing on the river Bhagirathee, which has an origin cast in Hindu mythology. Raja Sagar, of Ajodhya, who lived in pre-historic days, desirous of performing the great sacrifice of the horse, had entrusted a beautiful animal with his son, Asamanja, which, however, was stolen by Indra, Sagar ordered his sixty thousand sons to search and find out the horse. In their errands they entered subterraneous regions, where the fire of the wrath of Basudeva, disguised as Kapila, reduced them to ashes. For their salvation, Suparna, a maternal relative of the family, suggested oblations with the water of the

Ganges, which was then in heaven. Bhagirath, the great great grandson of Sagar, after one thousand and one years' of austere supplication, succeeded in propitiating Brahma and bringing down the Ganges, which flowed in seven streams, one of which followed the car of Bhagirath, who, bent upon effecting the salvation of his great grand uncles, proceeded, sounding his gong shell, to the regions underneath, where they had perished. This stream thence became known as the Bhagirathee, possessing great sanctity and credited for centuries without number as the great purifier of sins and the saviour of the fallen.

Apart from this pre-historic origin, the Bhagirathee is said to represent the old channel of the Ganges, which latterly took an easterly course and formed what is now known as the Pudma, a change which cut off the principal cities in Lower Bengal, reducing the river, which was the great trade route, through which the treasures of the country found their way to European marts, to a petty stream, barred here and there by sand banks. It is said that Serajuddowla, apprehensive that the English would in their ships of war pass up and down the river, caused immense piles to be driven into its bed, which facilitated the silting up of the river.

Near about Murshidabad, that is between it and Saidabad, the river was indeed circuitous. Towards the commencement of the last century, it left its old bed and from near Amaniganj, made a straight cut towards the south-west, leaving Cossimbazar, Kalkapur and Farrashdanga, on the left or east bank, a change which contributed to the downfall of those three European factories. The abandoned bed, which became a hot-bed of malaria, is traceable in the swamps now known as the Motijheel, Bansbarijheel, Bistoopoorbheel and Katiganga, down the relay house at Baharamganj.

Murshidabad was situated on what was known as the island of Cossimbazar, bounded by the Pudma on the north, the Bhagirathee on the west and the south, and the Jallangi on the east. The soil of this delta is soft as compared with that of the country lying to the west of the Bhagirathee, which is hard. The formation is, evidently, comparatively recent, which is confirmed by the discovery of sand during the course of the Railway excavations and the absence of any monuments of great antiquity, such as abound on the western bank, the most prominent among which are the temple of Kristeswari, and the ruins of Rangamati, Gysabad, Sagordighi, Mahipal &c.

The original foundation of the city of Murshidabad is involved in obscurity. Teiffenthaler says it was built during Akber's reign. The Afghans in the course of their rebellion in 1696 advanced as far as *Muksusabad.* It finds no mention in the Ain Akbari, though in the Akbarnamah, mention is made of one Muksus Khan, brother of a Governor of Bengal, who is credited by some with the foundation of the city.

Being more conveniently situated than Dacca for the collection of revenue and the supervision of trade and being protected by two natural barriers, Murshed Kuli Khan, the Great Dewan of Bengal, selected it as his head quarters and embellished it, giving it its present name after his own. It is supposed to be the *Madasoubazarki* of Tevernior mentioned in 1666. Muxudavad, Muksusabad, Muksudabad, Moorshoodabad, Moorsheedabad, Moorshedabad, Moorshidabad and Murshedabad are some of the forms of the name which the city has borne, while the current and authorized form is Murshidabad.

The capital extended along both banks of the river, from Amaniganj or Motijheel to Sadeqbagh and from Khoshbagh to Baranagor. Breadthwise, it extended towards the east up to Topekhana and towards the west, up to Kriteswari. Even distant Bhagwangola has sometimes been mentioned as the northern urban limit of the capital.

The town on the eastern bank was situated in Perganah Choonakhali, within Udambar or Urambar, one of the nineteen Sircars into which the great finance minister, Todermall, had divided Bengal. In 1759, two years after Plassey, Clive described the capital to be as extensive, populous and rich as London, with individuals possessing infinitely greater property than those in the English metropolis. One of its palaces, situated on the western bank, was described to be big enough to accommodate three European monarchs. Clive, after his victorious entry into the city, found that the inhabitants were so numerous, that if inclined to destroy the Europeans, they might have done so with sticks and stones.

Apart from income derived from land assessment, the variable revenue of Murshidabad, about the year 1725, which included the Syer Choonakhali or inland customs levied in the city and its environs, taxes on houses, shops, bazars, license fees for vending spirituous liquors, duties on export of raw silk and piece goods manufactured in or about the capital and tolls on bridges and ferries, amounted to Rs. 3,11,603. The mint duties of Murshidabad amounted to Rs. 3,04,000 at two per cent. on the bullion coined. Thus the taxes only amounted to over six lacs of rupees. To-day the Municipal income of the city falls far short of thirty thousand rupees.

Of seven hundred families of Lala Kayeths or Behari Scribes, who inhabited the portion of the city known as Chitakhana, which is now a desolate jungle, and found remunerative occupation in the departments of the Nizamut, hadly seven male representatives yet live in Murshidabad. From the pinnacles of the turrets of seven hundred mosques, the voices of seven hundred shouters of the *azan* simultaneously rent the atmosphere of the crowded city. Of these places of worship, hardly seventy now stand, and of these seventy hardly seven are in proper repair. Who can tell how many hundreds of thousands of the citizens of Murshidabad, who sat down to pray in these mosques, are now, wrapt in their winding sheets, and bedecked with the *tusbi* of Mecca or the earth of Kerbella, lying in repose in their deep dug cells, awaiting the awful day of judgment !

The population, which was very large, was cut down considerably by the great epidemic of small pox of 1770, which followed the great famine of 1769, calamities which spread universal devastation. The mortality was great and in and around the capital it became necessary to keep several sets of persons constantly engaged in removing the dead. Instances were not rare in which entire families became extinct. In 1815, the population had come down to 1,65,000. In the year of grace, 1904, the second centenary of the foundation of Murshidabad, it is only 15,000. The old capital of Bengal, Behar and Orissa is now confined within the nut-shell of a town not six miles in circumferenee.

Hardly a century and a half have elapsed since the days of Plassey, yet few monuments stand in tact to tell the tale of Murshidabad's departed glory. It is to-day the great graveyard of buried greatness. The great scene of mighty revolutions is now covered with the dust of crumbling monuments. Yet these tell most eloquently the history of Murshidabad for the eighteenth century, the history of the Suba Jinnat-ul-Belaod Bengala, the Suba of Bengal, the Paradise of nations, as Aurengzebe called it. At every step, the visitor treads on historic ground and meets with marks full of meaning.

From 1704, the year of its foundation or re-embellishment, to 1793, when the remnants of sovereign authority disappeared, Murshidabad was the arena of mighty events. Its importance went down gradually. The sunlight of former days is passed and its glory vanished, but, in the significant words of its Prince, there is a faint crescent still visible through the unparalleled generosity of the British Government.

PART I.

SYNOPSIS OF THE HISTORY OF MURSHIDABAD.

A list of the Nawabs with their titles &c.

No.	Names.	Titles.	Year of Accession.	Year of Death.
1	Murshed Kuli Khan	Motaman-ul-Mulk, (Guardian of the country.) Alauddowla, (Promoter of the State.) Noser Jang, Noseri, (Helper in War, the Defender.)	1704	1725
2	Shuja Khan	Motaman-ul-Mulk, (Guardian of the country.) Shujauddowla, (Hero of the State.) Asad Jang, (Lion in War.)	1725	1739

A list of the Nawabs with their titles &c.—contd.

No.	Names.	Title	Year of Accession.	Year of Death.
3	Serferaz Khan	Motaman-ul-Mulk, (Guardian of the country.) Alauddowla, (Promoter of the State.) Hyder Jang, (Lion in War.)	1739	1740
4	Ali Verdi Khan	Shuja-ul-Mulk, (Hero of the country.) Hashemuddowla, (Sword of the State.) Mahabat Jang, (Horror in War.)	1740	1756

5	**Serajuddowla**	**Munsur-ul-Mulk,** (Victory of the country.) **Serajuddowla,** (Light of the State.) **Hybut Jang,** (Horror in War.)	**1756**	**1757**
6	**Meer Jaffer**	**Shuja-ul-Mulk,** (Hero of the country.) **Hashemuddowla,** (Sword of the State.) **Mahabat Jang,** (Horror in War.)	**1757**	**1765**

(DEPOSED IN 1760 AND REINSTATED IN 1763.)

A list of the Nawabs with their titles &c.—contd.

No.	Names.	Title.	Year of Accession.	Year of Death.
7	Meer Kasem	Nasir-ul-Mulk, (Victor of the country.) Etmazuddowla, (Politician of the State.) Ali Jah, Nasrut Jang, (Of high rank, Victorious in War.)	1760	1763
8	Najmuddowla	Shuja-ul-Mulk, (Hero of the country.) Najmuddowla, (Star of the State.) Mahabat Jang, (Horror in War.)	1765	1766

9	Syefuddowla	Syef-ul-Mulk, (Sword of the country.) Shujauddowla, (Hero of the State.) Shahamat Jang, (Arrow in War.)	1766	1770
10	Mobarukuddowla	Motaman-ul-Mulk, (Guardian of the country.) Mobarukuddowla, (Auspicious to the State.) Feroze Jang, (Victor in War.)	1770	1793
11	Babar Ali	Nasir-ul-Mulk, (Helper of the country.) Azududdowla, (Arrow of the State.) Delar Jang, (Brave in War.)	1793	1810

A list of the Nawabs with their titles &c.—contd.

No.	Names.	Title.	Year of Accession.	Year of Death.
12	Ali Jah	Shuja-ul-Mulk, (Hero of the country.) Mobarakuddowla, (Auspicious to the State.) Ali Jah, Feroze Jang, (Of higher rank, Victor in War.)	1810	1821
13	Wala Jah	Baeran-ul-Mulk, (Administrator of the country.) Ihtishamuddowla, (Dignifier of the country.) Wala Jah, Mahabat Jang, (Of high rank, Horror in War.)	1821	1824

14	Humayun Jah	Shuja-ul-Mulk, (Hero of the country.) Ihtishamuddowla, (Dignifier of the State.) Humayun Jah, (Of auspicious rank.) Feroze Jang, (Victor in War.)	1824	1838
15	Feredun Jah	Muntizam-ul-Mulk, (Ruler of the country.) Mohsenuddowla, (Benefactor of the State.) Feredun Jah, (Of high rank.) Nasrut Jang, (Helper in War.)	1838	1884

(ABDICATED 1881. DIED 1884.)

A list of the Nawabs with their titles &c.—concld.

No.	Names.	Title	Year of Accession.	Year of Death.
16	Hussan Ali	Ali Kadr, (Of first rank.) Ihtisham-ul-Mulk, (Dignifier of the country.) Raesuddowla, (Premier of the State.) Amir-ul-Omrah, (Noble of Nobles.) Mahabat Jang, (Horror in War.)	1881	Long may he live !

I.

MURSHED KULI KHAN, 1704—1725.

Haji Safi, a merchant of Ispahan, brought up the son of a poor Brahmin of the Deccan and named him Mahomed Hadi. During his early years Hadi served as an assistant in the revenue department under the Mahomedan Dewan of the Berars, and was then appointed by Aurenzebe Dewan of Hyderabad.

In 1701, the Emperor appointed him Dewan of Bengal and with the title of Kurtulab Khàn, posted him to Dacca. There he fell out with Prince Azemoshan and removed to Muksudabad.

The Emperor being pleased with the collection papers prepared by him conferred upon him valuable Khilluts and the title of Murshed Kuli Khan. He changed the name of the city to Murshedabad ; opened a mint ; introduced the "Zurbe Murshedabad" coin ; threw open the responsible revenue offices to none but Bengali Hindus and materially improved the administration of revenue, which secured to him the imperial title of Motamul-ul Mulk Alauddowla Jaffer Khan Noseri Nasir Jang.

He was then appointed Subadar of Bengal, Behar and Orissa, after which he assumed an attitude of independence, never sending any remittances to Delhi.

He appointed his daughter's daughter, Nafisa Begum's husband, Syed Rezi Khan, his Dewan, who in order to enforce payment of the revenues, caused the defaulting Zemindars to be drawn by a rope under their arms through the infernal pond of filth which he called Baikunt or paradise.

Murshed Kuli Khan reduced the expenses of the militia, forbad the exportation of grain, gave great encouragement to learning, remitted the pressing imposts, effected great financial reforms and took delight in feeding the poor. He was sober and temperate and had but one wife.

During his reign rice sold at five maunds the rupee and a man with an income of one rupee a month could have two meals a day with pollao and kalia. He died in 1725.

Murshed Kuli Khan, who possessed all the qualifications of a legislative financier, administered the most brilliant period of the financial history of Bengal.

II.

SHUJA KHAN, 1725—1739.

Shuja Khan or Shujauddeen, whose father was an important officer of State in the Deccan, came of the celebrated Turkish family of Khorasan. He was brought up by Murshed Kuli Khan, who married to him his only daughter, Jinnatunnissa or Azimannissa Begum and appointed him Naib-Dewan of Orissa and then Naib-Nazim.

Ali Verdi Khan came about this time to Shuja Khan, who was his mother's relation. Shuja Khan obtained the title of Matamul Mulk Shujauddeen Bahadur Asad Jang, together with the insignia of rank, namely Hufthazari, Mahimoratub and other honors.

He liberated the defaulting Zemindars who had been kept in confinement, upon their giving security for the regular payment of revenue in future, conferred the office of Dewan upon his son, Serferaz Khan and the administration of Orissa upon his other son, Mahamed Taki; confirmed his son-in-law as Deputy Governor of Dacca and gave to the three sons of his chief counseller, Haji Ahmed, brother of Ali Verdi Khan, namely Nawazesh Mahomed, Syud Ahmed and Zainuddeen, the posts of paymaster General, Fouzedar of Rangpore and Fouzedar of Bengal, respectively.

Upon his old servant, Shuja, he conferred the office of Fouzedar of Hoogly. In 1739, the last year of his reign, he gave the Governorship of Patna to Ali Verdi Khan, and formally appointed his son, Serferaz Khan, his successor, enjoining upon him to follow the advice of Haji Ahmed, Alam Chand and Jagat Sett.

Shuja Khan was a charitable, just and impartial ruler, and gave great encouragement to learning. On his death-bed he asked forgiveness of his attendants and passed away in 1739.

III.

SERFERAZ KHAN, 1739—1740.

Serferaz Khan, the son of Shuja Khan by Azimannissa Begum, daughter of Murshed Kuli Khan, on his accession to the Musnud fell out with his Dewan, Haji Ahmed, who having brought over to his side Jagat Sett Fatteh Chand and Rai Rayan Alam Chand, planned the Nawab's deposition and with that object in view, visited Ali Verdi Khan, then at Delhi, asking him to secure the imperial firman and then to march against Serferaz Khan.

Ata Ulla Khan, intercepted all correspondence and thus kept the preparations of Ali Verdi Khan concealed.

Serferaz Khan marched out with his cavalry to Khamra, when he heared of Ali Verdi Khan's advance through the defiles of Teliagarhi and Sakrigali. Through Jagat Sett's help, the Nawab's men had been suborned and he found in his magazines bricks and clods in the place of cannon balls and powder.

The Nawab superceded the men and gave Panchu Feringee, the son of Antony Feringee, the Portuguese physician, the charge of his artillery. At Giria, the attack began. The Nawab finished his prayer, took up his Koran, and mounting his elephant, advanced towards the enemy, when a bullet struck him in the head and put an end to his life.

His son-in-law, Gazanffar Hossein, and Hussan Mohomed Khan, reached the city the next day and made preparations to defend the capital; but all was useless.

Haji Ahmed and then Ali Verdi Khan entered the city and laying hold of the treasures, which were seventy lacs in cash and fifty crors in jewels, placed them in charge of Yeasin Khan.

Serferaz Khan was a man of valour and of a religious temperament. His short career ended in 1470.

IV.

ALI VERDI KHAN, 1740—1756.

After his victory over Serferaz Khan at Giria, and a halt of three days near Gobranala, Ali Verdi Khan entered the city and proceeded to the residence of Azimannessa Begum, Serferaz Khan's mother, and alighting from his elephant, sent to her a most respectful message to solicit her forgiveness. She returned no answer. Thereupon he proceeded to the Chehel Satoon and ascended the Masnad.

Ali Verdi Khan appointed his sister's husband, Meer Mahommed Jaffer Khan, already conspicuous for his valour, his Commander-in-chief and retained all old officers in service.

After suppressing two revolts in Orissa, he defeated forty-five thousand Maharattas under Raghuji Bhonsla near Burdwan. The defeated army meanwhile reached Dahaparah and looted Jagat Sett's house of two crores of rupees. On Ali Verdi Khan's arrival they fled.

The Maharattas were continually devastating the country and after completely exterminating them, Ali Verdi Khan directed his attention to the internal administration of the country. Upon Dullavram he conferred the title of Rajah and sent him as Governor of Orissa.

The Afghans in Behar having insulted his daughter, Amena Khanum, her sister, Ghasiti Begum and others came to his help and he proceeded against them and rescued her.

The Mahrattas again began their raids and at last peace was purchased by ceding Berar and twelve lacs as the *chout* or a fourth of the Bengal revenue. Ali Verdi Khan imposed abwabs to the extent of Rupees 22,25,554 in order to meet the extravagancies of his favourite grandson, Serajuddowla. A dispute arose with the French factors at Cossimbazar and it was compromised for fifty thousand rupees. In 1755, his nephews, Nawazesh Mahomed and Syud Ahmed, died. The Nawab too became bed-ridden and his young grandson, Serajuddowla, began to manage the affairs of State. Nowazesh Mahomed's widow attempted to secure the throne for Serajuddowla's younger brother, Ekramuddowla.

Ali Verdi Khan was regular in his habits. He rose early and after ablutions and prayer drank coffee with his select companions. At day-break he gave public audience, when the public servants were admitted without reserve. After two hours he received his particular friends and relations. Poems were now recited or history and anecdotes read to him. He ate with his friends and many shared his bounty. He sometimes gave directions to his cooks and often had victuals prepared before him according to his palate. After meal, the company retired to repose. At this time, the story-tellers attended to relate some amusing narrative. After his afternoon seista, he performed his ablutions and read the Koran till four. He received learned men, in whose company he spent an hour daily. Buffoons and jesters also entertained him with their repartees.

Ali Verdi Khan offered high offices to Hindus. He thought like Murshed Kuli Khan and others who patronized Hindu revenue officers that a Mahomedan was like a seive, much of what was poured in went through, while a Hindu was like a sponge, which retained all, but on pressure, gave back as required, what it had absorbed.

Ali Verdi Khan had no son. He married his three daughters to the three sons of his brother, Haji Ahmed. He adopted and declared his favorite grandson as his heir.

At five in the morning of Saturday, the 9th Rajab, 1169 A. H., corresponding with April, 1756, Ali Verdi Khan died in the eightieth year of his age. His principal servants and relations after having purified his body, wrapt it up in a winding sheet and taking it up at midnight, they carried it in pursuance of his appointment to the feet of his mother, entombed at Khoshbagh, "on the side of the river opposite to Motijheel." It has been said that he was perhaps the only prince in the east whom none of his subjects wished to assassinate.

V.

SERAJUDDOWLA, 1756—1757.

Serajuddowla, who has been described as a monster of cruelty and lust, young in years but old in vice and a weak, pampered despot, was born in 1738. He was the son of Hybut Jang, by Amena Khanum, a daughter of Ali Verdi Khan. While the latter was engaged with the Mahrattas, Serajuddowla started with his wife, Lutfunnissa Begum, for Patna in a cart drawn by a pair of bullocks which could go eighty miles a day. Being defeated in a skirmish with the Naib of Patna, he came back to Murshedabad and killed Hossein Kuli Khan, the favorite assistant of Nowazesh Mahomed Khan, the husband of Ghasiti Begum, as also his blind brother. In 1752, he was sent by his grandfather to Hughly, where he received various presents from the Dutch, the French and the English.

On ascending the throne, he expelled Ghasiti Begum from her palace and kept her in confinement. All her treasures were confiscated. The valiant Meer Jaffer Khan was dismissed and Meer Khadem appointed in his place. Mohan Lal was promoted to be prime minister. These supercessions caused great mortification to Meer Jaffer and Rajah Dullavram. On receiving intimation of Drake's refusal to break down certain fortifications that were in progress at Calcutta, Serajuddowla attacked the English fortification at Cossimbazar and imprisoned all the English officers. He then attacked Calcutta and Fort William surrendered. The Black Hole tragedy was then enacted. The verdict of modern historians has exculpated Serajuddowla from his being an active accomplice of this wholesale murder. Four of the survivors of that night to horror, that added its gloom to the sufferings of the victims, one of whom was Holwell, were sent up by boat to Murshidabad. On arrival they were being led in chains through the streets of the city. Serajuddowla on his return, while passing in his palanquin, noticed the prisoners and at once ordered their release.

Serajuddowla required Jagat Sett to raise three crores of rupees from the European merchants trading in the country and on his refusal to comply with the requisition, the latter received a blow in open durbar.

The Nawab then marched against Souket Jang of Purneah and killed him in battle. Meanwhile the news of the English reverses at Cossimbazar reached Clive at Madras. Secret conferences were held at Jagat Sett's house and the deposition of Serajuddowla was decided upon. A mental division of the treasury was made, in which the share of Omichand, one of the confederates, was put down at thirty lacs. The plan of the white and the red treaty was then devised.

The Nawab, apprehensive of the designs of the English had located his army at Plassey. This greatly offended Clive who sent Scrafton with a request that Serajuddowla should no longer keep his army at Plassey, the whole of which under Meer Jaffer was recalled to Murshidabad. Foolishly secure of his position, the Nawab insulted Meer Jaffer in open durbar and replaced him by appointing Khaja Hadi as Commander-in-chief. Subsequently when the designs of the English began to ooze out, he effected a reconciliation with Meer Jaffer. On the 21st of June, 1757, the Nawab's army took up their former positions at Plassey. On the 22nd, the English army crossed the river and advanced towards it. The battle that decided the fate of India was then fought and won by the English. Serajuddowla mounting his camel and escorted by two thousand horsemen, left the field for Murshidabad, which was reached before midnight of the 24th With his favorite wife, Lutfunnissa, he left the deserted palace. Meer Jaffer reached Murshidabad on the 25th of June and Clive on the 29th.

Meer Jaffer received him in State at the Palace of Mansurganj, where the Nawab's Darbar had assembled. Clive placed him on the throne, and as representative of the East India Company, presented him with a nuzar of gold mohurs and congratulated him as Nawab Nazim of Bengal, Behar and Orissa. He informed the assembly that it was fortunate that in the place of a tyrant they had secured a good ruler. Walsh, Clive's Secretary, entered into the vaults of the palace and found stored there Rs. 17,60,000 in silver, and 23,00,000 in gold, besides chests of precious stones. The inner treasury contained eight crores. Clive and others went to Jagat Sett's house and there arranged for the payment of the stipulated amounts. Omichand did not get his share and fell down in a swoon.

On the eighth day of his flight, Serajuddowla was brought back to Murshidabad and put to death by Meer Jaffer's son, Miran.

Among Serajuddowla's acts of uniquity are related his attempts to secure Tara, the widowed daughter of Rani Bhowani and his walling up alive Faizi, the dancing girl of exquisite beauty who weighed only twenty-two seers and had been procured from Delhi at a cost of one lac of rupees.

VI.

MEER JAFFER, 1757—1760.

Meer Jaffer, whose grand-father came from Arabia to Delhi, was a direct descendent of the Prophet. He married Sha Khanum, Ali Verdi Khan's sister. On ascending the musnud of Bengal, he confirmed the various officers in their respective posts.

Clive returned to Calcutta on the 13th September, 1757. For assistance in repelling Sha Alum, Meer Jaffer granted Clive the jaigire of the Zemindaries of Calcutta, yielding three lacs annually. Clive wrote to the Directors in England under date the 6th August, 1757—"the Nawab's generosity has enabled me to live with satisfaction in England."

Meer Jaffer went to Calcutta to see Clive on the eve of his departure for England. His reception cost the Company eighty thousand rupees. A nazur of one hundred and one gold mohers was presented to the Nawab.

In the fourth year of his reign, Meer Jaffer issued in the following terms a perwana for the establishment of a mint at Calcutta—"To the noblest of merchants, the English Company, be the royal favour. In Calcutta a mint is established. You shall coin gold and silver of equal weight and fineness with the Asherfis and rupees of Murshidabad in the name of Calcutta. In the subas of Bengal, Behar and Orissa they shall be current."

Sha Alum having directed another attack upon Patna, the Nawab's forces were sent under his son, Miran, upon whose death by lightning, Rajballav became absolute in command.

Holwell, who had been placed at the head of the Calcutta Committee after Clive's departure, became prejudiced against Meer Jaffer and in concert with his son-in-law, Meer Kasem, planned his deposition. An agreement was concluded by which, though the old and grief-striken Nawab was to continue as Nazim, all real power was to be exercised by Meer Kasem. Meer Jaffer sent the royal seal to his son-in-law and then, under an English escort, proceeded to Calcutta.

VII.

MEER KASEM, 1760—1763.

Meer Kasem, the grand-son of Syud Imtiaz, Subadar of Guzerat, ascended the musnud on the dethronement of his father-in-law, Meer Jaffer. He reduced the expenditure of the several departments, confiscated the properties of wealthy citizens and realized large nazars from the Zemindars and was thus able to pay off the large arrear salaries of the soldiery.

Suspecting Nanda Kumar of intrigue with Sha Alum's agents, the Nawab imprisoned him. He then marched against the rebellious Zemindar of Beerbhoom and quieting him, proceeded towards Patna, where

Sha Alum was causing disturbances and making unreasonable demands. The Emperor demanded an interview with the Nawab which the latter refused.

Meer Kasem then demanded of Coote to remove the English guards from the gates of the fort of Patna and complained to Vansittart at Calcutta of the insolence of Coote and Carnac, who were in consequence recalled to Calcutta. The Nawab then imprisoned Ramnaraen and perpetrated other acts of cruelty at Patna. Raja Sitaram, whose sympathies were with Meer Jaffer, was put to death.

The reformation of the army and the administration of revenue next attracted his attention. Ram Kanta, the husband of Rani Bhowani, was ousted from his Zemindari of Rajshye, which however was returned to him at the intercession of Jagut Sett. In three years, the revenue of Bengal increased to an alarming extent. Meer Kasem's administration has been described as more a pillage than a system of Government. The arrests of Mansaram, Aratoon and Hay, the strictures passed by Ellis, the refusal of the keeper of the fort at Monghyr to admit armed European soldiers, the interception of letters at Cossimbazar and other circumstances caused great estrangement of feelings.

Amyatt proposed that the twenty lacs the Nawab had promised to pay to the Governor and the members of the Council at Calcutta at the time of his installation, should be demanded from him. Meer Kasem

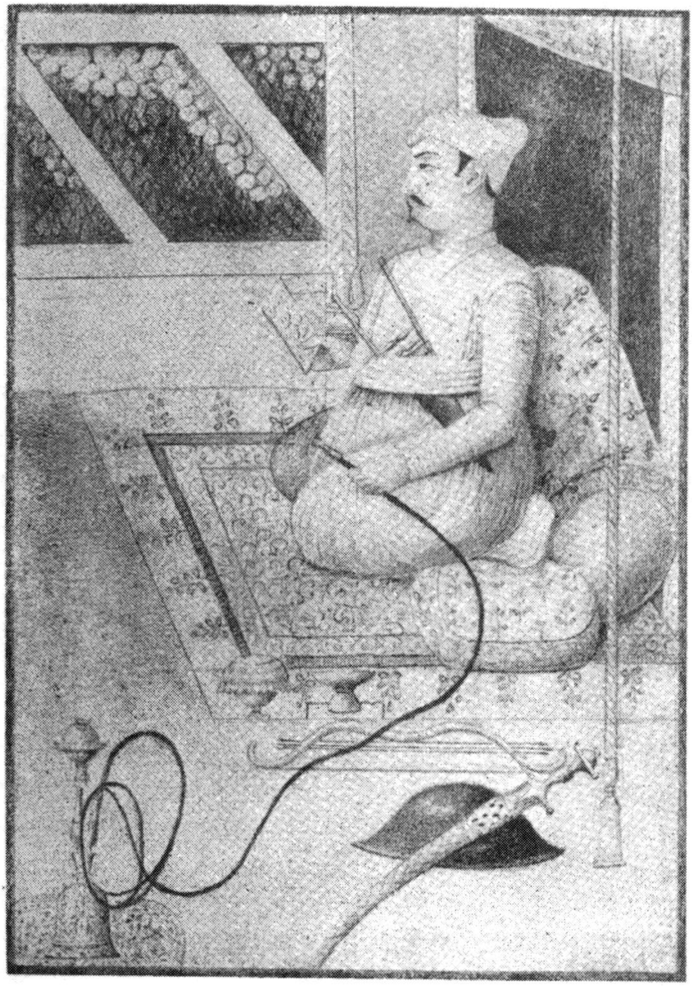

NAWAB MEER KASEM.

MAJUMDAR'S MURSHIDABAD.

FANCY PRESS.

replied—"I owe no body a single rupee nor will I pay your demand."

Meer Kasem complained of the English monopoly of trade. In 1763, he advanced towards Nepal and defeated the Nepalese soldiers. The Sett brothers, Rajah Rajballav, Ramnaraen and other Hindus of eminence were taken to Monghyr and kept under confinement. A few boats carrying arms for the English soldiers at Patna were seized. The English were taken prisoners. Carstairs and Amyatt were killed.

The Nawab's troops surrounded Cossimbazar and he wrote a taunting letter to the Calcutta Council demanding reparation for the damage caused by the English. On the 7th July, 1763, war was declared against Meer Kasem, and his deposition was announced.

An agreement dated the 10th July, 1763, was entered into with Meer Jaffer, stipulating *inter alia* that Meer Kasem should be deposed and Meer Jaffer reinstated. Meer Jaffer left Calcutta and joined the English forces on the 17th July at Agradwip. The Nawab's forces were routed and Meer Jaffer for the second time entered the capital with the English on the 23rd July, 1763. The English pursued Meer Kasem and at Giria a severe fight ensued and the combined forces of Meer Jaffer and the English then advanced towards Udhuanala. After putting to death Ramnaraen, Rajballav, the two Jagat Setts and others, Meer Kasem proceeded towards Bhagulpore.

The fall of Udhuanala disheartened Meer Kasem, who fled towards Patna. The English took Rajmehal and Monghyr. Meer Kasem fled and took shelter under Shujauddowla of Oudh, who stripped him of whatever was left to him and placing him upon a lame elephant, drove him out. He then visited Allahabad, Gwalior and Delhi and then, deserted by his friends and attendants, he died like a pauper and his funeral was performed with the proceeds of the sale of a pair of his shawls, the only property left by him.

VIII.

MEER JAFFER—(Reinstated), 1763—1765.

On his return to the capital on the 24th July, 1763, Meer Jaffer was reinstated on the musnud. Clive being informed of this wrote to Meer Jaffer—"this being the principal of my wishes, I returned thank to the Almighty and fired off the guns in celebration of this happy event. The province of Bengal is now reduced under your subjection and all the inhabitants of the country are blessed with tranquility and delivered from the oppression of the enemy."

At the repeated requests of the Council, Meer Jaffer repaired to Calcutta and though received with great honors, was met by heavy demands.

At Murshidabad, Dullavram was appointed Dewan, and Nandakumar was placed in charge of the Jaigires and the Treasury. Mahamed Reza Khan, naib at

Dacca, was summoned to account for the twenty lacs standing in his name.

Vansittart resigned in 1764, and Meer Jaffer, thinking Clive would come out to succeed him, went again to Calcutta with a view to see him. The Mayor and the Alderman and the civil and military officers of the Company presented nuzurs. Clive did not return to India and the old, depressed Nawab, then aged seventy-four, returned to Murshidabad and appointed Najmuddowla his successor.

Meer Jaffer died on the 17th January, 1765, leaving a legacy to Clive, *noorchashm*, "the light of his eyes," of five lacs of rupees, mohers and jewels, which had been entrusted with his wife, Mani Begum. With this money Clive created on the 6th April, 1770, a trust fund for the relief and maintenance of European officers and soldiers, invalid or superannuated, and their widows. The wealth which Clive had acquired brought him an income of forty thousand pounds a year.

IX.

NAJMUDDOWLA, 1765—1766.

Najmuddowla, the son of Meer Jaffer, by Mani Begum, ascended the musnud while yet a minor. This cost him £140,000, divided among the members of the Calcutta Council. Mr. Middleton and other European gentlemen attended the proclamation of the young Nawab, at the Killah. Francis Sykes arrived at Moradbagh as Resident at the Durbar and applied to the Nawab to disband his military rabbe maintained at a cost of eighteen lacs per annum. He explained to Najmuddowla the advantage of accepting a stipend and of being relieved from embrassing circumstances. It was arranged that Najmuddowla should get a stipend of Rs. 53,86,161 per annum and the affairs of Government should be placed in the hands of Mahamed Reza Khan, Dullavram and Jagat Sett, the former of whom was charged with the payment of the Nawab's sepoys, horse, servants &c., as also the following stipends, namely,

Syefuddowla, the Nawab's brother	Rs.	7,000	per month.
Mobarukuddowla do.	,,	5,000	,,
Miran's son, the Nawab's nephew	,,	5,000	,,
The Begum and her family	,,	6,000	,,

The young Nawab was extremely tractable and polite, and Sykes secured from him one hundred and six profitable perwanas, and the Zemindars were put entirely under the authority of the East India Company on whose behalf, the Governor and Council at Calcutta, engaged by a treaty to secure to Najmuddowla the Subadari of the three provinces of Bengal, Behar and Orissa, and to assist him with their troops in the defence of the provinces.

Najmuddowla confirmed the treaty entered into with Meer Jaffer. The Chuklas of Burdwan, Midnapore and Chittagong were confirmed to the Company

NAWAB NAJMUDDOWLA.

for defraying the ordinary expenses of the troops, besides the grant of five lacs annually, so long as the exigencies of keeping a large army continued. The business of the Sircar was to be transacted as heretofore at Murshidabad, which was to continue as the seat of Government.

Najmuddowla consented that an Englishman should reside at his Durbar as representative of the Company. He consented to pass rupees coined at Calcutta and to entertain no Europeans in his service. The entire military force passed into and remained in the hands of the Company and they began to exercise an extensive control over the internal affairs of the Suba.

The Directors of the East India Company, though glad of the triumphs, were not without anxieties, as they yet considered their position exposed to hazard. They induced Clive to come out to Bengal and, equipped with ample powers and placed beyond the control of the Calcutta Committee, he arrived in 1765, and negotiated for and secured the Dewani, the nature of which, according to him, was to collect the revenue and, after defraying the expenses of the army and allowing a sufficient fund for the expenses of the Nizamut, to remit the remainder to Delhi. This was not the office which the Company were willing to execute. They, therefore, entirely approved of preserving the old form of Government in upholding the dignity of the Subadar. An agreement, securing the annual stipend of Rs. 53,86,131, was signed in the presence of Clive. In accordance with custom, the Poonneah was held at Motijheel on the 29th April, 1766, the first Poonneah of the Dewan Company.

On the 8th of May of the same year, Najmuddowla died of fever caught at a party given in honor of Clive on his way through Murshidabad to Lucknow.

For the annual stipend of fifty-three lacs, Najmuddowla abandoned with a light heart a revenue estimated at two crores and fifty-six lacs and a total income from all sources of three crores and thirty lacs. He accepted Clive's proposal with joy and exclaimed—"Thank you, I shall now have as many dancing girls as I like."

The imperial firman of 1765, conferring upon the East India Company the Dewani of Bengal, Behar and Orissa, was confirmed by Najmuddowla by the agreement of the 30th September of that year.

X.

SYEFUDDOWLA, 1766—1770.

Syefuddowla, a younger brother of Najmuddowla, was placed on the musnud, while a youth of sixteen. The management devolved upon Mani Begum. A treaty was concluded on the 19th May, 1766, in which

SYEFUDDOWLA.

MAJUMDAR'S MURSHIDABAD. FANCY PRESS.

the Company engaged to pay him the reduced stipend of Rs. 41,86, 131-9-0, namely Rs. 17,78, 854-1-0 for his household and Rs. 24,07, 277-8-0 for the support of the Nizamut. Mahamed Reza Khan, Dullavram and Jagut Sett were allowed to continue in their offices.

Of the sixteen lacs of rupees which in 1765, his brother, Najmuddowla, had paid to the Company upon bond, three lacs were repaid to Syefuddowla and the balance, which remained due to the Nawab, he gave as a fund, to be disposed of in the same manner as the five lacs bequeathed to Clive by Meer Jaffer.

Though the old musnud remained in the Nawab's palace at Murshidabad, real authority passed into the Chamber of the Directors in London. They considered, however, that the majesty and the dignity of the Government still resided in the Nawab and his ministers and these only were known to the inhabitants as the power to whom they were accountable.

Jonoji Bhonsle, the Mahratta chief, ceded the province of Orissa which had been given to the Maharattas by Ali Verdi Khan.

A Nizamut custom house was established at Murshidabad to check the private importation of arms and ammunition by Europeans.

In 1769, a great epidemic of small pox raged in Murshidabad and sixty-three thousand of its inhabitants died, one of the victims being Nawab Syefuddowla.

The amount of the stipend fixed was possibly in consideration of the yield of the Jaigire or akta lands, which lay dispersed throughout the province in small dismembered allotments, which had been assigned for the maintenance of the dignity and household of the Nazim.

XI.

MOBARUKUDDOWLA, 1770—1793.

Mobarukuddowla, the son of Meer Jaffer by Bubboo Begum, became Nawab, when a boy of only twelve. Hastings appointed Mani Begum, the Nawab's stepmother, his guardian; though his mother, Bubboo Begum, was alive. The reason why the guardianship was not given to his mother has never been satisfactorily explained. In the subsequent examination of her accounts for the period of her guardianship, a large sum was discovered to be unaccounted for. Mani Begum was placed under restraint and in the inquiry that was held she stated that a considerable sum had been paid to the Governor General.

The charge of taking money was originally preferred by Nandakumar. Hastings stated he had anticipated such a charge and addressing his Council he said—"The chief of this administration, your superior, Gentlemen, appointed by the Legislature itself, should I sit at this Board to be arraigned in the

NAWAB MOBARAKUDDOWLA.

MAJUMDAR'S MURSHIDABAD. FANCY PRESS.

presence of a wretch whom you well know to be the basest of mankind, I believe I need not mention his name, but it is Nuncoomar."

On the 21st March, 1770, a treaty was concluded with Mobarukuddowla and the East India Company and the stipend was further reduced to Rs. 31,81,991-9-0; of which Rs. 15,81,99-9-0 were allotted for the Nawab's household and rupees sixteen lacs for the support of the Nizamut. The Directors of the Company, while not disapproving the preserving of the succession in the family of Meer Jaffer, and while admitting that both justice and policy recommended a measure which at once corresponded with the customs and inclinations of the people of Bengal, disapproved of the continuance of so large a pension, which was accordingly further reduced in January, 1772, to sixteen lacs only, representing the income of the imperial Jaigires once enjoyed by the Nawabs Nazim. The savings thus effected were to form a fund to provide for military exigencies.

Hastings visited Murshidabad in 1772, and Mahamed Reza Khan having failed to collect the revenues properly, was imprisoned and sent to Calcutta. Nandakumar's son, Gooroodas, a youth of twenty, was appointed Dewan.

The revenue offices were now transferred from Murshidabad to Calcutta. Dullavram's son, Rajah Rajballav, was appointed by the Company their first Roy Royan to supervise the work of collection. The

Council of Calcutta took into their hands the criminal jurisdiction hitherto exercised by the Nizamut, but this was, after four years of experiment, transferred to the Nawab's officers. Nandakumar having been hanged on a charge of forgery, Mahamed Reza Khan attained a triumph and was reinstated at Murshidabad and Mani Begum and Gooroodas were removed.

Mobarukuddowla announced his intention of visiting Calcutta in 1786, and the Governor General issued orders, requiring the Zemindars to present nuzurs, which the Nawab, who was naturally kind, refused to accept.

Rana Chhattar Sing of Gohud sought Mobarukuddowla's friendship and alliance and requested the Nazim to recommend the Company to be on good terms with him.

Lord Cornwallis visited Murshidabad in 1787 on his way to Lucknow.

In 1790 criminal jurisdiction again began to be exercised by the English Government and the Nizamut Adalat was removed to Calcutta. In 1793, all power virtually passed into the hands of the English, to the ordinary jurisdiction of the English judiciary, the Nawab's Killah alone remaining an exception. The last of the *treaties* was made with Mobarukuddowla.

In 1790, the Begum of the Emperor Sha Alum wrote to Lord Cornwallis to pursuade the Nawab Nazim to give his daughter in marriage to her son.

NAWAB BABAR ALI.

MAJUMDAR'S MURSHIDABAD.

FANCY PRESS.

Nothwithstanding the Governor General's request, Mobarukuddowla declined to give away his daughter to one who, though of the royal blood, was not a Syud.

Mobarukuddowla died in 1793, mourned by a large family and a very large number of friends, relatives and dependents, to whom he was always kind and generous.

The military power and the revenue admistration had already been transferred to the Company before his time and civil and criminal jurisdiction passed over to them during Mobarukuddowla's Nazimship. The transfer of civil, criminal, revenue and military jurisdiction was thus complete within thirty years of the battle of Plassey, during which there were no less than six successions to the musnud, half the number of which were during the nonage of the Nazims.

XII.

BABAR JANG, 1793—1810.

Babar Ali Delair Jang succeeded to the musnud on the death of his father, Mobarukuddowla, in 1793. Lord Wellesley, the Governor General, assured him that he had his welfare at heart and that he would be ready at all times and happy to exert his interest to promote the peace and comfort of the Nizamut and to maintain the splendour and uphold the dignity of the Nawab's exalted court. Sir John Harrington was instructed to attend the auspicious assembly of the Nawab's succession to the Nizamut Musnud and to acknowledge His Highness on behalf of the Government as Subadar of the three provinces.

In 1802, Viscount Valentine had an interview with Babar Jang and Mani Begum. He found the Nawab wearing magnificent jewels, which were taken out of pawn for the occasion and he saw the creditors waiting downstairs to watch and remove them again on his departure. Babar Jang died in 1810.

The Nizamut Stipends under the old scheme of Mr. Harrington, dated May, 1796, were as follow during Babar Jang's time :—

The Nawab Nazim, with Akrobas &c.		Rs. 16,00,000
The Nawab Nazim with Akrobas and sons and Bubboo Begum	Rs. 1,16,335	
Nawab Begum	,, 12,000	
Saleha Begum	,, 1,000	
Syud Murtaza Khan	,, 3,000	
Fazilatunnissa Begum	,, 1,000	
The sons of Mahamed Reza Khan, Delawar Jang and the widow of Baharam Jang		,, 1,44,000
Mahomed Saleh Khan of Purneah		,, 14,400
Syud Reza Ali Khan of Rajmehal		,, 75,000
Rajah Dhiraj Naraen Kamla Pershad	,, 450	,, 7,200
Roy Sing Lall	,, 150	
Fateh Ali Khan		,, 6,000
Shamsher Ali Khan		,, 4,800
Nizamut		,, 12,000
Lungerkhana, Motijheel		,, 1,800
TOTAL		,, 18,65,200

THE

MUSNUD OF MURSHIDABAD

(1704-1904)

BEING

A SYNOPSIS OF THE HISTORY OF MURSHIDABAD

FOR THE LAST TWO CENTURIES

TO WHICH ARE APPENDED

NOTES OF PLACES AND OBJECTS OF INTEREST

AT

MURSHIDABAD

COMPILED BY

PURNA CH. MAJUMDAR

GYAN

Published by

Gyan Publishing House
5, Ansari Road
Daryaganj, New Delhi-110002
Phone: 011-47034999, 9811692060
E-mail: books@gyanbooks.com

Distribution Network
gyanbooks.com
India, USA, Canada, UK, Australia, France

ISBN: 978-81-212-9124-8 (PB)
First Published, 1905

2nd Impression 2023

Printed at: Gyan Press, Delhi.

THE MUSNUD OF MURSHIDABAD (1704-1904)
COMPILER: PURNA CH. MAJUMDAR

NAWAB ALI JAH.

MAJUMDAR'S MURSHIDABAD FANCY PRESS.

XIII.

ALI JAH, 1810—1821.

Zainuddeen Ali Khan, known as Ali Jah, eldest son of Babar Jang, succeeded his father and received from Lord Minto, the Governor General, letters of congratulations and friendly assurances. His succession was not without dispute, as Mani Begum had nominated Abul Kasem, second son of Mobarakud-dowla. Mr. Richard Roche, who was then in charge of the Nizamut affairs, was directed to attend at the musnud and to invest the Nawab with the Subadary of Bengal, Behar and Orissa. The 5th June, 1810, was the auspicious day fixed for the ceremony, when in the presence of all the nobles of the city, the proclamation was read in open Durbar and it was announced that the Company would not flinch from helping the Nawab. The usual presentation of Khilluts then took place. The stipend of sixteen lacs was continued and the Governor General offered to give his best counsel and to exert his friendly aid in supporting the rank, dignity and welfare of the Nawab.

Latterly Ali Jah was in indifferent health and proceeded to Monghyr on excursion for a change. Returning thence he went to Champa-pukur, and then to Furrabagh, where he resided in a bunglow close to the river bank for seven or eight days, during which he appeared greatly emaciated from his protracted illness. His Highness used to go out in his Chowpala, amuse himself with seeing wild fowls sporting in the tanks and shoot dear, resting his gun on the shoulder of his orderly sepoy. He wrote for permission to go to Calcutta. Mr. Russell, the agent to the Governor General and Dr. Smith, the Civil Surgeon, came to see him, and were fetched from the opposite side of the river by a boat which the Nawab had directed Rajah Udwanta Singh, the Dewan, to send. Mr. Russell delivered to His Highness the Governor General's letter conveying His Lordship's assent to the Nawab's proceeding to Calcutta.

On the 31st July, 1821, His Highness left the Bunglow and as soon as the pinnace had been fitted up, he embarked about sun set and was rowed down towards Amaniganj. On the 4th August, he performed the religious exercises of seeking pardon of God and directed that those Khawases, who attended upon him, should wash and purify his corpse and after clothing him with the winding sheet of Kerbella should inter him. His Highness then ate of some earth brought from Kerbella. On the day following, he desired Basant Ali Khan to fetch an elephant for eleemosynary purposes, which was brought and with some penetential ceremonies was bestowed upon a Brahmin, with two gold mohers; but as the Brahmin did not seem to be satisfied, the gift was increased to five gold mohers.

NAWAB WALA JAH.

MAJUMDAR'S MURSHIDABAD. FANCY PRESS.

On the morning of the 6th August, Mr. Russell and Rajah Udwanta Singh were by the side of the expiring Nawab. He sent for his brother, Wala Jah, who came to the pinnace and fell down at his feet, shedding tears. At that time, putting his hand on the back of Wala Jah and ordering a chair, the Nawab said that he forgave him his past offences. Dr. Smith arrived later and Ali Jah asked the people to retire and at seven in the evening expired, after making testamentary dispositions in favor of some of his faithful servants and relinquishing pecuniary claims against others. Like Mobarakuddowla, Ali Jah was very fond of music.

XIV.

WALA JAH, 1821—1824.

Syud Ahmed Ali Khan, known as Wala Jah, second son of Babar Jang, succeeded to the musnud on the death of his brother, Ali Jah, in 1821. The Marques of Hastings lost no time in writing a letter of condolence to the Nawab and issued instructions to Mr. Russell, the Agent to the Governor General at Murshidabad, to repair to the Court of the Nawab for investing him with the Subadari. The fixed stipend and the mutually established points were allowed to continue.

Wala Jah framed some queer rules of etiquette. The akrobas or bood relations were required to dismount from their horses or carriages after advancing only a few hundred paces from the main entrance gate of the Killah. Jagat Sett was to dismount at fifty paces and the Roy Royan or Dewan at twenty-five. Others had to dismount at the gate. Few could use the sun-shade or umbrella within the Killah. Every morning a small procession was drawn up, which danced attendance all day long.

Certain disputes arose between Wala Jah and Amir-un-nissa Begum, the widow of Ali Jah, regarding the valuable jewels and other moveable property left or bequeathed by Ali Jah. Mr. J. Ahmuty, who bore the oriental title of Hamid-ul-Mulk, Fukhrud-dowla, Ihtesham Jang, was deputed as a Commissioner to inquire into the matter. Referring to Mr. Ahmuty's Report, which noted several points calculated to produce good results, the Governor General wrote to Wala Jah—"In all matters I hope your Highness will consider me as your well-wisher." Wala Jah died after a short rule of three years.

XV.

HUMAYUN JAH, 1824—1838.

Mobarak Ali Khan, better known as Humayun Jah, ascended the musnud of Bengal, Behar and

NAWAB HUMAYUN JAH.

MAJUMDAR'S MURSHIDABAD. FANCY PRESS.

Orissa on the death of his father, Wala Jah, in 1824. On the 14th January, 1825, Lord Amherst wrote to him a letter in Persian, which rendered runs thus:— "Truly on the receipt of the joyful intelligence of the happy installation of your Highness on the throne of ancestral authority, the budding of joy of this friend so bloomed with delight that to describe one of its thousand blossoms or to draw a single rose from the bough in just array is beyond the flowers of rhetoric." The same allowance continued to be paid.

Humayun Jah purchased from the East India Company the old Court houses at Findallbagh and converted the grounds into a garden which is still known by his name. The present Palace at Murshidabad was erected during his time, and a miniature of it in ivory, prepared by Sagore Mistri, together with portraits of His Highness and his son, and other presents were sent to King William IV., who honored the Nawab with the present of a full size portrait of His Majesty and an autograph letter and conferred upon him the badge and insignia of the Royal Guelphic and Hanoverian order, still preserved in the Palace.

Humayun Jah delighted in being painted in different costumes. He died on the 3rd October, 1838, leaving behind him his son, Mansur Ali and his daughter, Sultana Ghetiara Begum.

XVI.

FEREDUN JAH, 1838—1881. *(Abdication)*

Syud Mansur Ali Khan, known as Janab-e-Ali and Feredun Jah, whose life is full of melancholy interest, succeeded his father, Humayun Jah, while yet a minor and only eight years old, ascending the musnud on the day of the Idul Fitre in 1838. The Acting Governor General at once wrote a letter of congratulations and assurances and published a Proclamation notifying the Nawab's succession to the heriditary honors and dignities of the Nizamut and Subadari of Bengal, Behar and Orissa.

Of the sixteen lacs assigned to him, His Highness's personal allottment was seven and a half lacs and from the remainder, provision was to be made for the other members of the family, any unexpended balance going to the formation of a fund, known as the Nizamut Deposit Fund, which latterly became the subject matter of great controversy.

In 1850, His Highness sent to Her Majesty the late Queen Victoria certain articles of State decoration of local manufacture, which Her Majesty publicly exhibited in London and which were much appreciated by her and the British public.

Feredun Jah founded the Nizamut School and the Nizamut College, now known as the Nawabs' High School and the Nawabs' Madrassa, respectively.

NAWAB FEREDUN JAH.

MAJUMDAR'S MURSHIDABAD. FANCY PRESS.

In 1853, the death of two servants in the Nawab's shooting camp having caused some suspicion, his attendants, chief among whom was Aman Ali Khan, the principal eunuch, were prosecuted for murder. All the eunuchs were acquitted by the Supreme Court and they were received back in the Nawab's service. But Government ordered their peremptory dismissal.

In the same year, it was declared that the Nawab Nazim had no treaty rights. This was followed in 1854 by the abrogation of all the former priveleges of the Nazim. The Nawab's salute of nineteen guns was reduced to one of thirteen and the four Regulations and Acts of 1799, 1805, 1806 and 1822, securing to him certain priveleges, were repealed and the Nazim's right of control over the Nizamut Deposit Fund was denied.

After the great Indian mutiny, in which His Highness had rendered material assistance, the salute was restored. In 1860, Feredun Jah memorialized the Secretary of State for India in Council about his numerous grievances. His Highness then said—"It is my desire to be to Her Majesty the Queen, the first as I have always been the most loyal of Her Indian subjects"

Receiving no redress, the Nawab Nazim went to England in 1869, against the advice of his Dewan, Rajah Prosanno Narain Deb, accompanied by his Private Secretary and chief counsellor, Mr. W. D. Fox, to prefer his complaint in person to her Majesty's

Government. His grievances were ventilated in Parliament but with little success.

Meanwhile the Nizamut at Murshidabad became involved in heavy debts and several claims were preferred against the Nawab Nazim and attachments were issued against his property. The Government of India, thereupon, actuated by a desire of freeing the Nawab and his property from suits and attachment and of discharging such portions of the claims as were proper to be paid, and with the further object of exempting him from the jurisdiction of the Civil Courts, passed, in 1873, an Act (XVII of 1873) and appointed thereunder a commission for the purpose of carrying out the objects of the enactment.

On the 13th December, 1875, the Commissioners, one of whom was Mr. Beaufort, formerly Judge of Murshidabad, submitted their Declaration with regard to Nizamut State Property, that is property held by the Government of India for the purpose of upholding the dignity of the Nawab Nazim for the time being.

In April, 1876, the Nizamut Commissioners completed and made their awards with respect to the pecuniary claims of the several creditors.

In 1880, while yet in England, His Highness entered into an Indenture with the Secretary of State, agreeing to receive ten lacs of rupees, which was to be paid out of his arrears of pension, in full satisfaction of his personal claims of whatsoever kind. Feredun Jah expressed a desire to retire from the

HIS HIGHNESS THE NAWAB BAHADUR OF MURSHIDABAD,
AMIR-UL-OMRAH, G. C. I. E.

Photo by Johnston & Hoffmann. KUNTALINE PRESS. CALCUTTA

Nizamut and a personal stipend of ten thousand pounds sterling per annum was granted to him, with option to reside where-ever he pleased.

In the October of 1881 he returned to Bombay and came latterly to Murshidabad, where he died at the Palace on the 5th November, 1884. His remains were deposited at the family cemetry at Jaffraganj, with strange coincidence, in the only available space left in the line of the tombs of the Nazims, and were subsequently removed for interment at Kerbella in Arabia, in pursuance of his will.

Of his one hundred and one children by more than twenty wives, he left him surviving nineteen sons and twenty two daughters.

The Nawab Nazimship of Bengal was buried with Feredun Jah, the last Nawab Nazim of Bengal, respected and renowned for his many private virtues.

XVII.

NAWAB ALI KADR BAHADUR.

1881—*May he live long !*

Nawab Ali Kadr Syud Hussan Ali Meerza Bahadur, who succeeded his father, Syud Mansur Ali Khan, the last Nawab Nazim of Bengal, Behar and Orissa, on his retirement in 1880, was born on the 25th August, 1846. He is seventh from Meer Jaffer,

Nawab Nazim of Bengal ; ninth from Syud Hussan Najafi, Chief of Najaf in Arabia ; twenty-eighth from Ahmed, entitled Nasiruddeen Alla, ruler of Yemen (315 A. H.) ; twenty-fifth from Imam Hussan ; thirty-sixth from Ali, the Amir-ul-Momin and Fatema, the Prophet's daughter ; thirty-seventh from Mahamed, the Prophet of Arabia ; thirty-ninth from Abdul Mottalleb, head of the Koresh tribe and chief of Mecca ; sixty-third from Ismail and sixty-fourth from Abraham of the old Testament, of whom, in verse 6, Chapter XVII, of the book of Genesis, it is said—"and Kings shall come out of thee."

Imam Hossein, the brother of Imam Hussan, the grandson of the Prophet, married Shaharbanoo, the daughter of Yezdegherd, the last of the Saffanides Kings of Persia, who reigned between 202 and 636 A. D., the founder of that family being Ardeshar Babegan, the son of Sassan. In 1636, Yezdegherd was overpowered by the Arabians and his daughter married Hussan, the issue of which marriage was a child, named Fatema Soghra, who married Hussan Masanna, the son of Imam Hossien, thus uniting both branches of the Prophet's descendants. Nawab Hussan Ali Meerza has, therefore, an uninterrupted pedigree, extending backwards for nearly four thousand years.

Ibraheem, the great grandson of Ali, was called Taba Tabi, meaning pure, unsullied and excellent and from him is traced the descent of the Murshidabad family, of which Hussan Ali is the present head.

Syud Hussien Najafi, Taba Tabi, the grand-father of Meer Jaffer, was the first to rise in prominence in India. He was much respected by the Emperor Aurengzebe, who gave his niece in marriage with him. The Emperor offered him a Subadarship, which he, however, declined. He thereupon appointed him his Darogah Byutat or the Lord Steward of the Empire.

Najaf Khan, Meer Jaffer's uncle, was Deputy Steward and also Governor of the fortress of Gwaliar. Najaf Khan, another uncle of Meer Jaffer, was Deputy Governor of Orissa.

Meer Jaffer married Sha Khanum, the step-sister of Ali Verdi Khan, who belonged to the Afsar tribe of Turks, the same tribe to which belonged Nader Sha and Shuja Khan. The latter married Azmatunnissa, alias Jinatunnissa, the mother of Serferaz Khan and daughter of Murshed Kuli Khan.

Burra Saheb, the name by which young Hussan Ali was known, shewed, in his boyhood, signs of extraordinary intelligence and received his early lessons in English and Persian and the Arabic scriptures, in which he shewed marked progress. Accompanied by his two younger brothers, Wala Kadr alias Mujleh Saheb and Humayun Kadr, alias Ameer Saheb, he was, in 1865, sent to England, to complete his education, in charge of Colonel Herbert. All kinds of instructive amusements were provided for the young princes. They put up in the South Kensington Hotel.

They attended the Prince of Wale's Levee, to which the right of private entree was .granted to them. They subsequently removed to Pembroke Square but latterly reverted to the Hotel. Ali Kadr met Lady Williams, a grand daughter of Lord Clive and received attention from all sides. He was introduced to Her Majesty the late Queen Victoria by the Secretary of State. Sandgate, Dover Castle, Southsea, Portsmouth, Birmingham, Coventry, Kidderminister, Worcester, Chester, and Manchester were visited in turn. Leaving London in December of the same year, the party travelled back through France, Italy and Malta, visiting Paris, Bologna, Genoa, Florence, Leghorn, Rome, Naples and Pompeii *en route* and landed in Calcutta in March, 1866. Ali Kadr's second English visit was in company with his father in March, 1869. After a stay of three years, he returned to India.

Upon the Nawab Nazim's retirement in 1880, Nawab Ali Kadr succeeded to the musnud of Murshidabad in the life-time of his father. His installation ceremony was performed in the Throne Room of the Palace on Tuesday, the 27th March, 1883, at 6 P. M., by Sir Rivers Thompson, the Lieutenant Governor of Bengal, who delivered to him in a Durbar the Sanad of the Viceroy dated the 17th February, 1882, conferring upon him the heriditary title of Nawab Bahadur of Murshidabad.

On the 16th February, 1887, Nawab Hussan Ali Meerza Bahadur was created a Knight Commander of the most eminent order of the Indian Empire.

On the 28th May, 1887, the oriental titles of Ihtisham-ul-Mulk, Raes-ud-Dowla and Amir-ul-Omrah were conferred upon him.

Sir Hussan Ali was made a Knight Grand Commander of the above order on the 20th May, 1890, under a Royal Warrant, bearing the sign Manual of Her Majesty the late Queen Victoria.

He set himself with assiduity to the settlement of Nizamut affairs. His labours for the regeneration of the house of Meer Jaffer resulted in an agreement with the Secretary of State, dated the 12th March, 1891, to which validity was given by an Act of the Indian Legislature, securing to him the heriditary titles of Nawab Bahadur of Murshidabad and Amir-ul-Omrah, carrying with them the precedence, rank, dignity and priveleges of the Primier Noble of the three provinces of Bengal, Behar and Orissa, descendable to his male lineal heirs, according to the right of primogeneture, and a stipend payable from the revenues of the Government of British India, besides the income of the Nizamut State lands. This Indenture settled the controversy and discussion, which had risen to their height under his father, and which had embarrassed the Nazim's position with those difficulties, which proved so full of disaster to His late Highness.

Ever since his assumption of the charge of affairs, the Nawab Bahadur worked with great deligence, effecting vast improvements in all branches of the administration of the Nizamut. His work has been one of steady progress. His successful administration of the estates, his extensive charities, his broad sympathies, catholic in their character and not limited by caste, creed or nationality, his readiness to help the poor and to succor the distressed, his liberal hospitality, his devotion to public good, his humility, simplicity, kindness, generosity and benevolence, his keen sense of justice tempered with mercy and his amiability have made up a career for him, which every one admires and respects. He is the receipient of the good wishes of the Suzerain and the subject, of the rich and the poor, and of the high and the low, such as no Nawab on the musnud of Murshidabad had the fortune to won. The whole of his resources is for the good of others. In charity he gives, and gives liberally, but silent tears trickle down his cheeks, because he feels he cannot give more.

Old fossilized ideas, that a Nawab need do nothing in the world beyond spending his time and resources for his personal enjoyment, never found encouragement from Nawab Sir Hussan Ali Meerza Bahadur. His Highness has always thought of others before thinking of himself. Even in the most insignificant daily affair of the distribution of betel, the Nawab Bahadur has his spoon of pestled *pan*, after that leafy luxury in spicy cubes has been served out to all his visitors.

To all loyal and benevolent movements, the Nawab Bahadur has always extended his patronage. In his evening drives, he has stopped to hear the wails and cries of want and poverty, of distress and privation, vouchsafing immediate relief. During floods and fires, he has thrown open the grounds and halls of the Killah for the shelter of thousands of afflicted persons, not fearing for one moment the possibilities of the outbreak of disease from overcrowding and the dangers of contagion. To persons suffering from such distress, he has given food and shelter alike. Few appeal to him in vain. Few tales of sorrow do not readily strike the chord of his sympathetic heart.

The Koran and the Tusbi hang above his pillow. He never neglects his prayers and benedictions. His daily practices are a silent but most eloquent lesson to many. The mere mention of Imam Hossein's name, not to speak of his martyrdom, invariably draws forth his tears. The Nawab Bahadur attends the Moharram Mujlis and pnts on the chain of humiliation. On the eighth day of the ceremony, he distributes purses to persons in real distress.

In the daily functions of his examplary life, he is punctual to the minute. His durbar is open to all persons of respectability. His Highness receives visitors daily, and for every one he has a kind word of enquiry. Considerate, amenable to reason, devoid of ostentation, loyal to the backbone, the Nawab Bahadur lives for the good of others and considers a day lost on which he does not do some good to his people.

His Highness went on improving the resources and status of the Nizamut, when, in 1890, to the utter misfortune of Murshidabad, the fortunes of which occupied so large a place in his magnanimous mind, he was afflicted by a stroke of paralysis from which he has been suffering, in spite of which the Nawab Bahadur has all along been conspicuous for the good qualities which adorn him. Upon his staff, His Highness places implicit reliance and believes firmly that every one in his post is doing his duty. The two highest offices of State are held by two gentlemen of conspicuous merit, each an adept in his line: Khondkar Fazl Rubbee, Khan Bahadur, would have done credit to the seat of the great Dewan, Kurtullub Khan; while Babu Janaki Nath Paure is an ornament to the *Sanctorium* of the Secretariat, unhallowed by the misdeeds of Fox and his fraternity.

Since the great earthquake of the 12th June, 1897, His Highness had been living in a lowly Bunglow, within sight of the stately Palace, which together with other buildings were greatly damaged by that catastrophe. He has of late removed to the New Palace.

In the early part of 1902, His Highness had the unprecedented honor of a visit from the Viceroy of India. During His Excellency's stay at the Palace, where the Viceroy was a guest of the Nawab Bahadur, Lord Curzon made most frequent and solicitous enquiries regarding His Highness's health. At the

Bunglow His Excellency returned the Nawab Bahadur's visit, the first occassion the Viceroy of all India entered a straw thatched shed.

Close upon the first anniversary of Lord Curzon's visit, His Highness had the pleasure of receiving Lord Powis, the fifth in descent from Lord Clive, who had the inconceiveable pleasure of shaking hands with the seventh in descent from Meer Jaffer. Lord Powis coming to view the portrait of Meer Jaffer, which he had never seen before, intuitively recognized it and ejaculated—"That I think is Meer Jaffer."

A couple of months later, the Maharajah of Nattore had the honor of an interview with His Highness, who received the descendant of Rani Bhowani very cordially. The Brahmin aristocratic head of Bengal presented a nuzur of gold mohers, which were touched and remitted by the Amir-ul-Omrah, who at parting placed the garland of honor round his neck.

When the scheme of the Victoria Memorial Hall at Calcutta was first mooted, His Highness wrote unsolicited to the Viceroy to offer some of the beautiful and unique historical objects of interest in his possession, which His Highness had taken particular care to preserve or collect and which would, in themselves, provide the nucleus of a first class collection. This generosity is but one instance of the many voluntary offers of help which the Nawab Bahadur has made in various directions. The offer was gracefully acknowledged by the Viceroy in his speech at the Museum, where His Excellency held an Exhibition of the articles sent.

In pursuance of his father's will and at great cost, His Highness caused the remains of the last Nawab Nazim to be removed for interment at Kerbella in Arabia, where His Highness has founded an endowment for the maintenance of the tomb and the performance of the rites and ceremonies in connection with it.

The Nawab Bahadur's eldest son, Prince Wasif Ali Meerza Bahadur, was born on the 7th January, 1875. His Highness sent him to England for education at the early age of twelve, accompanied by his younger brother, Sahebzada Nasir Ali Meerza, and under the charge of Mr. Coles, the Principal of the Doveton College, Calcutta, as *ataliq*. He was educated at Sherbourne, Rugby and then at the Trinity College, Oxford. The Prince, after completing his courses, visited places of importance in England and travelled extensively in Scotland, Ireland, France, Germany, Italy, Austria, Turkey and Egypt, returning to Murshidabad with his brother on the 27th October, 1895.

The reception of Prince Wasif on his return from England was an affair of unprecedented grandeur. The Nawab Bahadur, accompanied by his friend, Mr. S. E. J. Clarke, the late lamented and talented Secretary of the Bengal Chamber of Commerce, proceeded as far as Jeaganj to receive him. On that occasion, the people of Murshidabad exhibited a spon-

THE HON'BLE PRINCE WAS!FALI MEERZA BAHADUR.

(From a London Photo)

MAZUMDAR'S MURSHIDABAD FANCY PRESS.

tanaety of feeling, which spoke well of their loyalty. The voluntary street decorations were on a superb scale, and the procession of carriages, which followed the four-in-hand, in which the Prince drove with his father, was the largest ever seen in Murshidabad, and marks of respect and attention were visible every where throughout the route. The meeting of the father and the son was one of mixed feelings, when, after eight years, the Prince, who had left his father hale and hearty, returned to find him afflicted with hemiplœgia. Every body present was visibly affected when the father embraced the son.

Shortly after his return, that is, in November, 1895, His Highness initiated Prince Wasif Ali Meerza Bahadur into the administration of the affairs of the Nizamut, investing him with authority over the several departments. In grasping intricate questions of State, the Prince has shewn commendable aptitude. His keen intelligence penetrates into everything, however complicated.

Into the younger generation of Murshidabad, the Prince has infused a spirit of activity, which is admirable. People, who do no more than waste their time in idle gossip, are engaged by him in healthy sports and games, and given occupations requiring skill and labour.

Prince Wasif respects the traditions of the House and is strict in his religious practices, being an ardent believer in the faith of his forefathers.

The Prince shewed his deep interest in public matters by accepting the Chairmanship of the Murshidabad Municipality in 1899. In 1901, he was appointed a member of the Bengal Legislative Council. His successful interpellations, regarding primary education in Bengal and accidents from overhead electric wires in Calcutta, bore ample fruit. On his elevation to the Bengal Council, he received an ovation at Murshidabad, on which occasion, he declared that in the administration of the affairs of the great House to which he belonged, he would follow the living example of his august father.

In 1901, the Hon'ble Prince Wasif Ali Meerza Bahadur was selected by the Viceroy to represent Bengal at the Coronation of the King Emperor in London, a complimentary message of which Lord Curzon was himself the bearer, on the occasion of His Excellency's visit to the Nawab Bahadur.

At the banquet given at the Palace, the Hon'ble Prince, in proposing the Viceroy's health, delivered an eloquent speech, which was much admired by Lord Curzon.

In public benevolent movements and institutions, the Prince takes the greatest interest. He recognises the fact that it is essential for the welfare of a country that the scions of its aristocracy, no matter if the royal blood flows in their veins, should not be divorced from public life, and that rank and position should not be a dispensation from work instead of a call to it.

As a guest of the Government of Bengal, the Hon'ble Prince attended the Delhi Coronation Durbar of the first of January, 1902. There he was introduced to His Royal Highness the Duke of Cannaught, who recognized him as one of the Government guests at the Coronation in London. His splendid mein, majestic gait, noble bearing and remarkable address attracted universal attention at Delhi.

The Prince was married to the daughter of his uncle, Nawab Wala Kadr Syud Hossein Ali Meerza Bahadur, the second brother of the Nawab Bahadur and his life-long companion. On the 14th November, 1901, a son was born to the Prince, who has been named Wares Ali Meerza, a loveable boy, who is a joy to his father and to his grand-father as also to those who behold him.

Of the numerous brothers of the Nawab Bahadur of Murshidabad, all but a few have, one by one, been gathered unto the great majority. Of the few survivors, the next in age to His Highness of Murshidabad is Nawab Wala Kadr Syud Hossein Ali Meerza Bahadur, whose genial temper, coupled with a strong desire to do good and a sense of disinterestedness, is the admiration of all. In prosperity and adversity, in health and sickness, in happiness and despondency, Nawab Wala Kadr has been the constant companion of his friends and relations. He is a keen sportsman and an intelligent conversationist. His *beaux esprits* have cheered up many a sorrowing home and his jocundity has brightened up many a sombre hearth. He is one of those members of the Nizamut family, who have not, in their lives, touched coin. Nawab Wala Kadr enjoys a reputation as a good Persian scholar and is a poet and vercifier besides.

Of His Highness's other younger brothers, Dara Kadr Syud Khakan Meerza and Soleman Kadr Syud Vahed Ali Meerza have been useful members as Chairmen of the local Municipality and Honorary Magistrates of the local Bench, while Fluk Kadr Syud Nasir Ali Meerza, who was the manager of the affairs of his grand-mother, Her Highness the late Nawab Raesunnissa Begum Saheba, has, since her death, been living a life of absolute seclusion at Murshidabad, going occasionally out of the city for change; and Asman Kadr Syud Asad Ali Meerza utilizes his time as an amateur artist of no inconsiderable merit.

Besides two daughters, His Highness the Nawab Bahadur has three other sons, namely Sahebzadas Iskander Kadr Syud Nasir Ali Meerza, Wasif Kadr Syud Asif Ali Meerza and Syud Mohsen Ali Meerza.

The old family coat-of-arms, adopted by the Nawab Bahadur of Murshidabad with a slight modification, consists of the shield, protected by a royal Bengal tiger on one side and the unicorn on the other, on which is a fish representing the Mahi Murateb, the rank bestowed upon His Highness's ancestors by the Emperors of Delhi; on the top or crest is a Zulfekar, or the double bladed sword of Ali, which is the family insignia. The motto on the riband is *Nil Desperandum.* The color of the standards resting on either side are red and green, emblemetic of Hussan and Hossien.

If there is one sincere prayer, more animated than another, which rises daily from the heart of Murshidabad, *it* is that God in His Infinite Mercy may prolong the days of the Nawab Bahadur of Murshidabad and give him health, happiness and comfort.

PART II.

PLACES AND OBJECTS OF INTEREST AT MURSHIDABAD.

Chemen ka tukt pur shahe gulka tajammul thha,
Hazaron bul bulonke fouj thhee shore thha o'ghul thha,
Khenza ke din jo ja dekha, na thha juz khar gulshunme,
Dekhata baghban, ro ro, ihan gulcha ihan gul thha.

THE SOUTH GATE OF THE KILLAH.

FANCY PRESS.

THE KILLAH NIZAMUT.

Situated on the left or eastern bank of the Bhagirathee, the Killah or Fort commands a delightful landscape. It contains the Palace, the Imambara, the Medina, the residential quarters, three mosques, a clock tower, Bunglows and other innumerable buildings.

The Killah is entered by many gates, the principal one of which is the Dakshin Durwaza or Southern Gate. The Chowk Gate and the Imambara Gate are also magnificent gates. All these are sufficiently high to admit elephants with *umbaries* to pass through.

The main gates are surmounted by Nowbut Khanas, where kettle drums, hautboys, trumpets, cymbols and other instruments produce an animating music, which can be heard from miles afar. Ordinarily the Nowbut plays once in the early morning, once at sunset and once at midnight. But on Sundays and days of festivities, such as the Id, it plays every three hours, day and night. However discordant the music may seem to ears not accustomed, the midnight and the early morning strains are indeed sweet. The speaking trumpets, which invariably follow the musical portion of the performances are, like the morning gun, useful in arousing people for early prayer and early work.

The river front of the Killah is about a mile in length. The embankment is studded with sentry boxes and lamp posts. There are several ghats, some made of stone. The one near the Imambara is called the Mint ghat. That to a little south of it is the Lat ghat, while the ghat, with a picturesque wooden and corrugated iron shed, near the residential Deori, is a recent addition, which has enhanced the beauty of the embankment.

At the South Gate, every morning and evening, a small guard of honor, with fife and tambourin, is drawn up to present arms, and from the battery two guns are fired, remnants of the military character of the Killah Nizamut.

On the embankment, stand two mosques, looking like two gold and silver crowns, one near the Palace and the other near the Southern Gate.

THE PALACE.

The Palace, called the Burra Kothee or Hazardooari, is a large and imposing pile of buildings in the Italian style, the proportions of which are preferred by some to those of the Government House at Calcutta. It is the chief object of attraction in Murshidabad and has more points of interest than probably any other secular building in India. It is a most magnificent edifice, holding a most distinguished place in works of architecture. It is 424 feet long, 200 feet broad and 80 feet high. The first floor is reached by an external flight

THE PALACE.

KUNTALINE PRESS, CALCUTTA.

of stairs, perhaps the largest in India. Thirty seven steps of stone, the lowermost one of which is 108 feet long, lead up to the upper portico; seven stately pillars, the perimeter of each of which, at the base, is 18 feet, support the pediment, in the tympanium of which is the Nawab's coat of arms and unicorn in ultra relievo. On either side, at the foot of the grand staircase, is a masonry lion in sitting posture, at the back of which are stone slabs imbedded in the walls of the pedastals for triple lamp posts, one bearing an inscription in Persian and the other in English, which runs thus:—

THE FOUNDATION STONE OF THIS PALACE WAS LAID ON THE 29th AUGUST, A. D. 1829, BY HIS HIGHNESS THE NAWAB NAZIM HUMAYUN JAH BAHADUR, IN THE PRESENCE OF THE AGENT OF THE GOVERNOR GENERAL, THE COMMANDANT OF THE BRITISH TROOPS, ALL THE EUROPEAN INHABITANTS OF THE STATION AND A LARGE CONCOURSE OF NATIVES.

THE EDIFICE WAS COMMENCED UNDER THE ADMINISTRATION OF THE RIGHT HONOURABLE LORD WILLIAM CAVENDISH BENTINCK, G. C. B., AND COMPLETED IN DECEMBER A. D. 1837, DURING THE ADMINISTRATION OF THE RIGHT HONOURABLE GEORGE AUCKLAND, G. C. B., GOVERNORS GENERAL OF INDIA.

DESIGNED BY COLONEL DUNCAN McLEOD, OF THE BENGAL CORPS OF ENGINEERS AND EXECUTED ENTIRELY BY NATIVES UNDER HIS SOLE SUPERINTENDENCE.

The concrete bed for laying the foundation of the Palace was dug so deep that Nawab Humayun Jah, in descending to it, had to step down a ladder and the close atmosphere, consequent on the depth of the excavation and the large concourse of people that, like a thick wall, stood surrounding it, were responsible for an awkward incident, for His Highness fainted away and had to be helped up, when he had laid the foundation stone and declared it to have been well and truly laid. The propinquity of the Palace to the bank of the scouring Bhagirathee, from the edge of which it is within 40 feet, has been censured by some as an act of engineering indescretion. But the foundation walls, laid so deep, are supposed to afford sufficient protection.

This remarkable building, unique in design, embodying most artistic work, and which may be called an architectural triumph, elicits universal admiration. Its stately dimensions cannot be realized from the illustration, in which a facade of fifty lacs of square inches have been miniatured into one of fifteen square inches only. Each of the four facades is different. The perimeter is therefore different on the four sides.

There are four inner stair-cases of peculiar construction, consisting of seventy-six steps each, all but two of which are paved with stone and protected by rails topped by well-polished mahogany. The steps and the stairs are, to all appearances, supportless at the exterior ends. These lead up to the corridors. At the corners, are four spiral stair-cases for servants. The uppermost stair-case leads to the roof, from which a beautiful panoramic view is obtained of the Killah and the surrounding country. The top of the dome is about 15 feet above the topmost roof and standing on it, of the city beyond the Killah, little meets the eye except a dense green forest, the monotony of which is broken by the white-washed tops of a few brick-built houses.

The exterior walls of the ground floor are over 6 feet wide. The Toshakhana, the Armoury, the Record room, and various offices are located on the ground floor.

On the first floor are the throne room, the drawing room, the banqueting hall, the billiard room, bed and office rooms, chambers, sitting rooms and the boudoir. On the second or topmost floor are the Library, the Ball room, ante-rooms, bed rooms &c.

The whole building is divided into three blocks, connected by corridors and rooms. Between the central and each of the two blocks, on the east and the west, are two open quadrangles planted with crotons.

An iron railing runs round the edifice, the ground between being laid out in gardens or lawns.

The halls, corridors and rooms, throughout, are commodious and handsome and are fitted up with matchless splendour. The decorations are rich and gorgeous ; the embellishments and furniture are of corresponding elegance and unite every thing that is good and lovely.

The DURBAR or THRONE ROOM is a round room fifty feet in diameter, surmounted by a dome 63 feet high, from the centre of which hangs by three massive chains a superb chandelier, with one hundred and one branches. The floor is one of well polished marble. Magnificent candelabras, bearing numerous lights, and statues add to the unique splendour of the room. On opposite sides, facing each other, are two marble stands, one worked or inlaid with gold, on which, on occasions of State, are placed the State Chair or Throne. The ceiling of the dome is done up and ornamented with sky blue enamel, pink and gold. When lighted up, the room presents a scene of surpasing beauty. The marble underneath reflects the lights above. The eye loves to linger on every object in the Palace, but on none more than the Throne room, with its superb dome dazzling overhead, the admiring spectator seeming lost in its beauty, its majesty and its vastness.

The equipments of the DRAWING ROOM, every article of which is in keeping with its surroundings, are as rich, comfortable and magnificent as can be conceived. The floor is covered with a beautiful carpet upon which, besides two round tables of massive marble, are innumerable couches, sofas and chairs of ivory, (which is solid and not veneered), velvet and plush. Splendid chiffoniers stand against the lower walls, while the upper portions are hung up with life-size pictures in massive gilt frames, one of

A NICHE IN THE ROUND ROOM.

which is the celebrated portrait of King William IV, presented by His Majesty to the Nawab Nazim Humayun Jah. Valuable vases and beautiful marble figures, some under glasses, adorn the mantle pieces, and side tables.

The BOUDOIR, now used as a bed room, is fitted up most luxuriously. Of the beds, the largest one is that which was used by the Nawab Nazim Humayun Jah. Netted within its curtain and sunk in the softness of its mattresses, one may well consider himself lost.

The FIREPLACES are cosiest and most delightful, with mantlepieces of marble, surmounted by beautiful pictures.

The BILLIARD ROOM contains one of the best and well set tables in India.

The BANQUETING HALL is 189 feet long and 27 feet broad, with a floor of exquisite marble. Sliding doors, which have been substituted for those of mirror, when adjusted, divide the hall into three appartments.

The CHINA ROOM of the Palace, located on the topmost floor, contains a collection of old and rare specimens of great variety and value, with which the stands and tables are studded and the walls decorated in various devices. Stoneware and earthenware, glazed, enamelled, vitreous, translucent fabriques, belonging both to the old China porcelain and modern European manufacture, such as Dresden, Sevres and Worcester and majolica and several classes of faience make up a really facinating collection, which it is a delight to behold, and which, like the armoury and the picture galleries, is unrivalled in India.

The LIBRARY contains a large and varied collection of books and most rare and valuable oriental manuscripts. Graphical embellishments of various kinds, brilliantly colored inks, gold, enamel, highly finished ornamental and floral designs, of every conceiveable fanciful and elegant description, make the Korans and other books gorgeous and artistically beautiful. Some are mere perfections of the caligrapher's art. The collection of Korans is unique in India. The total number of volumes in the Palace Library, Arabic, Persian, Urdu, English, &c., is considerable.

The following are only a few specimens. Books marked with an asterisk * have been sent for the Victoria Memorial.

KORANS.

1. Koran, written in Nastaliq character by Hossein Tabrezi for Nawab Sha Beg Khan. Bears, on the second page, the Persian royal *Sher Khurshed* or Lion and Sun Coat of arms, which is also painted on the last page of the book, which bears impressions of several seals, indicating ownership at different times, namely the seals of—

(*a*) Sultan Mahomed Soleman Meerza Safavi, Sha of Persia (1153 H.) with the crown of Persia.

THE DRAWING ROOM.

(*b*) Abul Fazl of Akber's Court.

(*c*) Nizamul-Mulk Moniruddowla Khadem Hossein Khan, Nasir Jang.

(*d*) Momtazuddowla Shujaul Mulk Sadat Ali Khan Bahadur, Nawab of Oudh.

(*e*) Iftekharuddowla Mokramul Mulk Syud Hussan Ali Khan Bahadur, Feroze Jang.

(*f*) Serferazuddowla Nazim ul Mulk Hussan Reza Khan Bahadur, Jaffer Jang.

2. Koran Alumgiri, owned by the Emperor Alumgir for his personal use. Copied in 665 H. by Yaqoot Mustasimi, the celebrated caligrapher, who improved the present Arabic character from the Koofi style. He was the slave of Mostasem Billa, Khalipha of Bagdad. A very old Koran, well written and illuminated. Bears the great seal of the Emperor Aurengzebe, in the middle of which is engraved—"*Aul Mozaffer Mohiuddeen Aurengzebe Bahadur Alumgir Badsha Ghazi*, 1076 H.", and around it are engraved the namas of his ancestors.

3. Koran, written by Faizulla Mashadi in the time of Aurengzebe (1105 H.) for Meerza Mahomed Kuli Beg. The cost, Rs. 4,515, is endorsed on the book.

4. Koran, caligraphed by Mahomed Abdul Baker Huddad, known as Huddad, the best caligrapher; 1118 H.

5. Koran, the whole book copied on sixteen pages only.

6 Koran, caligraphed by Yaqoot Raqam Khan. Very rare and one of the oldest properties of the Nizamut.

7. Koran, Khatthkoofi, that is, written in Koofi character, on parchment, before the invention of paper or the present Arabic character, probably in the first century of the Hejeira. Some pages are missing.

8. Koran, written in gold ink. Very old and rare.

9. Koran, written in red ink by Mahamed Mostaqim. Profusely illuminated.

10. Koran, caligraphed by Mahomed Areff Yaqoot Raqam Khan, written on gold leaf. Very fine and rare.

11. Koran, caligraphed by Mahomed Afzul, son of Mahomed Ali, on blue paper, with gold ink. (1099 H.)

12. Pansoora, a small volume containing five chapters of the Koran, written on gold leaf.

13. Koran, written in Cashmere. Beautifully enamelled.

14. Koran, belonging to the Library of the Emperors of Delhi and bearing the seals of Alumgir and Sha Alum.

15. Koran, written in 1709 by Ahmed Nairees, one of the best caligraphers of the Arabic character; very rare.*

16. Koran, a small volume, two inches by two inches.

17. Koran, a large volume, twenty-four inches by twelve inches, written for Nasiruddeen Hyder, King of Oudh; cost Rs. 30,000.*

THE BANQUETING HALL OF THE PALACE. FANCY PRESS.

18. Koran, in the handwriting of Ali, brought from Arabia by Shuja Khan at a cost of one lac of rupees. Originally kept in the mosque at his mausoleum at Roshnibagh. Brought to the Library but removed for safer custody and better care to the Nizamut Imambara. An object of great veneration of which the *Zayaruth* is performed by devout Mahomedans.

19. Koran, written by Yaqoot Mustasimi.*

SECULAR BOOKS.

1. Morocca, caligraphed by the celebrated Persian, Meerza Vesal, known as Haji Durbesh, who was unrivalled in the Shafia character. Ornamented with floral designs, much admired as a work of art.

2. Moroccajat Alamgiri, or Selections from the writings of celebrated caligraphers and the works of celebrated painters. Prepared for Aurengzebe before his accession to the throne of Delhi.

3. Tofeh Asafia, caligraphed by Hafez Nurulla, written by Mahomed Mohsen, the son of Fokruddeen Ahmed Khan Bahadur, for Nawab Asfuddowla, Subadar of Oudh.

4. Timurnamah, written in 1,000 H. Illustrated. Old. Writing good. Gilt and enamelled.

5. Dewan-e-Laqueeth, caligraphed by Yaqoot Mustasami in 682 H.

6. A volume containing the following books written for Amir Jelaluddeen Khalilulla Bostani in 870 H.,—

(*a*) Dewan Amir Khusroo.

(*b*) Dewan Hafez.

(*c*) Dewan Hussan.

(*d*) Dewan Kasem.

(*e*) Dewan Maghrabi.

(*f*) Dewan Moulana Saeed.

(*g*) Dewan Toosi.

(*h*) Dewan Resala Anisul Arifin.

(*i*) Resala Maqasemath.

(*j*) Resala Anisun Ashekin.

(*k*) Resala Sawal Jawab.

7. Anwar Sohli, caligraphed by Mahomed Yusuf Samarcandi in 940 H., in the time of Humayun, the Emperor of Delhi, in very good Nastaliq character, containing many good illustrations. Belonged to the Emperor Akber. Bears his seal and his signature in the form—"*Dida Shud Allah Akber.*"

8. A volume containing the following books, caligraphed in 992 H. by Abul Kasem, son of Sultan Hossein.

(*a*) Mukzunul Asrar.

(*b*) Sekundarnamah.

(*c*) Sekundarnamah Behri.

(*d*) Khusroo Sheereen.

(*e*) Laila Majnoo.

(*f*) Bostan Sheik Sadi.

(*g*) Khumsa Nizami.

9. Khumse Nizami, caligraphed by Syud Ali in 898 H. Very good writing. Illuminated. Gilt. On the first page there is an endorsement, from which it appears that the book was "purchased at Aurangabad at the time of the Dewani." It seems that Murshed Kuli Khan purchased it when he was Dewan in the Deccan and brought it with him to Bengal.

10. Tuzuk Timoori, written by the celebrated Hafez Ibraheem by order of Sha Alum.

11. Selections from Poets, very good handwriting. Bears the seal of Sha Alum, to whose library it belonged.

12. Tuzkurah-ut-Shora or the Lives of Poets. By Doulat Sha, son of Alauddowla Bakht Sha Ghazi Sumarcandi. Caligraphed, in 892 H., for the author, by Mahomed Amen, son of Syud Mahomed. Writing good. Matter enclosed by lines of gold.

13. Akbernamah, in two volumes. In the handwriting of Abul Fazl Allami, minister of Akber. On the first page is written—

"*Khutteh Allami Sehi danund*," meaning "know for certain that this is written by Allami," that is Abul Fazl. On the same page are the seals of several Emperors, but most of these have been erased out and are illegible. One seal reads—"Hum dum o hum raz Jehangir Badsha," meaning friend and private companion of Emperor Jehangir. In the second volume is a seal in which is engraved "*Afzul Khan bandae Sha Jehan.*" *Bandae* means servant of.

This is the original manuscript work in the handwriting of the author himself, namely, Abul Fazl, one of the *Nabaratna*, or Nine Jewels of the Court of Akber.

14. Dewan Maghrabi, caligraphed in 883 H. Bears the seals of the Emperors and belonged to the Imperial Library of Delhi.

15. Tufsir Molla Hosseini, by the son of Ali-ul-waez-ul Kashefi. Written in 897 H.

16. Subhutool Abrar, by Molla Jami, written in Nastaliq character in 949 H.

17. Mustaphanamah, or Universal History, in verse, a very big volume, written for Sha Shuja, the son of Emperor Sha Jehan.

18. Bostan Sadi, in very good Nustaliq character, gilt, enamelled and decorated with floral designs. Very old and valuable. Caligraphed by Meerza Mahomed, son of Sha Mahomed Turkestani.

19. Huft Paikur, by Nizami. Illustrated, good handwriting.

20. Huft Band Kashi, writing very good. Written for Khan Khanan Monaim Khan, Subadar of Bengal in 1574.

21. Shanamah, in Nastaliq character. Gilt. Illuminated and illustrated throughout. On the last page there are endorsements which are translated thus :—"Presented by Sultan Sha Safivi on the 14th Rajab, 975 H. in the capital of Ispahan. Received into the treasures of the Library."

AKBER'S NOWRATN DURBAR.

1 Hakim Haman 2 Raja Toder Mall 3 Raja Man 4 Raja Birbal 5 Mollah Dopeaza
6 Faizy 7 Abul Fazl 8 Mirza [illegible] 9 [illegible] Khan Khana.

"Allah Akber dated the 31st of the month of Urdi Bahesht, the 21st year, made over to the custody of Khajeh Ambar."

"Dated Tuesday, the 22nd Shawal, 1015 H., corresponding to the 2nd month of Isphandar, year 2; seen by the Emperor."

"Belonged to Shazada Daniel; made over to the custody of Mollah Saleh Ketabdar (Librarian). Signed by Sheik Sadr."

A Persian endorsement translated as follows, appears in the handwriting of Emperor Jehangir—

"Belonged to Daniel deceased. Received by humble Jehangir."

This book was written in 829 H. for Shazada Baisanker Khan, the son of Amir Timur, as appears from the preface of the book. Sha Tamash, the second King of Persia of the Saffi dynasty (975 H.) presented the book to Akbar, who presented it to his third son, Sultan Daniel, upon whose death it was inherited by Jehangir. All this appears from the preface and the endorsements and seals on the first and the last pages.

22. Poetical works of the celebrated poets of Persia, compiled and written in 870 H.

23. Pandanamah Jehangiri, in seven volumes, caligraphed by Mir Emad in 1607 for the Emperor Jehangir in unique Nastaliq character. Mir Emad was a great caligrapher who came to India from Persia in the time of Akber. These volumes were

taken by the English from the Imperial Palace Library of Delhi, during the great Indian Mutiny of 1857 and afterwards sold by Messrs Hamilton and Company, the celebrated jewellers of Calcutta, and purchased by the late Nawab Nazim for Rs. 7,000.*

24. The Sanskrit Drama of Nala Damayanti, translated by Abul Fazl for Akber, pp. 185, with thirty one beautifully painted scenes.*

11. Seir-ul-Mutaqherin. There is in the Palace Library a manuscript copy of the Seir-ul-Mutaqherin in Persian with marginal notes in the author's own handwriting. The Seir-ul-Mutaqhrin which means the Review of the times is a very comprehensive history of the period 1118 to 1195 H. and in its details rivals Roussuae's Confessions or Sully's Memoirs. The author was Syud Golam Hossein Khan, descended from a Tabatabite of the race of Hussan, and related to Serajuddowla, though not quite friendly to him. He commenced the book on Tuesday, the 1st Safar, 1194 H. and completed it in one year; "trusting to my personal knowledge and to what I have been gathering from persons of eminent rank and credit, I have strung the whole together in a plain unornamented style." He wrote both as an author and spectator. Of this interesting work, from which subsequent writers of history have so freely drawn, the first and the third volumes were recovered at Murshidabad by the gentleman who translated them and who was known under the assumed name of

Golam Mustapha, while he found the second volume at Lucknow. The translator describes his stay in Murshidabad as follows :—

"Living myself in the centre of Murshidabad wearing an Hindustani dress and making practice in the evening to walk the streets with only a servant either to listen to or to mix with any company I meet with either there or in the market place I necessarily get a variety of information."

It is worthy of note that the incident of the Black Hole finds no mention in the Seir-ul-Mutaqherin.

The Seir-ul-Mutaqherin was inscribed to Warren Hastings two years after his departure from Bengal.

12. Pandnameh Aristotalis, being a translation of the sayings of Aristotle. Written by Prince Dara Shoko in 1051 H.*

PICTURE BOOKS.

Among the picture books lying on the tables of the Library, the following deserve special notice :—

1. Recollections of the great Exhibition, 1851.
2. Views of Rangoon, 1825.
3. Zoological Researches in Java, 1824.
4. The Ilaid of Homer, the Odyssey of Homer, the Theogony Works and Days and the Days of Hesoid, Compositions from the Tragedies of Aeschylus, designed by John Flaxman and engraved by Thomas Peroli and Frank Howard, 1805-31.

5. Original designs of the most celebrated masters of the Bolognese, Roman, Florentine and Venetian Schools including works of Michæl Angelo, Raphael, Leonardo da Vinici, Lorraine &c. Dedicated to His Majesty of England, 1705.

6. Old English Universities and Chapels, 1814.

7. Layard's Monuments of Ninevah, the palace of Senucherib and the ruins of Nimroud, 1853.

8 The works of William Hogarth from the original plates. Restored by James Heath (1697-1764) with explanations of the subjects of the plates by John Nicholas.

9. Picturesque Representation of the Naval and Military and miscellaneous costumes of Great Britain.

10. Boydell's graphic Illustrations of Shakespeare, 1790.

11. Early Portraits of Queen Victoria.

12. Liber Studiorum of Claude Lorraine. By F. C. Lewis, 1840.

13. Imitations of Claude Lorraine. By do.

14. Interiors and exteriors in Venice. By Lake Price.

15. Household Furniture and Interior Decoration, 1807.

16. Mansions of England in the olden time.

17. Compositions of the Acts of Mercy. By Flaxman, 1831.

18. Antiquities of London and its Environs, 1791.

19. The Cottar's Saturday Night, 1853.

20. Picturesque Voyage to India by way of China, 1810.

21. Wilkin's Sketches in Turkey, Syria and Egypt, 1840.

22. Views and Monuments of Rome.

23. Willyam's Views in Egypt, Palestine &c. 1822.

24. Compositions from Hell, Pergatory and Paradise of Dante Alighiere. By Flaxman.

25. Views of London, 1834.

26. Portraits of the Game and wild animals of Southern Africa, 1840.

27. Twenty-five Imitations of Sir Thomas Lawrence's finest Drawings, Sovereigns, Statesmen, Ladies &c. Dedicated to the Queen. By F. C. Lewis, 1839.

28. Character and Costumes of Afghanistan. By Willis Hart.

29. Smyth's Sketches of the Canadas.

30. English Scenery. By F. C. Lewis.

31. Himalayan Botany, 1839.

32. Eighty-two Prints engraved by F. Bartolozzi.

33. Panorama of Dacca, containing, among others, the site of the Dacca branch of the banking house of Jagat Sett of Murshidabad, after whose death a rumour spread that a large amount of treasure was buried under the house. An extensive excavation was made but only two measures of oil were found to repay the trouble and expense of the search.

34. Plantæ Asiatical Rariores. Presented to the Directors of the East India Company, 1830.

35. Sketches of the Danube, 1838.

36. Illustrations of Constantinople, by F. C. Lewis, 1835.

37. Vie Politique et Militaire de Napolion, 1826.

38. Descriptions and Figures of two hundred fishes of the Coromandel Coast, 1803.

39. Sketches and Drawings of Alhambra, 1833.

40. The Coronation of George IV., 1839.

41. Illustrations Conchyliologiques.

42. Panorama of History.

43. Birds (plates 24 in. by 20 in. colored.)

44. Windsor and its Environs.

45. Dresses of Different Nations, ancient and modern, after the designs of Holbern, Vandyke, &c., 1772.

(*N. B:—In volume IV. of this work, on plate 36, appears the "Habit of Ally Verdi Cawn, Grand-father and predecessor of Serajuddowla."*)

46. The Costume of Hindustan, 1798-99.

The ARMOURY, which is located on the ground floor of the Palace, contains many valuable specimens. The walls are profusely decorated with pieces of armoury, military instruments and accoutrements, curiously arranged and swords, shields, pistols, lances, spears and daggers ingeneously displayed and forming various devices. Many valuable trophies, mostly Indian, cover the walls in delightful abundance.

The guns are mostly (1) *toradar* or match lock, of which there are two kinds, namely *Hindi* or Indian and *Roomi* or Turkish ; and (2) flint lock, made in

STATE CHAIR.

ARMOURY.

FANCY PRESS.

Europe and Monghyr in the sixteenth century and later. The Carabines and *Sherbacha* are mostly of that period. The pistols, which are match lock, flint lock and percussion cap, are both Indian and European and include among them many presented to the Nazims by the East India Company. Of Burchhas, Bhalas and Nezas, there are many, some of which belong to the Hindu period. The swords are of all kinds and periods and countries. Damase swords made at Khorasan by artizans from Damascus in Timurlane's time ; Ispahani swords manufactured by Asadulla, the great sword-maker of the time of Sha Abbas, King of Persia (1582-1638), many of which were made for him ; Daggers of every kind, namely, Afghanistan Chhoras, Peshkubz (Persian), Koroli (Turkish), Qama and Khagar (Arabic); Katars, Bichhooas, Ramdaos, Kukris and Bhoojalis (Indian) ; Shields, Bows and Arrows ; Mohalas or iron pieces for tusks of fighting elephants, Tabrs and Zafer Takias and other varieties make up a collection which is unequalled in India.

Most of the arms in the Palace Armoury are those actually used in battle by the Nazims, their generals, Omras and men. Many of these saw Plassey, Giria, Uduanala &c.

The swords in the Armoury may be classified as follows :—

1 Khorasani	2 Ispahani
3 Magrabi	4 Jenoobi

5 Alamani	6 Dakhni
7 Scinde	8 Dhope
9 Tega Burdwani	10 Nagdaman
11 Salawa	12 Neemcha
13 Katti	14 Soroi
15 Dumtamacha	16 Saif
17 Mahratti	18 Lakai
19 Sowsanpatta	20 Langercut

21 Khanda.

The following are some of the most interesting objects in the Armoury; those marked with an asterisk* having been sent for the Victoria Memorial :—

1. The Peshraw Burchha, a spear, originally belonging to Vikramadittya, taken by the Mahomedans from the Hindus, bearing on the blades the images of Vishnu on the one side and of Goroor on the other. Blade 18 inches long ; the weapon with the shaft and the *boori* (spike) is 8 feet long. Inlaid with gold. It is carried always at the head of processions as a trophy.* (Out of two, one sent for the Victoria Memorial.)

2. A broad blade spear, with a tiger and an elephant on either side of the blade in *bass relievo.* Blade 3 feet by 6 inches.

3 The Saang spear with an iron shaft, which belonged to a great dakoit who lived at Binodenala, north-west of the city, and infested that part of the country. He was killed by Murshed Kuli Khan. Blade 2 feet and 6 inches long.*

4. The sword which belonged to Timurlane. The pointed end is broken. Bears the Persian inscription in gold, *Amir-e-Saheba Keran.**

5. A very old Damask sword, with a groove along the blade, bearing inscribed marks.

6. Ali Verdi Khan's favourite sword, which he used always to keep by his side, even under his pillow at night ; the hilt studded with jewels and inlaid with gold.*

7. A Nakdaman sword, with waved edges, which belonged to Morad Ali Khan of Talpur, near Hyderabad, Scinde.

8. Several Persian swords made by Asadulla at Ispahan during the reign of Sha Abbas, King of Persia, (1582-1628), who made Ispahan the metropolis of Persia.

9. A very old Deccan Khandi (sword) which belonged to the Mahrattas. Blade inscribed and hilt inlaid with silver.*

10. Tehgi Burdwani, or executioner's sword made at Burdwan. 2 feet 6 inches long and 3 inches broad at the hilt.*

11. A sword made at Delhi which belonged to Alumgir, with the inscription—"*La hol bela qoouth ella billa al alial azeem Alumgir Shahi maka jo*"—meaning there is no power nor virtue but in God who is Great and High, belonging to Emperor Alumgir, longing for war.*

12. The Saif, an Arab sword, blade 3 feet 6 inches long, hilt worked in gold, bearing marks inscribed.

13. A straight blade European sword, 2 feet 9 inches long, with a double groove along the blade by Ferara, of the Elizabethan period, with the inscription—

A. H. D. R. E. A.
F. E. R. A. R. A.

14. The Shumsher Morassa, sword sent by Alumgir II., the Emperor of Delhi, with the Sanad, dated the 14th Rubiussani, of the Subadari to Meer Jaffer; reached the Nazim at Futwah, while he was proceeding to Behar.*

15. The sword of Sha Abbas, King of Persia, the very weapon used by him.

16. A Dutch sword, with the year 1762 inscribed thereon, presented by the Dutch to the Nawab Nazim.

17. Khorasani swords made at Khorasan for Timurlane.

18. A beautiful sword by Henry Wilkinson of Pall Mall, London.

19. An Indian sword, made at Delhi with the best steel, the blade, which is elastic, bears the inscription "*Mahomed Shah Ghazi*". 2 feet 6 inches long. One of the favourite swords of the late Nawab Nazim, who used to keep it near his pillow.

20. A Katar or triangular dagger, with a Roman and a modern combat represented on either side of

the blade. Presented to the Nawab Nazim by Warren Hastings.*

21. A dagger belonging to the Hindu period, with an elephant and a man-fight represented on either side of the blade.

22. Indian shields, with the central brass pieces inscribed with Nadeh Ali or benedictions.

23. A pair of pistols richly ornamented and worked in gold and silver, bought by Ali Jah for Rs. 12,000.* (One sent for the Victoria Memorial.)

24. A Dutch long bore cannon, 8 feet long, girth 2 feet 2 inches at the touch hole, diameter of bore at muzzle 2 inches, bearing the following inscription—

GRANS. IANSZ. AMSTELODAMI.

A. D. 1742. MEFECIT. CIPRIANUS.

805.

25. A handsome brass cannon, 7 feet long, with a girth of 2 feet, mounted on a carriage, the muzzle shaped like the head of a demon, with pointed ears, a human face and crocodile's jaws, decorated with floral designs. On a shield is an inscription in the Bengali character which reads thus—"*Jai Kalika Jantoo Tatsat Srijucta Krishna Chandra Rai Maharaja Mahashaia Srijucta Roopram Bandopadya Sri Rajkisore Das Karmokar,*" said to have been brought by Serajuddowla from Calcutta after the surrender of Fort William and the incident of the Black Hole.*

26. A long bore cannon, 4 feet 6 inches long with "*Fateh Azem*" and "Nawab Mir Nosiri Khan Bahadur" inscribed thereon. The gun is made of eight metals and belongs to the class known as shutarnals, which were made in India for the Emperors of Delhi. Mir Noseri Khan, better known as Khan Douran Khan Noser Jang, was a grandee of the time of Sha Jehan and Subadar of the Deccan (1055 H.) This gun, which belonged to him, probably came to Bengal with Prince Azeem Oshan or with Murshed Kuli Khan, both of whom came from the Deccan.

27. A long bore brass cannon, 5 feet long, with a *hashtpahal* or octagonal barrel.

28. A brass cannon, 4 feet 10 inches long, the muzzle shaped like the petals of a lotus. The touch-hole which is shaped like the ear, is by the side of the barrel and not on the top.

29. Guns, made of brass, for fighting boats.

30. A spear with the blade 3 feet 3 inches long.

31. The Toofang or a pipe, which is charged with sharp pointed needles, which are blown off.

32. An old musket, barrel, 6 feet 2 inches long.

33. The Nizamut standard.

There are some arms in the Toshakhana.

The Toshakhana is the repositary of jewels of great value, ornaments of pearls, diamonds, emeralds and rubies, such as singly would be prized as heirlooms in princely families. Some of the gems are famous alike for their size, color and history. Of colored

SOME PALACE JEWELS.

diamonds, there are great varities. Some of the diamonds, emeralds and rubies are gloriously brilliant and of extraordinary size. Their intrinsic value, which by itself is great, is enhanced by the associations which surround them. Some of these are connected with the Emperors of Delhi and have descended from the earlier Nazims, being still discernable in their portraits, which adorn the walls of the Palace.

The following are some of the objects of interest in the Toshakhana :—

1. State sword, Indian blade, 2 feet 7 inches long, bent, fine steel ; hilt, seven and a half inches long, enamelled white and gold, set with carved rubies. The jewels only were valued by Messrs Hamilton and Co. at Rs. 30,000. The history of this sword as to how it came to the Murshidabad family cannot be traced.

2. State sword, Indian blade, hilt, enamelled white and green, set with emeralds, rubies and diamonds. Presented by the Emperor of Delhi to the Nazim.

3. State sword, made at Damascus, blade bent and grooved at the thick edge ; ivory hilt, ornamented with gold, enamelled red and green, and set with diamonds. The scabbard is also set with diamonds. Travelled with the late Nawab Nazim to Europe and was a favorite sword of his and of his father.

4. State sword, blade bent and grooved at the thick end ; jade hilt, ornamented with gold and set

with emeralds and rubies. There is an inscription on the blade which is rendered thus—"Made by Asadulla Ispahani."

5. State sword, made at Damascus, thin blade, jade hilt, set with diamonds, emeralds and rubies. Very old. Presented by the Emperor Mahomed Sha of Delhi to Nawab Nazim Shuja Khan.

6. Katar or dagger, with representations on the blade in bass relievo of an elephant and a tiger and an elephant and a man combat; handle, enamelled and set with jewels. Belongs to the Hindu period. The man wears a *dhoti* and a cap on his head like the crown used by Hindus at the ceremony of marriage.

7. Peshkubz or Persian dagger, jade handle terminating in a horse head.

8. Peshkubz or Persian dagger, crystal handle, scabbard enamelled and bearing the figures of a Turkish man and woman.

9. Tabr or Persian axe. The point opposite the blade is a spiral tongue tapering to a sharp point.

10. Bridegroom's dagger, nine and a fourth inches long, with emerald handle. three and a fourth inches long; scabbard set with pearls and diamonds, carried by bridegrooms at weddings.

11. Big Tiara or Sirpench of diamonds, with three large diamond pendants, of which the middle one only was valued by Messrs Hamilton and Co. at Rs. 30,000. Said to have belonged to the Emperor Akbar.

12. Tiara or Sirpench of cut diamonds, set on petals of diamonds, with five diamond pendants, a unique ornament. It appears in the head dress of Nawab Nazim Najmuddowla.

13. Diamond kulgi or aigrette, set with a large ruby, with large ruby pendants.

14. Carved emerald kulgi or aigrette, gold, set with a large emerald and several large emerald pendants, very old and of fine color.

15. Diamond kulgi or aigrette with diamond pendants.

16. Diamond kulgi, set with five large rubies and three ruby pendants.

17. Aigrette of brilliant diamonds of all colors, white, rose, pink, yellow, green, black &c., set with a brilliant diamond star and two rubies.

18. Diamond aigrette with emeralds set round with diamonds, with pendants of fine colored and flawless emeralds.

19. Three pairs of Bhoojbands or bracelets, set with diamonds and rubies.

20. Two pairs of Dastbands, set with large rubies and diamonds.

21. A beautiful necklace of pearls, rubies and emeralds, with diamond pendants shaped like the petals of a flower. On one of the ruby beads is inscribed—"*Jehangir Sha ebn Akbar Sha* 1018."—Jehangir Sha, son of Akbar Sha, 1018. This is one of the jewels which Mahomed Sha, the Emperor of

Delhi, apprehensive of the invasion of Nader Sha had sent to the Subadar of Bengal for safe custody. Many of these were taken by Meer Kasem, when he fled across the Keramnassa to the dominions of the Vizier of Oudh, who, however, stripped him of those jewels and turned him out of his kingdom.

22. Three large emerald clasps for waist belts, set all round with brilliant diamonds, each emerald measuring two inches by one and a three-fourth inches, the largest size in India. Used sometimes as buckles. These jewels appear in the portraits of many of the Nazims, from Meer Jaffer down to Nawab Feredun Jah.

23. Necklace, set with good emeralds and diamonds.

24. Torra or tassel of pearls for the head dress, being several strings of pearls hanging from an emerald *tukti*, engraved with an extract from the *aitul kursi* Surah of the Koran.

25. A set gold spoons and forks, said to have belonged to Queen Elizabeth.

26. A set (eighteen) emerald buttons, worn by the late Nawab Nazim during his English visit. Very fine and old emeralds.

27. Silver State chair of Meer Jaffer, surmounted with a gold umbrella, with embroidered fringes.

28. Silver State-chair made by Nawab Humayun Jah.

29. Silver State Tonjon of exquisite design and workmanship, jewelled, resting on silver elephants

ELEPHANT WITH UMBARI.

MAJUMDAR'S MURSHIDABAD. FANCY PRESS.

and eagles, with the arms shaped as fish. Made at the time of Humayun Jah.

30. The insignia of the Imperial Order of the Mahi Meratib, consisting of four gold balls, one gold *alam* or standard and one gold head of a fish, all surmounted on poles, cased in gold embroidered cloth, with scales. Presented by the Emperor of Delhi to the Nawab Nazim. The whole set is carried on three elephants walking abreast in state processions. This order used to be given by the Emperors of Delhi to the Nawabs Nazim, as a mark of very great honor.

31. The collar, insignia and badge of the Royal Hanoverian Guelphic order. Presented by His Majesty King William IV. to His Highness the Nawab Nazim Humayun Jah, with an autograph letter from His Majesty.

32. The star, collar and badge of Knight Grand Commander of the most eminent Order of the Indian Empire. Presented by Her Majesty the late Queen Victoria to His Highness the Nawab Bahadur of Murshidabad, under a Royal Warrant bearing the Sign Manual of Her Majesty.

33. Silver and Ivory *Umbaries* for elephants, covered with richly embroidered velvet.

34. Kamalpukhri silver Howdah, surmounted with a silver umbrella.

35. Nalki or open palanquin, made of ivory.

36. Jhapanak or ladies palanquin, covered with gold cloth.

37. Gold embroidered *Kanats* or Tent purdah walls of great beauty and value, captured by Ali Verdi Khan from the Mahrattas in 1746.* (One sent for the Victoria Memorial.)

The RECORD ROOM, which is on the ground floor of the Palace, contains valuable treaties, engagements, firmans, *sanads* and letters, some in originals and some in photographic and manuscript copies.

The correspondence with Mobarakuddowla on the one hand and the Governor and officials and the nobles of the provinces on the other, is most interesting, having relation to the events which culminated in the transfer of the Nazim's powers to the East India Company.

In the list given below, the originals of the documents marked with an asterisk* have been sent to the Victoria Memorial. Of these, photographic copies have been substituted, which are as good as the originals.

There are eighteen firmans from the Emperors of Delhi to Meer Jaffer; two to Najmuddowla; fourteen to Syefuddowla and twelve to Mobarakuddowla.

Of letters to the Nazims, that dated the 19th Showal, of the fifth year of the reign of the Emperor of Delhi, is from Carnac, written from Mohobbelipur, near Patna, when he was fighting in the interests of the Nazim with the Emperor, congratulating His Highness on the victory obtained by him. There are six other letters. all written in the same fifth year,

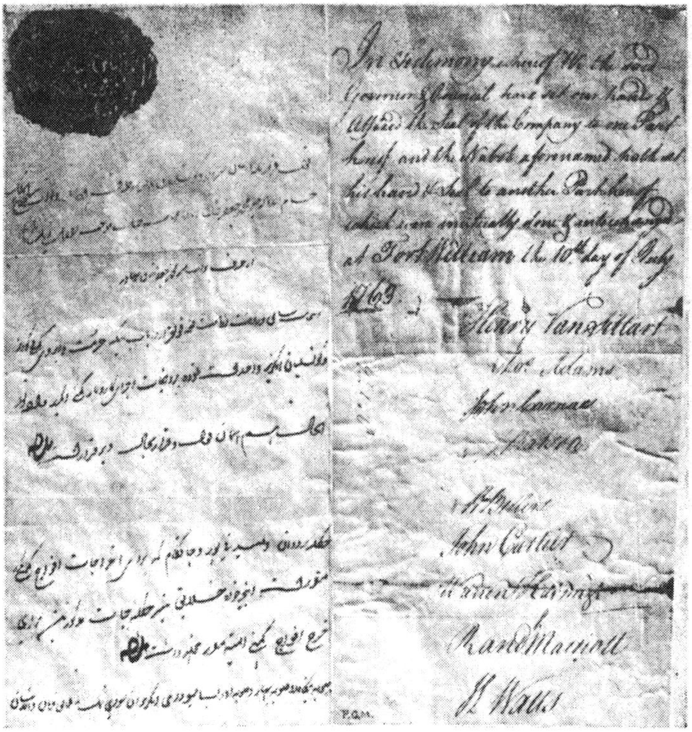
In testimony whereof We the said Governor & Council have set our hands & affixed the Seal of the Company to one Part hereof and the Nabob aforenamed hath set his hand & seal to another Part hereof which were mutually done & interchanged at Fort William the 10th day of July 1763.

Henry Vansittart

John Carnac

John Cartier

Warren Hastings

Rand Marriott

H. Watts

TREATY OF 1763.

which are equally interesting. The letter dated the 23rd Shaban, 1178 H., from Governor Spencer to Najmuddowla, condoles the Nazim on the death of his father, Meer Jaffer. Four other letters deserve perusal. Of the letters addressed to Mobarakuddowla, there are some from Cartier, Warren Hastings, Macpherson, Lord Cornwallis and Sir John Shore.

The letters written in reply to the above or otherwise addressed by the Nazims to the Governors, Presidents of the Calcutta Council and others, of which copies are preserved, are equally interesting.

Some interesting letters of later dates are those signed by Minto, Metcalfe, Auckland, Bentinck, Cobbe, Sykes, Wellesley, Amherst, Morrison, Beadon, Grey &c.

Of the contents of the Record Room, the following deserve inspection :—

TREATIES.

1. Treaty between the East India Company and Meer Jaffer, the duplicates of which were exchanged at Fort William on the 10th July, 1763, bearing the Company's large seal and the seal of Meer Jaffer and the signatures of Vansittart, Carnac, Billers, Warren Hastings, Marriott and Watts, the Company reinstating Meer Jaffer in the Subadari of Bengal, Behar and Orissa by deposing Meer Kasem, by which Meer Jaffer granted to the Company the *Chuklas* of Burdwan, Midnapur and Chittagong, which had been

ceded before for defraying the expenses of the Company's troops and which conferred upon the Company the privelege of carrying their trade free of duty, except salt, upon which a duty of 2½ per cent. was to be levied, giving to the Company half the saltpetre produced in Purneah and half the lime made in Sylhet and passing the rupees coined in Calcutta current like the *Siccas* of Murshidabad, without *batta*.*

2. Treaty between the East India Company and Najmuddowla, executed by the President of the Calcutta Council on the 20th February, 1765, and by the Nawab on the 25th of the same month ; the Company engaging to secure the Nawab in the Subadari and to support him with their troops against his enemies and the Nawab ratifying the treaty which his father had concluded with the Company; agreeing to take in Mahomed Reza Khan, Naib of Dacca, as Naib Suba, and to entertain no Europeans in his service.*

3. Agreement between Najmuddowla and the East India Company, dated the 30th September, 1765, the former agreeing to accept the annual stipend of Rs. 53,86,131—9—0 for the support of the Nizamut, namely Rs. 17,78,854—1—0 for his household expenses and Rs. 36,07,277—8—0 for the support of his dignity, which latter sum was to be disbursed through "Meeanuddowla," that is, Mahomed Reza Khan, Mozaffer Jang.*

4. Treaty between the East India Company and Syefuddowla, dated the 19th May, 1766, the Company

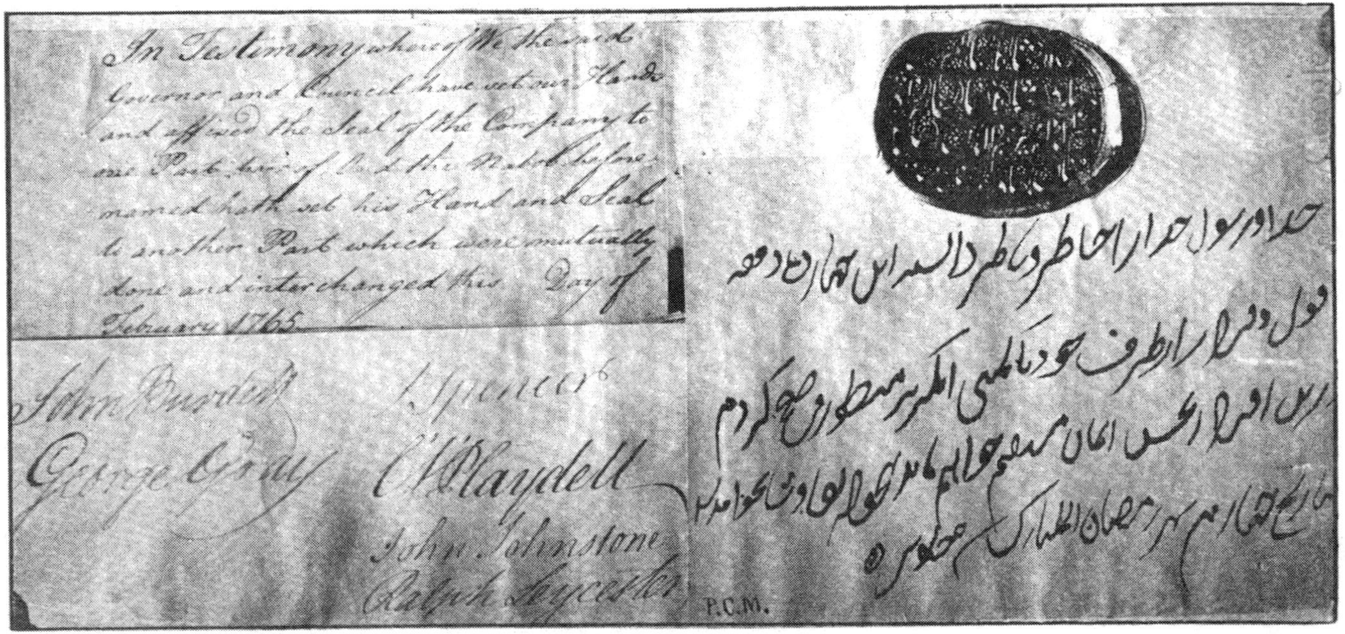
In Testimony whereof We the said Governor and Council have set our Hands and affixed the Seal of the Company to one Part hereof and the Nabob before named hath set his Hand and Seal to another Part which were mutually done and interchanged this Day of February 1765.

John Burdett
George Gray
J. Spencer
C. Playdell
John Johnstone
Ralph Leycester

P.C.M.

TREATY OF 1765.

engaging to secure the Nawab in the Subadari and to support him with the Company's forces against his enemies and the Nawab confirming the treaties entered into by his father and brother with the Company, leaving the protection of the country and the maintenance of the force, sufficient for the purpose, entirely to their discretion and management, in consideration of their paying by monthly instalments to the Emperor Sha Alum Rs. 2,16,666—10—9 and to the Nawab Rs. 41,86,131—9—0, namely Rs. 17,78,854—1—0 for his household expenses and Rs. 24,07,277—8—0 for the maintenance of his dignity, to be disbursed by Mahomed Reza Khan, who in concert with Maharajah Dullavram and Jagat Sett was to continue in his authority as Naib Suba.*

5. Treaty between the East India Company and Mobarukuddowla, dated the 21st March, 1770, the Company engaging to secure to the Nawab the Subadari and to support him with their forces against all his enemies and the Nawab ratifying the treaties entered into by the Company with his father and brothers, and agreeing to accept Rs. 31,81,991—9—0, namely Rs. 15,81,991—9—0 for his household expenses and Rs. 16,00,000 for the support of the Nizamut, which latter sum was to be disbursed through Mahomed Reza Khan.*

In these Treaties, appear the original signatures of Clive, Watts, Bussey, Vansittart, Adams, Drake, Carnac, Watson, Billiers, Cartier, Warren Hastings,

Marriott, Sykes &c. and the seals of the East India Company and the Nazims.

LETTERS.

In the letter from Lord Cornwallis to Mobarukud-dowla, the Governor General interceded on behalf of Sha Alam's queen, requesting the Nawab to give his daughter in marriage to her son. The offer was not accepted, the Nawab's reply to the Governor General being in these terms—"Please request the queen to pass over this matter, I cannot, by any means, accede to the proposal. There are many obstacles in the way. Moreover there is a long standing usage in my family that our daughters can never be given in marriage to any one other than a Syud. If I act contrary to this, my family custom, I shall be ruined. At all events, my mother and I cannot accept the offer."

The autograph letter from King William IV. accompanying His Majesty's present to Nawab Nazim Humayun Jah is as follows:—

"William the Fourth, by the Grace of God, King of the United Kingdom of Great Britain and Ireland, Defender of the Christian faith, King of Hanover, &c.

To

His Highness

MOBAURIK ALLI KHAUN,

Nobab of Bengal.

We have received your friendly letter and also the presents which your Highness has sent to us by the

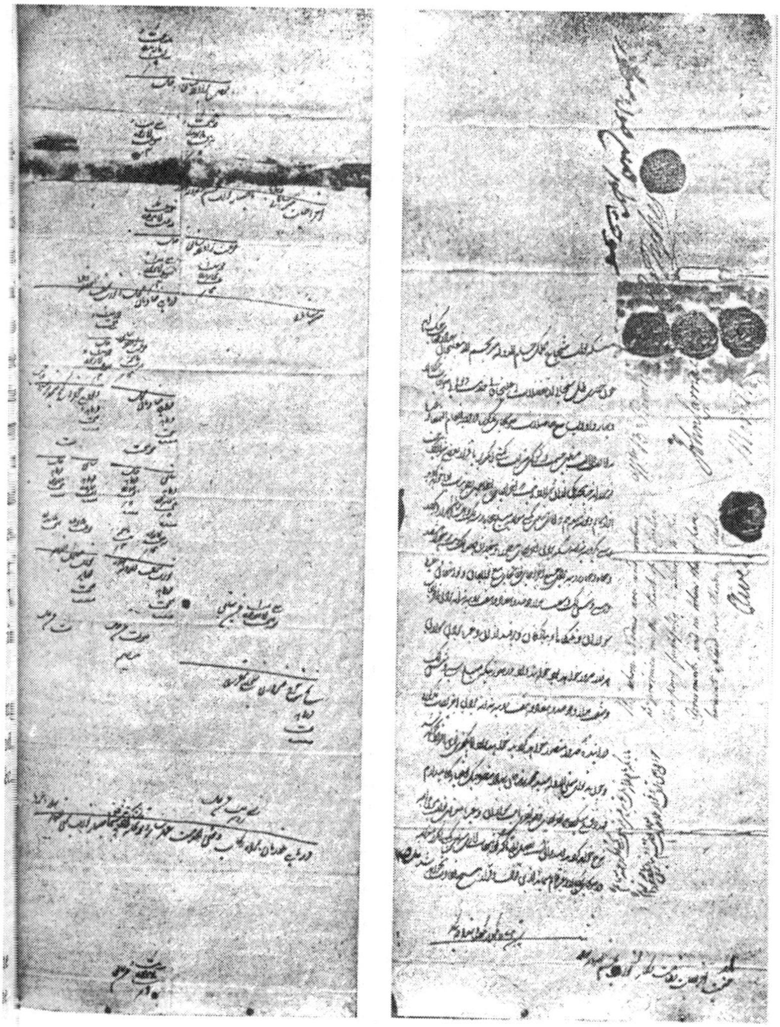

AGREEMENT SIGNED BY CLIVE.

MAJUMDAR'S MURSHIDABAD. FANCY PRESS

hand of Mr. Chinnery. Of these tokens of your esteem by far the most acceptable is that which contains the portraits of your Highness and of your son and we shall not fail to give to that valuable picture a place in our Royal Residence.

In order that your Highness may be fully aware of our satisfaction, we have commanded that our portrait at full length, and in original, shall be transmitted to your Highness. Moreover, we have determined to confer upon your Highness the Grand Cross of the Royal Hanoverien Guelphic Order and the Insignia thereof together with our portrait, will be duly conveyed to your Highness, by our trusty and well beloved Councillor, Lord Auckland, Governor General of India.

We pray Almighty God to give to your Highness many years of health and prosperity and bidding you hearty farewell, remain

Your Friend,

William R.

Given at our Palace at St. James, the fourteenth day of September, A. D. 1836, and in the seventh year of our Reign.

By His Majesty's Command

John Hobhouse."

Similarly interesting is another letter, bearing the

sign manual of Her late Majesty, Queen Victoria, of which the following is a copy :—

"To

His Highness Mohsenooddowlah Fureedoon Jah Syud Mansur Ally Khan Bahadur Nusrut Jang,

Nawab of Bengal.

We have to inform your Highness that Dr. Robert Young has faithfully executed the commission with which your Highness entrusted him and has carefully delivered to us the splendid articles of State Decoration which your Highness committed to his charge.

We are much gratified by the anxiety which your Highness has evinced that the beautiful workmanship of the natives of India should be shewn by such fitting examples at the Government Exhibition of Industry of all nations which is now displayed in the metropolis of our dominions.

A prominent position has been assigned to the presents received from your Highness and you will be pleased to hear that they have been beheld with the utmost admiration.

We shall take an early opportunity of transmitting to your Highness some token of our esteem and we desire to express our hope that it may please the Almighty to grant to your Highness many years of health and prosperity.

THE TREATY OF 1770 SIGNED BY MOBARAKUDDOWLA.

Given at our Court at Osborne the 21st day of August in the year of our Lord 1851, and in the fifteenth year of our Reign."

The following is a copy of another interesting letter from Lord William Cavendish Bentick, Governor General, addressed to Amiran-nissa Begum, known as Dulhin Begum, widow of Nawab Nazim Ali Jah.

"To

HER HIGHNESS NAWAB AMEERUN-NISSA BEGUM.

My Honored and Valued Friend,

Being desirous of returning to England, I sometime since expressed my request to be relieved from the charge of the Supreme Government of the British Possessions in India and it is my intention to embark for Europe about the middle of the next month.

I have not yet heard whether any individual has been appointed to succeed me from England, but should no one arrive in that capacity before my departure, Sir Charles Metcalfe, who has received a provisional appointment to that effect, will succeed me in the office of the Governor General and will exercise, until further orders, the important functions of this high office.

In like manner the Hon'ble Mr. Blunt will, in that case, exercise the powers of Governor of the Agra Presidency.

It is a source of great satisfaction for me to reflect that during my residence in India, the intimate connection which happily subsists between your Highness and the Honorable Company has been strengthened and confirmed, and of no less gratification to know that in my successor your Highness will experience the same disposition to cultivate and improve the existing harmony and good understanding between the two Governments, and an inviolable adherence to the engagements by which your Highness and the Honorable Company are indissolubly connected.

Your Highness may be assured that no distance of time, nor local situation will impair the sentiments of personal respect and esteem I entertain towards you, or diminish my solicitude for the continuance of your Highness's prosperity, happiness and welfare.

In conclusion, I beg to express the high consideration I entertain for your Highness and to subscribe myself

Your Highness's
Sincere friend

FORT WILLIAM
24th February, 1835. (sd.) W. C. BENTINCK."

The BALL ROOM is as large as the Banqueting Hall below it and has a floor paved with well-polished teak. There are numerous side-rooms and lateral halls which are fitted up with comfortable sofas and other seats and which afford a much sought for retreat for rest after the heat of the dance.

The PICTURE GALLFRIES of the Palace, of which there are several, form its most prominent featre. The collection of oil paintings, being at once rare,

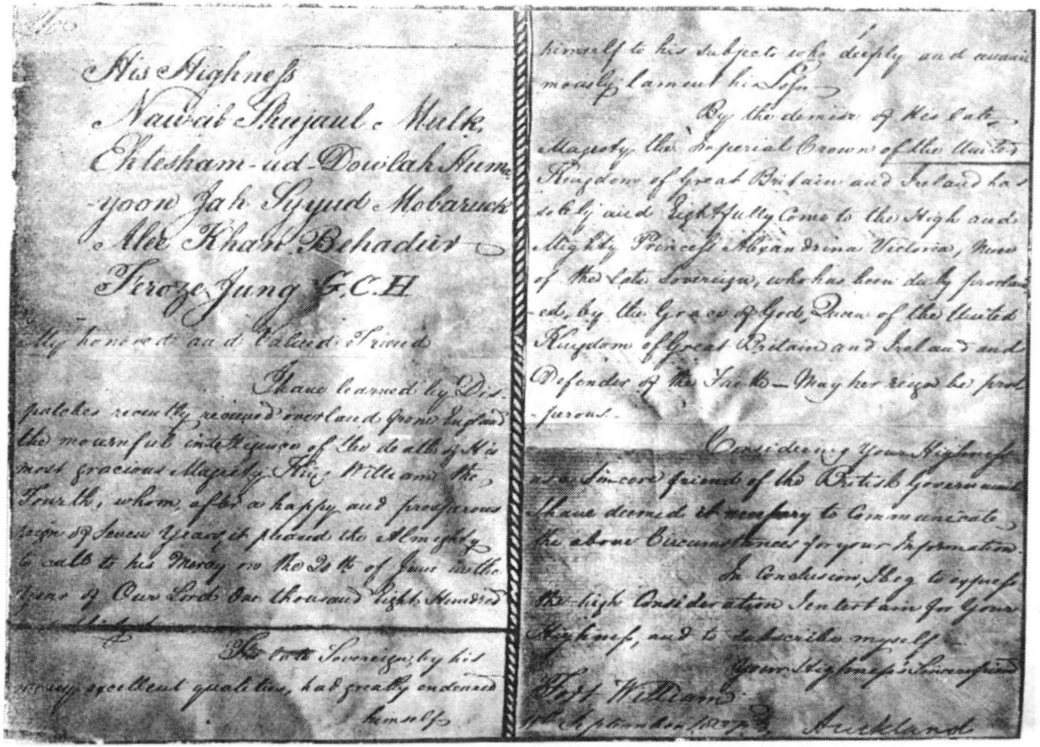
His Highness
Nawab Shujaul-Mulk,
Ehtesham-ud-Dowlah Hum-
-yoon Jah Syyud Mobaruck
Allee Khan Behadur
Feroze Jung G.C.H.

My honored and Valued Friend

I have learned by Despatches recently received overland from England the mournful intelligence of the death of His most gracious Majesty King William the Fourth, whom after a happy and prosperous reign of Seven Years it pleased the Almighty to call to his Mercy on the 20th of June in the Year of Our Lord One thousand Eight Hundred [illegible]

The late Sovereign, by his many excellent qualities, had greatly endeared himself to his subjects who deeply and unanimously lament his Loss.

By the demise of His late Majesty the Imperial Crown of the United Kingdom of Great Britain and Ireland has solely and rightfully come to the High and Mighty Princess Alexandrina Victoria, Niece of the late Sovereign, who has been duly proclaimed, by the Grace of God, Queen of the United Kingdom of Great Britain and Ireland and Defender of the Faith — May her reign be prosperous.

Considering Your Highness as a sincere friend of the British Government I have deemed it necessary to communicate the above Circumstances for your Information.

In conclusion, I beg to express the high consideration I entertain for Your Highness, and to subscribe myself

Your Highness's sincere friend

Fort William
[illegible] September 1837

Auckland

rich and beautiful, is the finest in India, consisting of many masterpieces, both ancient and modern and being principally strong in the Dutch, Flemish, French and Italian schools. One gallery leads into another and most valuable works of art are scattered about the Palace. The specimens afford ample study and many a connoisseur would be surprized to see such a variety of valuable paintings.

The following is a list of some of the noted pictures :—

GRAND STAIRCASE ENTRANCE.

1. His Highness the Nawab Nazim Humayun Jah consulting Col. Mc. Leod who is explaining the plan of the Palace.
2. Venice (after Tiepolo)
3. Bolton Abbey, by Alfred Wither.
4. Mary Magdalen, by Morghen.
5. Lorena, by Perux.

FIRST GALLERY.

1. The Scotch Warrior, by G. Campbell.
2. Cavaliers of Venice, by Marchatti.
3. Falstaff, by Marchatti.
4. Old Scotland, by J. S. Rowle.
5. Bohemian Landscape, by French.
6. Engel des Fegefeur, by Herlein.
7. The Judgment, by Sir E. Landseer, R. A.
8. Cindrella, by T. Young.

9. No Surrender, by Denham.
10. Tyrolean Landscape, by Joseph Dower.
11. The Ocean, by Pratt.
12. The Bera on the river, by Hudson.
13. Harold's Head, by Lorenz.
14. Bacchus and Adriane.

SECOND GALLERY.

1. H. H. Nawab Nazim Humayun Jah.
2. Swiss Landscape, by Malleure.
3. Landscape, by Delmora.
4. After the storm, by Leedham.
5. Italian Landscape, by Mareana.
6. The Marquis of Spinola, by Vandyke.
7. French Landscape, by Lacroix.
8. Scene of the Thirty Year's War, by Jorgenson.
9. The Sick Cupid, by Reni.
10. Linen Bleachers, by Perout.
11. On the Bosphorus, by D. Temper.
12. Sea View, by Schotel.

THIRD GALLERY.

1. German Landscape, by Frauz Hensner.
2. After School, by Meissen.
3. Winter scene in Holland, by Vermaillin.
4. Landscape in Tuscany, by Perugia.
5. The Lovers, by Arquin.
6. Landscape, by R. P. Bonington.
7. The Woman of Samaria, by Raphael.

8. Katrine, by Wolfe.
9. Peasants carousing, by Rembrandt.
10. Hunting Party, by Beechey.
11. The Music Party, by D. Tiniers.
12. French Landscape, by Courbet.
13. The Castle, by A. Cuyp.
14. The Rival, by Snyders.

FAMILY GALLERY.

CONTAINS THE PORTRAITS OF THE NAWABS NAZIM.
(FOR REPRODUCTIONS *vide* ILLUSTRATIONS, PART I).

BOUDOIR.

1. N. N. Humayun Jah, by Hutchinson.
2. Lt. Col. Colin Mackenzie, A. G. G., by Hudson.
3. Mrs. Mackenzie, by Hudson.
4. Major C. A. Thomson, A. G. G., by Hudson.
5. Hussan Ali and Hossien Ali, by Hudson (*N. B.* H. H. the Nawab Bahadur and Nawab Wala Kadr in their boyhood).
6. Rajah Prosanno Naraen Deb, Dewan, by Hudson.
7. H. H., N. N. Feredun Jah, by Hudson.
8. Major Macgregor, A. G. G., by Hudson.
9. Mr. Caulfield, A. G. G., by Hutchinson.
10. Col. McLeod, (the Architect of the Palace) by Hutchinson.

DRAWING ROOM.

1. William IV., King of England. (Presented by His Majesty to Humayun Jah).

2. Her Majesty the late Queen Victoria.
3. The Earl of Munster.
4. H. H. Prince Wasif Ali Meerza (equestrian).
5. H. H. The Nawab Bahadur of Murshidabad.
6. The Marquis of Wellesley.

BED ROOM.

1. Prince Wasif Ali Meerza.
2. Prince Nasir Ali Meerza.
3. Lord Cornwallis.

BANQUETING HALL.

1. Burial of Sir John Moore, by Marshall.
2. Several Pictures of the Nawab Nazim's Sons.
3. Bohemian Landscape, by Ernest.
4. Nadir Sha of Persia.
5. The Nawab Nazim's Durbar, by Lewis.
6. Meer Jaffer and Miran.
7. Humayun Jah's Dancing Party.
8. The Durbar of His Highness the Nawab Nazim of Bengal, by Lewis.

BALL ROOM.

1. Lilly (after Sir Joshua Reynolds).
2. The Holy Family, by Renardi.
3. Meditation (after Worth).
4. General Showers.
5. Lady Showers.
6. Retribution, by R. A. Sterndate.

THE DURBAR OF HIS HIGHNESS NAWAB NAZIM OF BENGAL.

7. Will He Return, by M. Claxton.

The stuffed skin of an alligator, 13 feet long, with a girth of 6 feet round about the middle, said to have been shot by Nawab Humayun Jah at the Kriteswari tank; a tortoise shell, with a girth of six feet and a piece of bamboo with a girth of two feet, placed at the inner stairs are among the objects of interest in the Palace.

Among the innumerable treasures of the Palace are some objects presented to Meer Jaffer by the East India Company (Vide Long's Selections from the Records of the Government, Vol. I., p. 144 *et seq*). The most interesting of these are the following :—

1. A marble Table.
2. An Organ Clock (Price Rs. 5,000).
3. A Musical Box (Price Rs. 2,080).
4. Curious cut Lustres (Price Rs. 9,216, the pair).
5. Many Pairs of large sized Looking Glasses.
6. Guns and pistols.
7. Several "lanthorns"(lanterns).

In the preservation of the equipments of the Palace and in the collection of articles of variety, His Highness the Nawab Bahadur of Murshidabad has evinced the greatest interest, books and manuscripts claiming his foremost attention.

Of the buildings within the Killah, those to be permanently maintained are the following :—

1. The Palace including the Sundial with iron railings.

2. The South Entrance Gate of the Killah.
3. The Body guard's quarters.
4. The Khansamani and Farrashkhana.
5. The Baitakkhana and Mahalsara.
6. The Clock Tower with iron railing.
7. The Imambara.
8. The Musjed on the river bank near the South Gate.
9. The Musjed on the river bank near the Palace.
10. The old Madina.
11. The Baburchi-khana quadrangle.

In the Killah there are several flagstaffs, but only two of these are generally used, the one near the Baburchi-khana and the other near the Dakshin Durwaza or South gate.

MADINA.

To the north of the Palace, only a few yards off, is the Madina, the central dome and only remnant of Serajuddowla's famous Imambara, which was burnt down by fire, during a display of fireworks. The area enclosed by the foundation walls was dug up five feet and six inches deep and was filled up with earth brought from sacred Kerbella, in Arabia. Serajuddowla himself carried on his head the first basket of materials. The costly treasures, which were lavished by him upon this Imambara with so much pride, were

OLD MADINA AND THE BACHAWALI TOPE.

turned into ready money by Meer Kasem, to help the poor of the city and to send indigent Mahomedans to Mecca.

THE BACHAWALI TOPE.

To the east of the Old Madina, stands on two masonry pedastals 5 feet high, a big gun, called the Bachawali tope, consisting of two pieces of different diameters. The smaller portion, which is the chamber, is 3 feet and 7 inches long, with a girth of 4 feet and 4 inches ; and the larger portion, namely the barrel, is 11 feet and 6 inches long, with a girth, at the muzzle, of 7 feet and 9 inches. The diameter of the bore at the muzzle is 1 foot and 7 inches. The touch hole has been plugged with melted iron. Eleven rings bind the wrought iron barrel, the inner surface of which bears ample evidence of the gun's great antiquity. The rim round the muzzle is ornamented with petals, while one of the rings resembles a string of beads. On the upper half of the barrel surface, near the muzzle, fourteen lines, seven on each side, are inlaid with brass. Eight smaller rings are attached, at various points. The breach plug is driven until its chamfered end dovetails and fits tightly into the chamber of the barrel, which are tied together with the rings attached to each.

The gun was made between the twelvth and the fourteenth centuries, probably by the Mahomedan rulers of Gour. It rested originally on the sand bank adjoining Ichhaganj, (how it came there is not known) protecting the city from attack from the north west. On the completion of the Imambarah, it was, at the suggestion of Mr. Henry Torrens, Agent to the Governor General at Murshidabad, removed to its present site by Sadeq Ali Khan, the architect of that sacred building.

It is said that the gun was once fired in Murshidabad and the sound produced caused many cases of abortion for miles round. Hence its name.

Mr. Syud Mahomed Hossein, the translator of Bernier's Travels, says that Mir Jumla brought from Assam 675 guns, one of which could take a ball weighing three maunds. Might it be this ?

THE IMAMBARAH.

Parallel to the north facade of the Palace, stands the Nizamut Imambarah, built in 1847 at a cost of upwards of six lacs, after the celebrated Imambarah of Serajuddowla had been destroyed by fire. It is 680' feet long, with varying breadths, that of the central block, being 300 feet. It took only eleven months in construction, under the supervision and direction of Sadeq Ali Khan, who was not a professional engineer. The workmen received food in addition to their wages, so that they could work day and

THE NIZAMUT IMAMBARAH.

KUNTALINE PRESS, CALCUTTA.

night without interruption. After the completion of the building, the workmen received presents of *doshalas* and *roomals*, that is, double shawls in pairs and square shawls (not handkerchiefs as *roomals* has been translated by the oriental scholar, Professor Blockman), so that at that time one could see those costly articles of luxury in every street and lane in Murshidabad.

There is an inscription on the top of the eastern gate, composed by Mollah Mahomed Sharif Shirwani, which is rendered thus :—

1. Inventors of the tide of destiny, with the pen of divine decree, have written this building on the first tablet.

2. The courage and firmness of Feredun Jah, for honor and greatness, have taken upon themselves, the servitude of the son of Zohora.

3. A Nowbutkhana, Musjed and Imambarah are built on one and the same ground. He has therefore established a place of both worlds.

4. The management and labour of Sadeq Ali of high origin have tried hard to complete this heart-pleasing edifice.

5. His power and ingenuity have laid the foundation in this world of heaven and a place of sorrow combined together.

6. The messenger of God placed on thy Jesus like palm this epigrammatic verse "Behold another Kerbella is erected in India."

The Imambarah, which is the largest in Bengal and perhaps the largest but one in India, is divided into three large quadrangles, in the central one of which is the present Madina, the plinth of the raised floor of which is decorated with ornamental China tiles. Its massive pillars and arches are surmounted by a dome of magestic proportions, the roof of which is painted sky blue and which is crowned with a golden *kuls*. The space within the pillars and arches is in the shape of a moat in which fountains have been provided and which encircles the shrine of Madina, surmounted by a dome of dazzling tinsel, gold and silver. On the top of the arches and the spaces between them, the walls are decorated with extracts of texts from the Koran. The floor is reached by marble steps, placed in opposite directions.

The eastern hall of the central block is called the *memberdalan*, where there is a pulpit from which elegies are recited. The floors of this spacious hall and its verandah are covered with polished marble. There is a spacious side-room for ladies.

Between this and the Madina is a vat in which there are several fountains provided with silver head pieces, which work when the singing of the elegies is over. The colonnades, with the entablatures and stylobates are majestic.

The corresponding hall, to the west and its rooms, all paved with polished marble, are the repositories of Tazias, Alams and Punjas of gold and silver and standards encased in shawls, embroidered with texts from the Koran.

At each corner of the two remaining wings or halls of the quadrangle is a structure, called a *pahar* or mountain, of bamboos, more than a hundred years old, covered over with dyed cotton, in the centre of which is a Burag, meaning literally the bright one, being a representation of the animal with human face and peacock's tail on which the Prophet ascended to Miraj or heaven. The tail reaches the ceiling of the first floor and is over fifty feet in height. At the foot of this structure is a reservoir, round which are placed date trees and camels, made of sola and cotton, to remind one of the plains of Arabia. At the back of the Burag is a large mirror. Well polished Indian shields and China and tin plates are fitted into the feathers of the tail to represent the eyes of the peacock's feather. Swords, sabres, daggers and lances, used by Serajuddowla for similar purposes, are arranged in different designs round the shields and the tongues of the structure; and thousands of candles their light reflected on the mirror, make the whole a dazzling scene. Uniform splendour is visible in all the four gigantic structures at the four corners of the central quadrangle. The split bamboo of these structures is over a hundred years old.

The two other quadrangles are equally spacious. The eastern quadrangle is reached from the streets through a big gate, of what is called the Imamia architecture, which is surmounted by a Nowbutkhana. The western quadrangle terminates in a two storeyed mosque, standing on the mint ghat and rising almost from the river.

The enclosures are entered through seven large gates. Besides these, there are two inner gates, as large, between the quadrangles.

The parapets all round are studded with innumerable minarets with colored glass panes, red alternated with green, emblamatic of blood and poison. Screens of painted glass run round the upper rooms. These when lighted up produce a marvellous effect.

With its large proportions, its stately pillars, its spacious marble floors, its innumerable large chandeliers, some of which form part of the presents of the East India Company, and its other magnificent equipments, the Nizamut Imambarah stands unrivalled. The whole place is brilliantly lighted during the ten nights of the Moharram, when *Mujlises* are held and Mursia Khans, Soze Khans, Ketab Khans and Hadis Khans flock from every part of the country to read, recite or sing the elegies.

The Moharram is the principal religious ceremony performed and observed by the Sheas of Murshidabad, among whom the Nawabs, have always evinced an ardour and enthusiasm, quite consonant with the religious devotion and fervor which characterized Ali, the Amir-ul-Momin, though they have exercised a degree of toleration, which is admirable. It is the observance of the anniversary of the saddest event recorded in the history of early Islam.

Briefly told it is as follows :—

The Prophet of Arabia had all along evinced a great affection for his uncle's son and son-in-law, Ali, the husband of Fatema. He had on several occasions indicated Ali as his successor. At the assembly of Khum Ghadir, situated between Mecca and Medina, Mahomed declared—"Thrice hath the angel Gabriel appeared unto me and thrice hath he commanded me to declare unto all my followers, be they white or be they black, that Ali is my Caliph, Wasi and Imam ... and that he shall be your guide after my death; that my followers are to obey him when I am departed hence, as they did me while yet among them. They who shall disobey Ali shall disobey God and His Prophet. Such, O friends, are the commands of Allah...After Ali, his sons, Hussan and Hossein, are to succeed."

Three days before his death, Mahomed said "whosoever loves me, let him regard Ali as his friend." Mahomed died and his second wife, Ayesha, succeeded in obtaining the Caliphate or leadership for her father, Abu Bakr, who, on his accession, sent Omar to Ali to fetch him to do him fealty. On his deathbed, he nominated Omar as his successor.

The Moslem world had already divided itself into two factions, the one upholding the superior right of heridity and the other maintaining the superiority of election.

On Omar's death, Osman became the third Caliph. The Arabs determined to get rid of him, and he was slain. Their representations now asked Ali to assume the reins of Government. On his accession, Ali dismissed Moaviah, a near relative of Osman. Ayesha placed herself at the head of a faction but her generals were slain and she herself fell into the hands of the conquering Ali, who now directed his attention towards Moaviah, who rebelled in Syria. The dispute was referred to arbitration. The award was to depose Ali. He and his followers retired to Cufa and succeed in regaining Arabia, while Moaviah established his authority in Syria and Persia.

It was the 17th day of Ramzan (27th January, 661) when Ali was offering prayers at the mosque of Cufa that the poisoned dagger of an assassin struck him. On his death, his eldest son, Hussan, was proclaimed Caliph and Imam. But he was forced to resign in favor of Moaviah, who granted him permission to retire on pension. Nine years after, Hussan was poisoned by his wife at the instigation of Moaviah.

Moaviah died shortly after and was succeeded by his son, Yezid. His cruelty compelled the people to send a requisition to Hossein, who was living at Medina, asking him to stand on his heriditary rights. When Hossein appeared on the scene, the insurrection had been put down. He found himself in the midst of hostile multitudes, who showered upon him numberless arrows. Of his seventy two followers, all fell, one after another; Hossein himself was struck by an arrow in his mouth, while drinking a cup of water at the door of his tent. His young son and nephew were killed in his arms. Hossein fell dead at the stroke of Shemar. The enemy trampled over his body and then cut off and carried his head to Cufa.

These tragic events are chanted during the observance of the Moharrum and their pathos has not unfrequently drawn the tears of even those who are beyond the pale of Islam.

THE CLOCK TOWER.

Between the Imambarah and the Palace, corresponding or rather contrasting with the rounded cupola of the old Madina, is the tall tower of great architectural beauty and majestic height which affords a magnificent frame work for purposes of effective illumination. It is surmounded by a heavy sounding bell which can be heard from a great distance. The pinnacle terminates in a rod to which is affixed a metallic fish in the form of a crescent. On the four corners of the roof of the ground floor are placed four masonry shields, supported by four masonry lions. The dial faces towards the river, the handles and figures are visible from the opposite bank and the clock may be called the Big Ben of Murshidabad, except that it does not chime quarter hours.

The tower was designed by Sagor Mistri, the native assistant of Col. McLeod, the architect of the Palace, and stands upon a foundation of tall Sal logs.

THE SUN DIAL.

To the South of the Palace is the Dhoopghari or Sundial, very accurately placed, with a metallic gnomon and a stone dial, with the equation of time and calendar engraved round the rim in bold figures and letters.

THE ZURUD MUSJED.

Within a few feet of the north west corner of the Palace, is the Zurud Musjed, situated on the banks of the river with foundation walls running deep into the embankment, built by order of Serajuddowla in one night. It is washed yellow, while the corresponding Musjed to the south, near the South Gate, is washed white. They look like two gold and silver crowns adorning the embankment.

THE TRIPAULIA GATE.

This massive gate, with three arch-ways, situated to the east of the Palace, was built by Nawab Shuja Khan. It is surmounted by a Nowbutkhana and is known as the Chowk Gate of the Killah.

The three single arch gates, near the chowk, the one at the entrance of the Bakrigully Road, the other on the Thana Road and the third near Ambakhana, are jointly called the Tripaulia gates, also built by Shuja Khan.

KHURSHED DULA'S DEORI.

The range of irregular buildings, between the Palace and the public road to the west of Noseri Banu Begum's Tomb at Jutapatty, is occupied by the descendants of Nawab Zainul Abideen Khan Bahadoor, Feroze Jang, deceased, son-in-law to the late Nawab Nazim, and an enlightened Mahomedan, who took great delight in matters of science, and was for many years a great supporter and promoter of technical education in Murshidabad. He was the son of Safdar Ali Khan alias Safdar Jang, a son of Abul Kasem, called Mir Mangli, the second son of Mobarukuddowla.

The present representative is Syud Abul Hossien.

A portion of the buildings has been demolished, being in dangerous proximity to the Palace.

THE CHOWK MUSJED.

The Chowk Musjed is now the largest mosque in the city in proper repairs, situated to the south-east of the Palace, abutting the walls of the Killah. It was built in 1767 by Meer Jaffer's wife, Mani Begum, on the site of the Chehel Satoon or the forty-pillar audience hall of Murshed Kuli Khan. Five roads through arched gateways lead to the pavement in front of the mosque, which with the shops round is called the Chowk, the principal market-place of the city, by which the city itself is called by neighbouring towns.

The corpses of respectable persons are taken to the pavement and placed before the entrance gate of the mosque, where prayers are offered for the dead before removal for interment.

This mosque is used on occasions of the Idul Fitr and the Iduz Zoha for public prayer.

The ceremony of Idul Fitr is performed on the completion of the thirty days' great fast of the Ramzan, the ninth month of the Mahomedan year. The fast is from dawn to sun set each day and more than one meal may be taken at night. The observance of the fast is enjoined in Surah ii, verse 179-184 of the Koran. The fast begins when the new moon is visible, the appearance being proclaimed by the fire of a salute from the Killah. The daily fast is broken at sunset when a single gun is fired from the Killah and several

THE EED PROCESSION.

FANCY PRESS.

CHOWK MUSJID.

guns are fired at intervals proclaiming hours for meals or prayer.

The day after the close of the month's fast is one of universal rejoicing and mutual salutations and congratulations. The gayest garments are worn and the sweetest perfumes used. After prayer, there is embracing in token of forgiveness.

Before noon, before which the prayers must be said, a state procession starts from the Killah and proceeds to the mosque. On its arrival and at the conclusion of the prayer salutes are fired from the Killah. An immense crowd gathers at the Chowk and the shopkeepers do brisk business.

The Iduz Zoha, known locally as the Bukreed, or the feast of the sacrifice, is celebrated on the tenth day of the month of Zilhejj. It is authorized by an injunction of the Koran contained in Surah XXII, verse 33-34. It was instituted in the second year of the Hijera. At Murshidabad many animals are sacrificed, one of which is a camel, the sacred meat being distributed generously and even European gentlemen are not forgotten. The ceremonies observed are similar to those at the Idul Fitr.

As the two Ids, so the Nowroze or the Mahomedan new year's day, the first day after the sun has crossed the vernal equinox, when Ali, the grandson and son-in-law of the Prophet, succeeded him in the Caliphate, is a day of great rejoicing at Murshidabad. At night, various presents are spread in a well-lighted room, where a flower is thrown in a saucerful of rose water and it is said that, when the sun passes the equinox, the flower whirls round in the cup. At dawn, a salute is fired from the Killah in honor of Ali's succession to the Caliphate.

The Shub-be-berat is another Mahomedan ceremony which is observed with great solemnity in Murshidabad. The tombs are whitewashed or laped with mud, decked with flowers and garlands and fenced round with mica tattis for illumination. At night fireworks are displayed and several kinds of victuals, but mostly hallooa and roti, are offered to the dead, in honor of whose departure, a salute is fired before daybreak.

Mani Begum, the founder of this Mosque, was high in favour with Clive and Hastings and on account of her lavish presents was styled the "Mother-e-Company." She in her turn received several, one of which was from Rani Bhowani, being a palki with thirty bearers gifted with service tenures, which they were to enjoy in lieu of wages. The lands so given are still in the possession of the Nizamut.

Mani Begum was the first of a class of chief ladies to whom separate deoris or allowances were assigned. These were called Gadinasheen Begums. From the time of Meer Jaffer, there have been six such ladies of the first class and three of the second class. Until 1769, the chief ladies were Mani Begum and Bubboo Begum, both widows of Meer Jaffer, who were on receipt of Rs. 12,000 and Rs. 8,000 respectively per month as their separate allowances. Faizunnissa or Waleda Begum, widow of Mobarukud-dowla, Bohu Begum and Amirunnissa alias Dulhin Begum, wives of Ali Jah, Najibunnissa Begum, widow of Wala Jah, and Raesunnissa Begum, widow of Humayun Jah, were Gadinasheen Begums. The present holder of the Deori is Her Highness Nawab Shams Jehan Begum C. I., a widow of Feredun Jah.

The following are the dates of the deaths of the five deceased ladies :—

Mani Begum	..	April, 1812.
Bohu Begum	..	24th October, 1849.
Dulhin Begum	..	21st January, 1858.
Najibunnissa Begum	..	23rd August, 1858.
Raesunnissa Begum	..	4th May, 1893.

Warren Hastings writing to his wife from Bhagul-pore said—"I forgot to tell you that Mani Begum expressed her regret of your departure in terms which seemed too natural to have proceeded from mere civility, I was pleased to hear her say that she grieved on my account as much as for her own loss in your departure and the necessity which occasioned it."

Anent Mani Begum's removal from interference with Nizamut affairs, Warren Hastings wrote to Mr. Lawrence Sulivan under date 21st March, 1776—"They have dismissed the Begum from her office which I had arranged her for the express and sole purpose of guarding the Company's authority against encroachment or competition." She shared in the administration of the Government of her husband, Meer Jaffer, and acted subsequently as the guardian of her sons, the minor Nazims, Najmuddowla and Syefuddowla.

Mani Begum paid out to Clive the large legacy which Meer Jaffer had bequeathed to him. Her acts of munificence to the East India Company and their servants were numerous.

The Government of the East India Company treated Mani Begum with distinguished consideration and viewed her with cordial regard. On her demise, a salute was fired by Government corresponding to the number of years of her age.

The most worthy successor to the gadi of the "Mother-e-Company" was Her Highness the late Nawab Raesunnissa Begum Saheba, a most generous lady, whose private charities were as numerous as they were unostentatious.

KULHORIA.

To the east of the Palace, outside the limits of the Killah, is Kulhoria, the site of the Palace of Murshed Kuli Khan built upon his removal from Dacca. The mosque built in 1731-32 was rebuilt later. The terrace is reached by steps under which in a vault, lie buried the remains of his wife, Noseri Banu

Begum. On the gateway is a stone slab bearing an inscription, which is rendered thus :—

Thanks, with the help of God, the luxurious,
that shewed us benefit, you know ;
A mosque surpassing the graces of Paradise,
order to build a second Mary gave ;
Who she is, I tell you, that with her pure skirt
a great boon to the world shewed ;
Wife of the Nawab, entitled Noseri, he whom
Jumsh served as porter ;
Owing to his order with all the felicity of joy,
the contents of the firman were brought into
real existence ;
Wonder of wonders, the date of that, see how
fresh is on people's tongues.
Mind and heart both and all with one mouth
said "A second house of God was made."

The date of the construction of the mosque lies concealed in the concluding words which mean 1145 H.

On the mosque itself there is a slab, which evidently replaced the former, which appears to have been taken down and placed in its present position on the gateway. The slab reads :—

Syed Ali nasab Sadeq Ali
Reqth tur he Musjede ba arzu
Natamam Azi Jahan be sebath
Janabe dar ul baqa binhad roo
Kurde tamamush Zerooi ehteman
Khan Ala Shan Nazir nek khoo

Bahre tarikhush masiha behejab
Goft hatif in dakhal tum furjedo
1267.

It appears that Sadeq Ali Khan had commenced to rebuild the mosque but Nazir Ali Khan completed it after his death. The year 1267 is concealed in the last four words which bears the plain meaning—"enter the Musjed and pray."

JANG'S IMAMBARAH.

At the back of the Nizamut Imambarah, about a hundred yards to the north-west at Lobegang, is Jang's Imambarah, called after Shamshere Jang, the husband of Lutfunnissa Begum, who founded it. She was a daughter of Mobarukuddowla, and a grand-daughter of Meer Jaffer. On her death her daughter, Amirunnissa Alias Dulhin Begum, became its trustee. On Dulhin Begum's death, her properties, being the properties left by a Gadinasheen Begum, devolved upon the Nawab Nazim under the custom of the family, and with them the trusteeship also passed on to him. The Nawab Nazim, however, placed the management of the Imambarah in the hands of his mother, Her Highness the late Nawab Raesunnissa Begum Saheba, the late Gadinasheen Begum, upon whose death the trusteeship devolved upon His Highness the Nawab Bahadur of Murshidabad, her sole heir under the custom of the family. There is an allowance paid by Government for the maintenance of this Imambarah. It stands the risk of demolition on account of the proposed extension of the Madrassa.

Meer Jaffer

Mobarukuddowla

Baber Jang — Shamshere Jang — + — Lutfunnissa

Ali Jah — + — Amirunnissa Alias Dulhin Begum

RAJMEHAL DEORI.

Between the Nawab's Madrassa and the Imambarah is Lobegang, the site of the Rajmehal Deori.

Meer Jaffer had appointed his brother, Nawab Itramuddowla Syud Kazem Ali Khan, Deputy Nazim at Rajmehal. On the death of his great-grandson, Amiruddowla, on the 21st November, 1859, the rayasat of Rajmehal was abolished by order of Government and the members of the family, some of whose ancesters had married the daughters of Mobarukuddowla, lived at Lobegang.

The following is a genealogy of the Rajmehal family :—

Itramuddowla

- Momtazuddowla
  - Son + a daughter of Mobarukuddowla
    - Yusufudden
      - Ekramuddeen
        - Nawab Shams Jehan Begum, C. I.
- Ghalib Jang
- Rokunuddowla
  - Madaruddowla
    - Syud Mansurali Khan
    - Amiruddowla

NAWAB'S MADRASSA.

This institution was sanctioned by Government in 1825, the Governor General of India and the Nawab Nazim of Bengal being the patrons and the Agent Governor General at Murshidabad being its controlling officer. It was temporarily located at Mobaruk Mehal. The present building, which was designed by Col. McLeod, of the Bengal Engineers, was constructed at a cost of Rs. 76,500, paid from the Nizamut Deposit Fund, between 1838 and 1843. Mr. Y. V. Sedon, the great linguist, who knew thirty two languages and the site of whose house at Berhampore is still known as Sedon Sahebka hata, was the Principal from 1841 to 1845. The connection of the

Governor General's Agent ceased on the abolition of the Agency in 1882. The College was under the management of a Committee of which the Agent was the president and the following were the members—

H. P. Russell, District Judge,
The Collector of Murshidabad,
Captain Showers
Nawab Shamshere Jung
Nawab Safdar Jang and
Rai Sita Nath Bose, Dewan.

This free Institution which is designed for the education of the younger members of the Nizamut family and which for forty years (1842–1882) was under the head mastership of the veteran, Mr. J. Arrow, was known as the College. It has a free board attached to it and is now under the direct supervision of Government. The building is situated in the midst of a compound which may be called the northen extremity of the Killah.

NAWAB'S HIGH SCHOOL.

The building in which the School is held was originally the residence of Mobarukuddowla before he ascended the masnud and was known as the Mobaruk Mehal. The Moharrum which intervened between the destruction of the old Imambarah of Serajuddowla and the completion of the present Imambarah was held in this building. The Nizamut College, now known as the Nawab's Madrassa, was held here for some time.

The school was founded in 1854 under the name of the Nizamut school, designed for the education of the sons of the citizens of Murshidabad other than the Akrobas or relatives of the Nawab Nazim. It was under the management of a Committee of which the Agent to the Governor General at Murshidabad was the President. The money needed for its maintenance came from the Nizamut Deposit Fund.

The nomencleture of the school, after the abolition of the Agency and the Agent's Committee was changed into the Nawab's High School, which is as yet a most useful Institution imparting superior education gratuitously. The status of the school became much improved in 1874 under the head mastership of Mr. George Lorimer, M. A., who took the greatest interest in its welfare.

AZIMNAGAR MOSQUE.

At Azimnagar, about half a mile to the north of the Palace, are the remains of a Musjed, built by Azimunnessa or Azmutunnissa Begum, the daughter of Murshed Kuli Khan. She lies buried near the terrace. The beautiful workmanship of the building is evidenced by the portion of the shattered and roof-

JAFRAGANJ CEMETRY.

MAJUMDAR'S MURSHIDABAD. FANCY PRESS.

less standing wall, whose once white lime work is now green and livid with fungoid growth.

JAFFRAGANJ CEMETRY.

Within an enclosure of waved walls at Jaffraganj, about a mile and a half from the Palace, is the family burial ground of Meer Jaffer, containing the tombs of the Nawabs Nazim, from Meer Jaffer to Humayun Jah. The remains of the last Nawab Nazim of Bengal, Syud Mansur Ali Khan, were temporarily deposited in a vault and subsequently removed to Kerbella in Arabia under his testament. Meer Jaffer's father, Syud Ahmed, Ali Verdi Khan's sister, Sha Khanum, Meer Jaffer's widows, Mani Begum and Bubbo Begum, Sultana Ghetiara Begum, Nawab Raesunnissa Begum, Mahomed Ali Khan, the brother and Ismail Ali Khan and Ashraf Ali Khan, the sons-in-law of Meer Jaffer, lie buried here.

The total number of graves is large. The graves of the Begums are enclosed by walls. Unless objectionable on religious grounds, which seems hardly to be the case, each of the principal tombs should be provided with a stone, so that there may not be any confusion. Though a plan of the tombs is kept in the office of the cemetry, yet tomb stones would be a decided improvement.

The following is a plan of the principal tombs. Each Mahomedan corpse is laid low into the grave, resting on its right side, with the head towards the north and the face towards the west.

		Sultan Gheteara Begum	Shakhanum
	Dulhin Begum	Syud Ahmed Najafi	
		Mahomed Ali Khan	
	Najibannissa Begum	Meer Jaffer	
	Shahunnissa Begum	Ismail Ali Khan	
Raesunnessa Begum		Najmuddowla	
	Bohu Begum	Syefuddowla	
	Umdatunnissa Begum	Ashraf Ali Khan	
		Mobarakuddowla	
	Bubboo Begum	Babar Jang	
	Mani Begum	Ali Jah	
		Wala Jah	
	Faizunnessa Begum	Humayun Jah	
Maherlekha Begum		* Where the remains of the last Nawab Nazim were deposited before removal to Kerbella.	

JAFFRAGANG DEORI.

Almost opposite the cemetry is the Jaffraganj Deori, the residence of Meer Jaffer, before he ascended the musnud of Bengal, that is when he was Commander-in-chief of the Suba. It was fortified with towers and provided with cannon.

Meer Jaffer's audience hall, since turned into an Imambarah, and his dwelling house in the mahal serai, now called the Kusre Azem, still exists.

Here the last secret conference before the battle of Plassey, took place between Watts, the East India Company's chief factor at Cossimbazar, who entered the Deori in a palanquin, disguised as a purdanasheen lady of the harem, and Meer Jaffer and his son, Miran. Miran received Watts in one of the appartments of the seraglio. Then placing the Koran on his head and his hand on the head of his son, Meer Jaffer swore with great solemnity that he would faithfully perform all he had promised.

The place, where according to the Seir-ul-Mutaqherin, Serajuddowla was murdered is pointed out in the compound of the Deori, by the side of the public road, under a Neem tree (*Melia Azudirachta*). On the walls of a room could be seen the blood stains of the murder of Serajuddowla. The walls which witnessed Mahamdi Beg's act do no longer stand.

According to Orme, the scene of the murder would seem to be in the Mansurganj Palace, on the other side of the river, opposite to the Jaffraganj Deori. Orme was writing at Madras. Family tradition strongly supports the view of the Mutaqherin. Some are of opinion that the probability is that Serajuddowla was killed at Mansurganj, where Miran resided, and that his mangled body was crossed over and kept at Jaffraganj at night, when, next morning, it was placed on an elephant and paraded through the streets of the city past his mother's house and then taken across the river for interest at Khoshbagh.

A pension of Rs. 6,000 per month was granted by Lord Clive to Miran. Fifth in descent from him is Syud Mahomed Faiaz Ali Khan, the present representative of Miran's family.

Meer Jaffer

Merau (predeceased his father) | Other children

Murtaza Khan

Mustapha Khan

Asadulla Khan

Azem Ali Khan

Faiaz Ali Khan.

NASHIPORE RAJBARI.

The raj premises occupy a large area and comprises the Thacoorbari, in the principal temple of which is located the family deity, Sri Sri Ram Chandra Deb Thacoor. In the inner quadrangle of the Thacoor Bari a niche or room it allotted to each one of the countless images that receive their daily worship.

e Sheba is well managed by the present Sheba Rajah Ranajit Sinha Bahadur, who performs the several annual festivities in connection with the Sheba, especially the Jhoolun, with great splendour. Vast Zemindaries have been dedicated for the worship of the Thacoors. The fact of this endowment was communicated to the Governor General by a letter received in Calcutta on the 6th Decembar, 1819, and his consent was conveyed through the Agent at Murshidabad.

The main building of the Rajbari, which is a two storyed house with a grand flight of stairs, has an imposing facade. The large and spacious Drawing room is well-furnished and upholstered. Two valuable paintings, the portraits of Rajah Keertichand Bahadur and Kumar Udoy Chandra, adorn the walls. The Viceroy, Lord Curzon, who paid a visit to the Raj-Bari, is reported to have said—"I do not agree with you when you say yours is a humble house. It is better than ours. It is a princely abode."

The present Rajbari was constructed by Rajah Keertichand Bahadur. The founder of the family, namely, Debi Singh of history, settled in a village near the railway station of Bokhara, where his Thacoorbari still exists. Rajah Udwant Singh removed and settled at Gaisabad and thence removed to Nashipore. A range of Zenana apartments is now under construction.

Among the family records are preserved letters signed by Hastings, Minto, Moira, Prinsep, Metcalfe, Darlymple and others.

To the Nashipur Raj belongs the credit of having possessed a complete set of the eighteen Purans in manuscript, out of which some were supplied to the Maharajah of Burdwan, when he undertook the publication of that valuable work, and which he could not procure elsewhere.

The Nashipore Raj family is one of considerable antiquity and historical importance. It claims Rajah Sagor of the Solar dynasty of Koilkote as its founder. One member of the family, namely, Tarachand, settled at Paniput and among his descendants, Devi Singh migrated to Bengal in 1756, and rose to prominence by farming the districts of Purneah, Edrakpore, Rangpore and Dinajpore, under a lease dated the 18th May, 1781. On the formation of the Provincial Councils in 1773, Rajah Devi Singh became Secretary to the Provincial Council of Murshidabad. The office of Dewan of the revenue administration of Bengal, then newly created, was conferred upon him. The revenues increased considerably and it was alleged that Devi Singh had inflicted a variety of punishments to effect this. In 1783, the ryats of Rangpore broke out into open rebellion, Devi Singh was removed from official trusts and a commission was subsequently appointed to investigate into his matter. Sir John Shore was of opinion that many of the worst accusations preferred against Devi Singh had no foundation whatever. Warren Hastings in 1783 and John Macpherson and Lord Cornwallis shewed the most laudable and anxious desire to do strict justice to Devi Singh. On his death, Mr. T. F. Bevan, the Collector of Murshidabad, wrote to the Board of Revenue—"I beg leave to report to you the decease on the 18th instant (April, 1805) of Maharajah Devi Singh Bahadur, Zemindar of Huda Ekoori &c. The deceased has left no children. His property will devolve to (sic) his brother and his nephews."

Devi Singh was succeeded by his brother, Rajah Bahadur Singh Bahadur, who died in 1811. The eldest of his three sons, namely, Kumar Hanumanta Singha, died within a year of his father's death.

His son, Kishen Chand, being a child of tender years, was ignored by his uncle, Rajah Udwant Singh, who became the next representative of the house of Devi Singh. In 1812, he was granted the privelege of addressing himself direct to the Governor General and the Government authorized him to assume the title of Rajah, remitting the nuzur of five gold mohers sent by him, as the acceptance of pecuniary offerings was, in those days, contrary to the practice of Government.

Rajah Udwant Singh had immense wealth and large commercial dealings. The British Government, being compelled to take up arms against the hostile Rajah of Rewa, desired Rajah Udwant Singh to join his "troops" with those of Government.

In 1819, Udwant Singh made an absolute gift of the business and profits of his Burrabazar firm with the Poshta lands and his Hanspookhooria dwelling house in Calcutta, besides the sum of one lac of rupees and various Zemindaries, for the maintenance of his family diety, Raghunathjee, still worshipped in the Nashipore Rajbari, known as Rama Baikunta. The endowment was reported to and sanctioned by Government.

Rajah Udwant Singh was, for some time, Dewan of Nawab Nazim Ali Jah. A controversy having arisen regarding the disposal of certain Nizamut property, a Commission of enquiry was appointed by Government and the evidence of the Rajah having become necessary, he attended the Commission on the 5th August, 1822, and stated that he could not depose on oath, as he had never appeared as witness in a Court of Justice. Interrogatories were therefore furnished to him to answer them solemnly.

In 1818 Udwant Singh visited Baidyanath and made valuable presents to the shrine, spending money with a lavish hand. In September, 1822, he set out on a pilgrimage to Gya and paid a visit to the Maharajah Sirdat Nath Singh of Ramgarh, where he fell ill. He wrote to the Governor General to look with kindness upon his successor. Kumar Kissen Chand, who had been passed over, now assumed the title of Rajah, which Government acknowledged as belonging to the family. The Khillut of the title of Rajah Bahadur was conferred upon him by Major Cobb, the Agent to the Governor General at Murshidabad.

Upon his death in 1850, Rajah Keerti Chand Bahadur represented the Nashipore Raj. On the 16th November, 1852, a Durbar was held at the Murshidabad Agency to invest him with the Khillut of the title assumed by him. The architectural additions to the Rajbari were due to his taste. Keerti Chand died in 1864.

His son, Kumar Ranajit Sinha, succeeded to the family title and estates, in the management of which he has exhibited remarkable capacity. Within a very short time and though burdened with heavy litigation in which he found himself involved on taking over his estates from the hands of the Court of Wards, he made considerable additions to the family property. On the attainment of his majority, he gave to the city of Murshidabad its Victoria Jubilee Hall. At the Durbar held at Belvedere on the 4th March, 1892, Sir Charles Elliot in addressing him said—"It is a very great pleasure to me to convey to you the sanad of the tittle of 'Rajah' which the Viceroy has been pleased to confer upon you. The title is one which had been honourably borne by your family for many generations and it is committed to you to hold untarnished. One of your ancestors, Rajah Devi Singh, rendered very valuable services to Clive at Plassey, and the continued favour in which your family has been held and the honour which is to-day entrusted to you, is a proof that the Government of India is never too slow to recognise and never forget services rendered to it by the houses in this country. You have lately attained your majority and succeeded to your property. I trust you will manage your estate in a manner worthy of your ancestry and that your career may compare favourably with that of other Zemindars in the province; and that it will be so distinguished that further honours will be conferred upon you, not on account of the good work of those who have gone before you, but as a reward for your own merit and exertions."

Ten years later, on the occasion of the Diamond Jubilee of Her Majesty the late Queen Victoria, the title of 'Rajah Bahadur' was conferred upon Rajah Ranjit Sinha and at the investiture Durbar held at Belvedere, Sir Charles Stevens, the officiating Lieutenant Governor of Bengal, addressing him said—"Rajah, you are a scion of a very ancient and respectable family and the proprietor of extensive Zemindaries, have conducted yourself in a manner worthy of your origin and of your rank and responsibilities; you have the reputation of being a good and liberal landlord to your own ryots, but your desire to do good service to the public has led you to enter a more extended sphere of usefulness. As a Municipal Commissioner and an Honourary Magistrate you have rendered great assistance to the local authorities. It has been deemed just and proper that you should be raised to the dignity which your father enjoyed, you have therefore been created a 'Rajah Bahadur,'

RAJAH RANAJIT SINHA BAHADUR.

MAJUMDAR'S MURSHIDABAD. FANCY PRESS.

and it gives me great satisfaction to hand you the sanad and the Khilat which mark your elevation to that rank."

In 1899, Rajah Ranajit Sinha Bahadur was appointed a member of the Bengal Legislative Council. He more than justified his selection. The Press was unanimous in extolling his services and zealous work, and congratulated him upon his public spirit, his devotion to the interests of his countrymen and his fearless independence. In his anxiety to improve the Calcutta Municipal Draft Bill, though a member nominated by Government, he vied with the representatives of the people, and no land-holder from his seat in Council had ever displayed such courage. The most useful interpellations of the Rajah Bahadur, in regard to the supply of good drinking water to the people of the mafassal, received a very sympathetic response from the Lieutenant Governor. For his services in the Bengal Council, the Rajah Bahadur was regarded by many as worthily representing that efficient school of political reformers to which belonged the late Kristodas Pal and Rajendra Lal Mittra.

In 1902, Lord Curzon, while visiting Murshidabad, entered the Nashipore Rajbari to receive the Rajah Bahadur's congratulations and welcome.

Of his children, the eldest son, Kumar Bhupendra Naraen Sinha, the heir-apparent, is a smart and intelligent boy.

The following is a genealogy of the Nashipur Raj family :—

Rajah Sagor
|
Maharajah Rawat
|
Maharajah Tarawah
|
Kumar Madan Singh
|
Kumar Sadhu Ram
|
Rai Lahar Mal
|
Rai Kulchand
|
Rai Singh Rai
|
Rai Jat Mal
|
Rai Tarachand alias Rai Jhabali Rai
|
Rai Gorib Das
|
Rai Ajit Singh
|
Rai Amar Singh
|
Rai Dewali Singh

- Maharajah Debi Singh Bahadur
- Rajah Bahadur Singh Bahadur
  - Kumar Hanumanta Singh
    - Rajah Kissenchand Singh Br.
      - Rajah Keertichand Br.
        - Rajah Ranajit Sinha Bahadur + Rani Kamal Kumari Saheba
          - Kumar Bhupendra Naraen
          - Kumar Nripendra Naraen
          - Kumar Rajendra Naraen
          - Kumar Birendra Naraen
          - Kumar Jagadindra Naraen
      - Kumar Udoychand
  - Rajah Udwant Singh Br.
    - Ramchand (adopted) <— Ramchand
  - Janakiram
    - Ramchand

JAGAT SETT'S HOUSE.

At Mohimapur, a few yards from the Nashipur Rajbari, are visible the ruins and remnants of the old banking house of the Jagat Setts, whose history is connected with some of the most critical revolutions in Bengal. By Jagat Sett is meant the bankers of the world and their transactions have been characterized to have been as extensive as those of the Bank of England.

On the 26th June, 1757, Watts and Walsh met Meer Jaffer and Dullavram in this house and conferred about payment of the amounts stipulated for before the battle of Plassey. Three days after, Meer Jaffer having in the interval placed himself on the masnud of Bengal, Behar and Orissa, Clive, Watts, Scrafton, Miran and Dullavram again proceeded to the house and stipulated for payment by instalments. Omichand, the millionaire, whom the English had employed as an useful agent, was present but was not allowed to sit on the carpet on which the others were seated. When the arrangements for payment were concluded, Clive said, "It is time to undeceive Omichand." Scrafton, whose knowledge of Urdu was useful on this occasion, advancing said—"Omichand, the red paper is a trick, you are to have nothing." Omichand thereupon fell back insensible and his mind became lost for ever. He was removed home in a palki, and thence he was sent out on a pilgrimage.

The major portion of the house has been cut away by the river, which tradition says could one day be blocked with Jagat Sett's treasures, so vast they were.

Among things of interest to be seen at Jagat Sett's house are the following :—

1. The Hindu temple built of porcelain tiles by Harreck Chand in 1798.

2. The ruins of the Jaina temple containing an underground cell for concealing treasures built by Fateh Chand in 1702.

3. Detached pieces of granite slabs, pillar, arches &c., some of them perfect, and of exquisite workmanship.

4. Jaina images made of pebbles, crystals and other precious stones, one of them bearing date 1664 with the price, namely Rs. 80,000, inscribed thereon.

5. Firmans of the Emperor of Delhi granting the title of Jagat Sett.

The origin of the Setts of Murshidabad is traced to Heeranand Saho, who belonged to the Marwari tribe of Rajputs and who migrated from his native village of Nagor, in Jodhpore, in 1695 and settled in Patna. The eldest of his seven sons, Manick Chand, proceeded to Dacca, from where he followed the great Dewan, Murshed Kuli Khan, to Murshidabad. Here he became banker and councellor to the Nawab, and was charged with the remittance of Bengal's contribution to Delhi, namely one crore and fifty lacs. The Nawab's personal treasures used often to be kept with him. On Murshed Kuli Khan's recommendation, he got the title of Sett from the Emperor Furrokh Shyr, in 1715.

RANI BHOWANI'S HOUSE.

JAGAT SETT'S THAKURBARI.

On the same recommendation, his adopted son, Fateh Chand, got the title of Jagat Sett from the Emperor Mahmud Sha in 1724. Nawab Ali Verdi Khan gave Jagat Sett Sharup Chand the title of Maharajah.

In 1742 the Mahrattas robbed the Setts of half a crore of rupees. In 1749, the Setts advanced twelve lacs to the English.

Serajuddowla ordered Jagat Sett to raise three crores of rupees from the 'merchants.' On Jagat Sett's refusal to comply with the requisition, he got a slap in open durbar.

In 1759 Jagat Sett visited Calcutta and was entertained by the servants of the East India Company at a cost of seventeen thousand rupees.

On the 21st April, 1763, Meer Kasem caused the Setts to be seized and imprisoned in the palace at Heera Jheel. Notwithstanding the intercession of the English, they were conveyed to Monghyr and there flung into the river from the bastions of the fortress.

The Setts of Murshidabad erected several temples on the Poreshnath hills in Hazaribagh. The Majhli or Murshidabad temple founded by them is the richest, being still maintained by the Jainas of Murshidabad. The inscriptions on the pedestals of the images are as follow :—

1. Sthapit Shougal Chand Jagat Sett, Sambat 1822.
2. Sthapit Sougal Chand and Hoshiyal Chand Sambat 1822.
3. Sthapit Rupchand Jagat Sett Sambat 1873.

The following is a genealogy of the Setts, "that family who have suffered so much in our cause, are peculiary entitled to our protection" (Despatch, 1768) :—

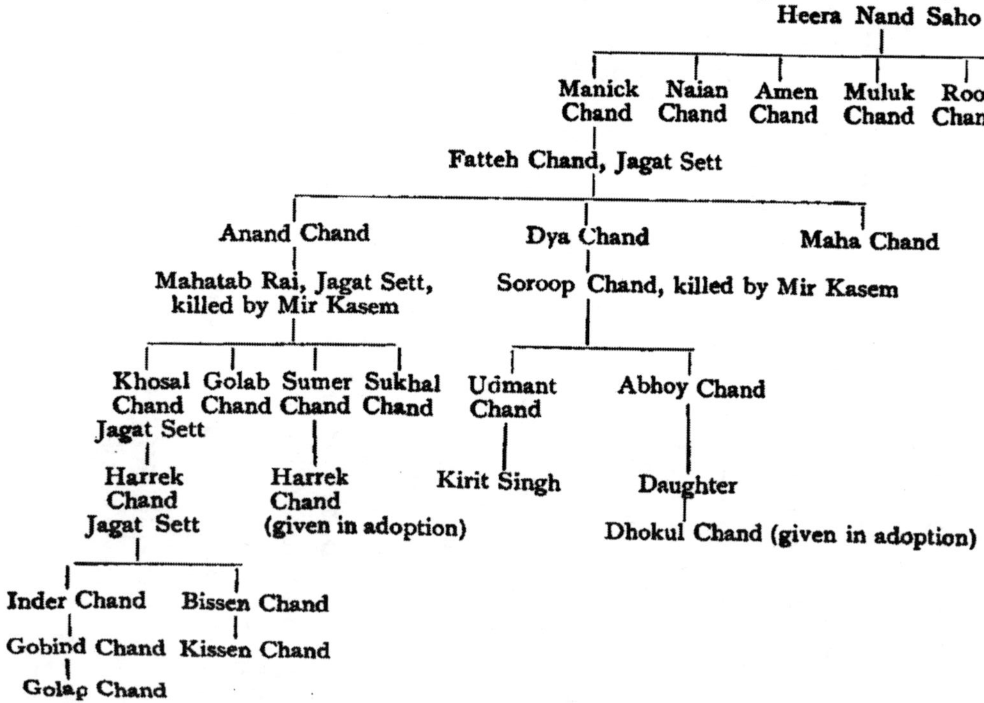

SUTTEE CHOWRAHA.

Two of the four roads which met a little to the north of Jagat Sett's house, from which the place takes its name, have been cut away by the river. Near the junction stands what is known as the Suttee Mandir, built to commemorate the death of a Hindu widow, who burnt herself on the funeral pyre of her husband. The temple is over two hundred years old. The stone door frames and commemorative slab have been removed and the temple is in disrepair.

When Ali Verdi Khan was the Subadar of Bengal and Sir Francis Russell was the Chief of the East India Company's factory at Cossimbazar, a case of sutee took place there, which was witnessed by Holwell, on the morning of the 4th February, 1743. The voluntary victim was the widow, aged seventeen, of Ram Chand Pandit, a Mahratta Brahmin, belonging to a family of great consequence at Cossimbazar. Lady Russell could not succeed in pursuading her to desist from self-immolation.

The remarkable isolated instance of a Mahomedan lady, burying herself alive with the corpse of her husband, is reported in the Calcutta Gazette of the 29th July, 1790, though the scene of occurence was elsewhere.

This revolting practice of burning alive Hindu widows is nowhere enjoined by the Shasters as an imperative duty and was declared in 1829 as illegal and punishable, by Lord William Bentinck, who, without intending to depart from the principle that all classes of the people be secure in the observance of their religious usages so long as that could be done without violation of the paramount dictates of justice and humanity, promulgated rules for its immediate suppression.

THE PHUTI MUSJED.

About three quarters of a mile to the east of the Palace, at Kumrapore, is the Phuti Musjed, reputed to have been built by Serferaz Khan in a single night. It is one of the largest mosques of the city, being 135 feet long and 38 feet broad. It is surmounted by five domes, some of which are incomplete, so that the sky is visible from the floor. At the four corners are four spiral stairs surmounted by four cupolas.

According to another account, masons were employed for several months in the construction of this huge pile. When the muster roll was called one day, the number that responded was one less than the number found actually to work. This mysterious fact was verified for several days, when it became so notorious that the mysterious excess workman suddenly disappeared, leaving the work incomplete, which the skill of the rest could not rectify.

An interesting relic is the mud which was used for the centering of the arches, to which for a century and a half, it has stuck fast and notwithstanding exposure, looks as if applied only yesterday.

MAHAMMAD TAKI'S TOMB.

A little to the south-west of the Kamaldaha or lotus lake, lies the tomb of Mir Mahammad Taki, the son of Nawab Mahabat Ali Khan, and nephew of Serajuddowla. He died in 1810. The Government has of late enclosed the tomb with a wall and put a tombstone bearing inscriptions in English and Persian.

The elevated land on the banks of the Kamaldaha is pointed out as the site of the Murshidabad residence of Manickchand, the Governor of Hughli, whom Serajuddowla left with a garrison of 3,000 men to command Alinagar, (as the Nawab called Calcutta), after the surrender of Fort William in 1756. On the arrival of the English armament from Madras under Clive, Manickchand fled to Murshidabad, where he was imprisoned by Serajuddowla and released on payment of ten lacs of rupees, as a fine for the plunder of Calcutta. After the victory at Plassey, Clive wrote to Manickchand from Daudpore, promising not to take him to task for his conduct in the plunder.

RAJABAZAR DEORI.

To the east of Serajuddowla's Bazar is the Rajabazar Deori, founded by Rowshanuddowla, a brother of Mobarukuddowla. The present representative of the Rajabazar family is Syud Mozaffer Ali Khan, the President of the Basant Ali Khan Endowment Committee, appointed under Act XX of 1863, whose descent is shewn below :—

- Mobarukuddowla
  - Rowshanuddowla
    - Gowharunnissa Begum
    - Syud Jaffer Ali
      - Amir Ali
        - Syud Mozaffer Ali Khan
      - Mobarak Ali
      - Azem Ali
      - Omda Begum
      - Abbasi Begum
      - Budrunnissa Begum
      - Sultani Begum

SERAJUDDOWLA'S BAZAR.

The site occupied by what is now known as Serajuddowla's Bazar was a large pit, the repository of unwholesome matter. By Serajuddowla's command, it was in one single night filled np and converted into a bazar or market place.

NAKTA KHALI.

Nakta Khali or Nangta Khali, now known as the Naginabagh, is the site of the palace of Serferaz Khan. The mosque built by his wife still exists. Near by is his tomb which has lately been enclosed by a wall.

Of the palace there are no traces. Serferaz Khan was killed at Giria and his dead body was hurriedly removed to the city upon an elephant and buried by his son, Mirza Amani, "darkly and at dead of night" (1740).

BEGUM MUSJED.

Close by the tomb of Serferaz Khan, at Naginabagh, known before as Naktakhali, is what is known as Begum's Musjed, constructed by Serferaz Khan's wife. The tablet on the central archway bears the following inscription, the last four words of which give the date in the hisab abejad or cryptographical form :—

"Khalaek Sijdagaheh urshe tarum
Behesht a in mokameh sakht Begum
Ta'al al Alla ajaeb masjedeh Sakht
Kebr firke malaek sa yah andakht
Cheh musjed az safa manand jinnat
Cheh musjed mania ijad rahamut
Batarikhush ze akhl emdad joostam
Hodooseh in nozool abad joostam
Khurud gofta makaneh faizi nust
Binaeh izzuteh, doonia o din ust
1131."

The above may be translated thus :—

This place of devotion for created beings is high like heaven,

The Begum has made this place like heaven;
God be thanked; she has erected a wonderful mosque;
She has thrown a shelter over the heads of God's messengers,
What a wonderful mosque, pure as heaven,
What a wonderful mosque, from which God's mercy is emanating;
I seek the aid of intelligence to find out its date;
I seek the origin of the permanence of this which has come down (from heaven);
Intelligence says this is the source of benefit,
It is the foundation of the honours of this world and of religion.

1131.

To the west of the mosque, is an enclosure of delapidated walls, said to contain the remains of the Begum herself.

THE MOSQUE AT BAHADUR ALI KHAN'S CHOWRAHA.

A little to the north west of the Subjail, at the junction of the four roads known as Bahadur Ali Khan's Chowraha, is an old mosque, the Persian distich of the stone slab on the middle arched door of which runs as follows :—

"Tah mir gusht Musjedeh pakiza khush shefat
Shaesta eejtehad Mohammed Amir Kurd

Uz Sha Kuli ke hust kherdmand nakezath
Tarikh Sal Mnsjed Kud Kamuthissellath.
1172."

The year, as usual appears in the cryptographic form in the last two words, which is admitted to have been very happily conceived. The distich is rendered thus :—

This pure and celebrated mosque is constructed,
Mahammed Amir constructed it well
Under Shiek Kuli who is intelligent and of good family.
Date and year of mosque, I truly raise up prayers.
1172.

MEHTER'S MOSQUE.

Mehter's mosque is situated a few yards off the north west corner of the Nizamut Stable compound. The following inscription appears on the slab, the cryptographic date being contained in the words "*Salath Khana neda*" which means "this is the house of prayer" :—

"Kurd ehdas Musjede zeba
Behtero mehter zerahe sedkth safa
Yaft anjam choon ze lutf e elah
Ukl e dad in Salath Khana neda
1173."

This distich is rendered thus:—

Constructed this beautiful mosque,
Good, great and in true and pure mind,
When construction was completed by mercy of God,
Intelligence said, this is the house of prayer.
1173.

KALIBARI.

The temple of Surbomongala Kali, over eighty years old, situated on what is known as the Kalibari ghat in city Murshidabad, with a flight of stone and masonry stairs and an embankment to protect the place from the errosion of the river Bhagirathee, was built by Joy Nath Ghosh Thacoor, who was the Ekjai Serishtadar of the Nizamut. The beautiful stone image of Kali is placed in a niche in the upper storey of the temple.

The Nawab Nazim pleased with Joy Nath offered him the Dewanship. But, while declining to accept it, he prayed that the post might be conferred upon his son-in-law, Ganga Dhar Rai, who got the appointment with the title of Rajah conferred upon him. The Sheba is now in the hands of his grandsons.

LAMPUT GHAT.

Opposite to the present Charitable Dispensary is the Lamput Ghat, the Ghat with stone steps constructed by Rajah Rajballav, the son of Rajah Dullabram, the major portion of which was been cut away.

The buildings occupied by the Charitable Dispensary were the Nautch ghar of Rajah Gangadhar.

Close by is the Victoria Jubilee Hall, on the site of the Shafakhana or old Nizamut Dispensary and a gift in commemoration of the Golden Jubilee of 1887.

RAI SAHEB'S HOUSE.

Between the Victoria Jubilee Hall and the Nizamut stables, is the house of Rai Udai Chand Majumdar, known as Rai Saheb's house. Udai Chand was one of those, who, towards the commencement of the last century, migrated to Murshidabad, even then a centre of learning and civilization, whither youthful aspirants might hie to rise to eminence. The founder of the family to which he belonged was Birat, one of the five kyasths who escorted the five Brahmins, versed in the Vedas, who came from Kanouj to Bengal at the invitation of Adisur, King of Gour, to perform his great sacrificial rites. Birat's descent is claimed from

Chitra Gupta of pre-historic days. About four centuries ago, Chandradwip was one stronghold of Kyastha influence and Kulinism, and Jessore was another.

Ramchandra, who with the multiplication of his sect, had settled at Chandradwip, served as an apprentice under his brothers-in-law, who held service in the office of the imperial canongoe of Sircar Satgaon. Of his three sons, the youngest, Sivananda, was appointed by Soleman Sha, King of Gour, Sadr Canongoe.

King Daud Sha conferred upon Sriharsha, Sivananda's nephew, known as Vikramaditya, the title of Maharajah. Upon his brother, Janakiballov, known as Basanta Rai, the king bestowed a similar distinction.

During the turbulent times of the close of the sixteenth century, about the year 1570, Sivananda retired to the interior of the country to pass his days in peace.

After Vikramaditya's death, his son, Maharajah Protapaditya of Jessore, asserted independence, but the imperial general, Man Singh, captured him, taking him in a cage a prisoner to Delhi. The Maharajah died at Benares and thus escaped further indignities at Delhi.

Haridas, the eldest son of Sivananda, Maharajah Protapaditya's grand uncle, married the daughter of Vaishnavdas, Zemindar of Perganah Chandraprotap.

Haridas's great grandson, Rajnaraen, held the highest post in the department of the Canongoe and obtained the title of Majumdar. Three generations intervened between his brother, Gopikanta, the founder of the family diety, and Udai Chand, who was born on Sunday, the 17th June, 1792, (corresponding to the 6th Asar, 1714 Sakabda).

Udai Chand entered the service of the Nawab Nazim as a moherer on a modest salary, and by the dint of his ability he rose to be Naib Dewan and defacto Dewan after the death of Dewan Rajah Poreshnath. The historic title of Roy Royan was conferred upon him and General Rapier, the Agent Governor General at Murshidabad, strongly recommended his confirmation as Dewan Nizamut; but the Agents death at Murshidabad and the working of conflicting interests at Calcutta resulted in the selection and appointment of Rajah Sitanath Bose as Dewan.

Rai Udai Chand spent in charities beyond his means. His house was the home of the needy and the poor. The *omedwars* and the *talblems*, who flocked to Murshidabad in search of employment or education, fed on his bounty. He bore the entire cost of marriages and sradhs in innumerable families. He was a man of great piety, of superior faculties, ardent in his affection, sincere in his sympathy, tender and generous under all circumstances, lavish in his commendation of others, humble in his estimate of himself and, above all, a faithful servant and a loyal adherent of his master, the unparalled generosity of whose royal house has, in recognition of his services, continued to his family, after his death on his return from pilgrimage to Gya, its help for over half a century now.

There are two most interesting objects jealously preserved in the family, a mandate from the Temple of Baidyanath and a small plant possessing extraordinary medicinal properties. The latter is supposed to have grown in the quadrangle of the Temple of Cufa in Arabia and to have been brought by a *faqir* who gave it to Rai Saheb. It is a small, dried up, shrunken, soot colored thing, which when thrown into water, exhibits signs of vegetable life and developes into a plant with distinctly visible roots, stem, branches, leaves, blossoms, flowers, petals and fruits. The water, in which it has been dipped, is efficacious, when drunk, in expediting labour and easy delivery. When withdrawn from the water, the plant dries up, shrinks and assumes its usual size and dark and dead appearance.

The mandate from the Temple of Baidyanath is written in the Nagri character upon Bhoojpatra, bearing the seal of the shrine, the signature of Isvariband Pujari and a representation of the Temple of Baidyanath. The sandal colored bark, speckled with small white spots and small chocolate colored lines, has cracked in many places, but the writing

NIZAMUT STABLES.

TRIPAULIA GATE.

FANCY PRESS.

is still decipherable. The story of the miraculous cure connected with this relic was confirmed by many eye witnesses, who lived within the last twenty-five years, among whom were Kantoo Sikdar and Kartiki two old servants of Rai Udai Chand, who belonged to that type of faithful and self sacrificing attendants which has now become extinct.

THE NIZAMUT STABLES.

The extensive range of stables, situated at the north east corner of the junction of the five roads known as Panchraha, is from its beauty and vastness not unfrequently mistaken by the unguarded visitor for the "Nawab's house." Attached is a spacious compound, walled round, with a large tank in the centre. The walls of the stables are cut high up into innumerable windows with sills for proper ventilation. The triple gate way is as spacious as beautiful. The large rooms of the upper storey are provided with sash doors and almirahs for the protection of harness and saddlery. The wings and the colonnades, as also the innumerable stalls and coach houses are all that could be desired.

Gram used to be ground and water from the tank drawn into a reservoir, and heated and distributed throughout the Stables, by an engine, located in a house with a large masonry chimney, not now in workable order.

A clock, with a prominent dial put up high on the wall, keeps time for the Stables.

LALBAGH.

Lalbagh is now the head quarters station of the Sub-Division of that name, and the seat of a Munsiff's chowki. The southern portion of the village has been cut away by the river.

The Court and offices of the Sub-Divisional officer are located in a building which is known by the name of Permit Kutchery, which was the Customs House established for the examination of boats, with which the river was continuously covered, being the route of great inland traffic.

During Murshed Kuli Khan's administration, Sultan Furrokh Shere, on coming from Dacca, was put up by the Nawab at his palace at Lalbagh, whence the prince removed to Rajmehal, where he settled. No trace of the palace now exists.

Of late a Bar Library was constructed with funds supplied by a public spirited Zemindar, at the instance of Mr. B. R. Mehta, C. S., the late popular and energetic Sub-Divisional officer of Lalbagh.

The Sanskrit Tol building constructed by public subscription stands close by.

THE KATRA MUSJED.

At Katra, about a mile to the east of the Palace, is the mausoleum of Murshed Kuli Khan, the founder of Murshidabad. In 1780 Hodges described Katra as a grand seminary of Mussulman learning, 170 feet square, adorned by a mosque which rose high above all the surrounding buildings.

The mosque itself, which is situated in a quadrangle, is 140 feet long and 25 feet broad, with five domes, of which the two next to the central one have collapsed. The central and the two last on either side have survived the great earthquake of 1897, which almost completely ruined the whole building. The parapet is overgrown with vegetation.

The two-storey cells round the mosque and the terrace, which accommodated seven hundred Karis or Koran readers, have nearly all gone. Between the mosque and the arched cells, there are open spaces 13 feet wide on either side and 42 feet wide at the back of the mosque. The cells are about twenty feet square, each having six arched doorways and windows. Fifteen steps, edged with stone, lead up to the gate, which has five arches on either side, through the central one of which, a pathway paved with stone runs up to the central door of the mosque, across the terrace, which in front of the mosque is 166 feet by 110 feet.

As a mark of humility, Murshed Kuli Khan lies buried under the stairs leading up to the terrace of the mosque. Marks of desolation are visible every where throughout the place, except the tomb which is kept in proper repair. A Kari is employed to read the Koran. A green silk canopy overhangs the tomb, which is covered over by a white sheet, upon which flowers are sometimes strewn and wreathes laid.

The only other thing which in this mosque, as in other old Musjeds, has cscaped the ravages of time or at least has not been materially affected, is the inscription, the crispness of which, being on basalt, has withstood with all freshness. The slab, which is on the middle door way, is rendered thus :—

"The triumph of Mahomed of Arabia is the glory of heaven and earth. Let the dust of his feet fall on the head of him who is not the dust of his door."

This latter portion is also rendered this :—"He who is not the dust of his door, dust on his head."

On the inner surface of the west wall of the mosque, there is a slab bearing a prominent inscription, which translated means there is one God and Mahomed is his Prophet.

The mosque is not an imitation of the mosque at Mecca, as is supposed by some. It was built in 1723, two years before Murshed Kuli Khan's death. The date, as usual, appears in the cryptographic form.

THE GREAT GUN AT TOPEKHANA. FANCY PRESS.

It is said that Murshed Kuli Khan pulled down the Hindu temples in the neighbourhood and utiltized the materials in the construction of this big mosque. This is hardly consistent with the fact that it was through his instrumentality that the neighbouring Hindu temple of Radha Madhub at Kowarparah and others received liberal grants of revenue free lands for their support. The uniformity of the materials also go to negative that allegation.

Murshed Kuli Khan is known as Jaffer Khan Zinda Pir, or the living saint. It is believed that cholera never breaks out in the vicinity of this sacred building, through his blessings and benedictions.

The river Pudma, lying at a great distance to the north east, was visible from the summits of the two high minars standing on either end of the compound, towards the back of the mosque. These were ascendable by spiral stairs. The upper portions of these minars have fallen down.

The Katra Jheel, as that portion of the Gobra Nala is called, was a trade route but is now silted up and hardly open for boat traffic.

THE GREAT GUN.

A quarter of a mile to the south east of Katra is Tope Khana, the site of the Nawab's Artillery Park and the east entrance gate of the old capital, protected on the east, throughout the length of the eastern limits of the city, by Gobra Nala, known locally as the Katra Jheel.

Here lies a great gun, called Jahan Kosha, destroyer of the world, which originally rested on a carriage with wheels and is now embedded in a pepul tree, which has grown by its side and holds it about four feet high from the ground, lifting it up *enmasse.* The wheels have disappeard. The iron work of the carriage and the trunions are still visible.

The gun is made of a composition of eight metals, namely gold, silver, copper, lead, zinc, mercury, iron and tin. It is 17 feet and six inches long, with a girth of 5 feet at the touch hole end. The diameter of the touch hole is one and a half inches. That of the orifice is six inches. The weight of the gun is 212 maunds and the powder required for the charge is 28 seers.

The gun was made at Dacca during the reign of Sha Jehan, when Islam Khan was the Subadar of Bengal, by Janardan Karmokar, under the instructions of Darogah Shere Mahomed and the supervision of Hara Ballav Das, in 1637.

The gun is an object of veneration by the lower classes of the people, who put oil and red mercury on it and offer presents of flowers, milk and sweets.

The muzzle points to the north and commands the whole length of the Katra Jheel.

On the gun are plated nine brass tablets with inscriptions, many of which cannot now be deciphered. The couplets in one of these is rendered thus—"During the just and equitable administration of Islam Khan, that accomplished ruler, by whom the large country of Bengal was brought into order, and whose generosity, like clouds, showered down blessings every where, and at whose door fortune attended as an insignificant slave, this dragon-like gun was manufactured for the destruction of the enemy of the Emperor of the time, Sha Jehan. When I was absorbed in thought in finding out the year of its manufacture, in the letters of the alphabet, the words *Tope Jehan Kosha* struck me." The letters of these *three* words will give the year.

The ninth plate is in prose and is rendered thus:—"This Cannon by name Tope Jehan Kosha was manufactured at Jehangir Nagar alias Dacca under the supervision of Shere Mahomed and the clerkship of Haraballav Das by Jonardan Karmokar in the month of Jamadiussani of the year 11 of the joloos. The cannon weighs 212 maunds and the charge of powder is 28 seers."

. To the north-east and the east of the great gun are still visible in the high mounds of earth the remnants of the Morcha or mud ramparts. The broad embankments are now covered with jungle and planted with trees. A few guns found here were removed and may still be seen at the corners of the Burra Laldighi tank at Berhampore.

A little to the north-east of the Tope Khana is Takia Sha Meer, a shrine held in great reverence by the community of wrestlers.

KADAM SHARIF.

About a quarter of a mile to the south of Katra is Kadam Sharif, by which name the mosque and Imambara of Itwar Ali Khan, Nawab Nazir of Meer Jaffer, are known. It was founded in 1194 H. Basant Ali Khan, a eunuch in the service of the Nawab Nazim, was appointed the first Mutwalli. A stone, held in very great reverence, is pointed out as bearing an impression of the feet of the Prophet of Arabia. Hence the name, Kadam Rasool or Kadam Sharif. It lay formerly at Gour, from where it was removed to Murshidabad with some other relics, such as the hair of the Prophet.

There is an inscription which is rendered thus:— "This mosque was erected in the reign of Saifud Dunyauddeen Abul Mozaffer Firoze Sha by his grand vizier. This engraving was done on the 2nd Moharram, 896 H." (1490 A. D.)

The establishment is maintained by the endowment of Basant Ali Khan, the chief eunuch in the establishment of Mani Begum, after whose death, he was appointed in that capacity to the Deori of Dulhin Begum and Bohu Begum. On the 24th June, 1833,

Basant Ali Khan wrote to Major Cobb, the Agent to the Governor General at Murshidabad, of his dedication of two thirds of his property to the Kadam Sharif and Imambara at Begumganj, and of his appointment of Bahar Ali Khan and Bahoo Begum as trustees. The endowment was approved by Government on the 23rd January, 1834, and due intimation was given to Nawab Nazim Humayun Jah, who as the master of a purchased slave, was Basant Ali Khan's heir, failing any relative or disposition by will.

In the administration of the affairs of the household and the control of the Zenana, the eunuch slaves of Murshidabad exercised no inconsiderable influence. The term slave, in its ordinary acceptance, was hardly applicable to them, having been considered as members of the household and often held in great esteem. They sometimes held other important and responsible charges. In their treatment, the Nawabs of Murshidabad have never been forgetful of the status they held in Islam. They have been fed and clothed and housed as relations and have been permitted to acquire property, though slavery was not dealt with so as to give slaves the power to hold property, until the enactment of Act V. of 1843.

Of this class of eunuchs, drawn from Abyssinia and other places on the east coast of Africa, the names most familiar in Murshidabad are those of Itwar Ali Khan, Almas Ali Khan, Basant Ali Khan,

Bushir Ali Khan, Nazir Ali Khan, Darab Ali Khan, Feroze Ali Khan, Arjumand Ali Khan, Aman Ali Khan, Aman Gong, Tahsen Ali Khan &c.

The chief eunuch was called the Nawab Nazir and was a personage of importance in the eyes of all. The more wealthy of these were imbued with a spirit of piety and benevolence, which have kept their names alive. They have left their properties tied up for the service of God and the benefit of man. The religious and charitable endowments of Basant Ali Khan, Nazir Ali Khan, Darab Ali Khan and Arjumand Ali Khan deserve special mention.

MOBARAK MANZIL.

To the south east of Kadam Sharif, about a couple of miles from the Palace, is Mobarak Manzil called also Humayun Manzil. The main building and the out offices were built by the East India Company in what was then known as the Findalbagh. The Courts were held here from 1765 to 1781, when they were removed to Calcutta. Subsequently the Civil and Criminal Courts were located here, before Lord Cornwallis, in 1793, transferred the Supreme Courts to Calcutta.

By order of the Governor General, the buildings, with the Findalbagh, were sold, in 1831, to Humayun Jah for Rs. 10,5000 and the adjoining lands and buildings were purchased by the Nawab for Rs. 35,000 from the Rajah of Nashipur, who had purchased them from the East India Company. The whole was converted into a garden house and summer residence, when the beautiful building, with marble floors, on the north, by the side of the tank, known as Lal Bunglow, was added by Humayun Jah.

On the terrace in front of this building stood the Masnud or throne, used by the Nawabs Nazim of Bengal from the time of Sultan Shuja, brought here by Humayun Jah. It was a round table made of black stone (horn blende), six feet in diameter and eighteen inches high, with four thick pedastals, the whole hewn out of one block. The edge or rim is cut into sixteen facets and on one of them is an inscription in Persian which reads thus :—"Taiar Shud Takt Mobarak batarikh bistohaftum Shahere Shaban-ul-Moazzum 1052 bai ehtemam Kumtaneen banda Khaja Nazar Bokhari fimokam Monghyr Munsebe Behar." Translated it means "this auspicious throne was made at Monghyr in Behar by the humblest of slaves, Khaja Nazar of Bokhara, on the 27th Shaban, 1052 H." (1643). It belongs to the reign of Sultan Shuja, second son of Sha Jehan, and Subedar of Bengal (1639-47). There are some holes near the edge of the throne for the insertion of poles for the support of a canopy.

Clive placed Meer Jaffer on this throne at Mansurganj after the battle of Plassey in 1757; and Clive sat on it side by side with Najmuddowla at Moti Jheel when celebrating, in 1766, the first Pooneah after the acquisition of the Dewani by the East India Company.

Drops of reddish liquid issue from certain parts of the stone which when dried up leaves stains, due perhaps to the presence of iron, which are, however, popularly regarded as tears, which have flowed ever since the Subadars of Bengal handed the Dewani over to the East India Company and ceased to sit on it to hold the Pooneah. Lord Curzon, while visiting Mobarak Manzil, sat on this throne and it is believed it will no more shed tears. (This Stone Throne has of late been removed to Calcutta for the Victoria Memorial).

There are a beautiful lawn and a conservatory. As a lovely garden and park, Mobarak Manzil stands unrivalled in Murshidabad.

Close by is Barafkhana, perhaps the only place in Lower Bengal, where, during the winter, water kept out in shallow earthen saucers upon cushions of straw, is converted into ice.

The Batta talao is a deep tank well filled with water and fish, close to the out office buildings of the East India Company which still exist.

Mobarak Manzil, like many other gardens of the Nawab Bahadur of Murshidabad, produces very superfor mangoes, for the variety and excellence of which Murshidabad has always been famous. They are known and appreciated in Calcutta by the name of Choonakhali mangoes. But the fruits of the best qualities seldom go out of Murshidabad. While

MOBARUK MANZIL, WITH THE STONE THRONE.

MAJUMDAR'S MURSHIDABAD. FANCY PRESS.

planting, grafts are preferred to seedlings, as the former bear fruit earlier. The general qualifications of a good mangoe are *chhilkapatla* or thin skinned, *shiradar* or juicy, *gootlichhota* or small stoned, *turshi* that is of sweet-sourish taste, *mugzmolaem* or of delicate flesh and *beresha* or threadless. With pallao, meat dishes and preparations of ghee generally the mangoe best suited and most liked is the ananas, which in flavour and color very much resembles the legitimate fruit of that name, namely the pine-apple. Great precautions are taken to prevent the fruits from being purloined. The owners of the best gardens seldom sell them and hence the extreme difficulty of securing the best varieties in the bazar.

The Murshidabad fruit is unrivalled in color, flavour and taste. Subacid mangoes are generally preferred by the Mahomedans to very sweet varieties, so much in favour with the Hindus. The fruits are taken down from the trees, one by one, in what is called a thoosi, which is a thin bamboo pole with an open mouthed net bag at the top end, into which the fruits are received when drawn in with a slight jerk. No good mangoes are obtained by shaking the branches and collected on the ground. The slightest pressure or hurt spoils them. The parts affected become hard and bad of taste. The most delicate varieties, like the Kalapahar, are kept on a cusion of leaves and their position is changed many times a day, till they are ready for the knife. Mahomedans and appreciative Hindus eat mangoes in slices and seldom take its squeezed out juice with milk, so much valued by the Hindus. The best varieties, so jealously sent out as presents to Europeans, seldom find a place on their table and frequently find their way into the private store room of the butler or cook.

The Murshidabad crop is earlier than the Maldah and June and July constitute its season. Mangoe makes good sauce and jelly. Indigestion if ever caused by partaking mangoes is cured by taking the kernel of the stone of the fruit with milk. A half ripe mangoe, taken from the tree with its stalk, is said to retain its taste for two or three months, while the color will remain even for a year, if the broken end of the stalk be closed with warm wax and kept in butter or honey.

The best living authority on and connoisier of mangoes is Nawab Wala Kadr Syud Hossein Ali Meerza Bahadur, who owns some of the best trees or purchases them at fabulous prices during the season.

The best varieties of Murshidabad mangoes are the following, among which the Kalapahar is the sovereign fruit :—

- Ananas
- Anupan
- Bangajal
- Begumpasand
- Bhowanichowras
- Bimli
- Bira
- Daudbhog
- Dilpasand
- Doodhia
- Foucalbayan
- Gourjit
- Hilsapeti
- Kalapahar
- Kohitoor
- Misrikand
- Mirzapasand
- Nawabpasand
- Nazimpasand
- Nazookbadan
- Ranipasand
- Rougni
- Shadowla
- Shahi (bura)
- Sinduria (bura)
- Subza

FINDALBAGH.

The lands adjoining Mobarak Manzil and near the Battatalao were known as the Findalbagh, after Mr. Findal, the officer who was required to attach the moveable properties of Rajah Devi Singh, when a commission of enquiry was ordered in respect of the charges brought against him in connection with his farming of Rangpore and Dinajepore. Upon the Rajah's protest, no attachment however was made.

The Nizamut Adalat or Chief Criminal Court and the Dewani Adalat or Civil Court houses were situated at Findalbagh and at Mobarak Monzil. The jail was located at Aishbagh, on the opposite bank of the Bansbari Jheel, close by.

By Regulation V of 1793 was established a Provincial Court of appeal exeercising jurisdiction over city Murshidabad and the districts of Murshidabad, Bhagulpore, Rajshye, Rangpore, Dinajepore and Cooch Behar

Under Regulation XVII of 1793, in complaints in the city or Zillah Courts, in which it appeared either upon the application of the Nawab Nazim or of the Complainant or Defendant, that both parties were servants or relations of the Nawab Nazim, or the widow or female descendants of the former Nazims of Bengal, the parties were to be referred for justice to the Nazim. Upon complaint against any servant of the Nawab by a person of a different description, the courts were to refer it to His Highness, or to hear it in the ordinary manner, taking care at all times and in all matters, to pay every proper attention to the dignity and long established rights of the Nawab.

Regulation XIX of 1805 defined the form of addressing and the channel of application to be observed by public officers in the judicial, revenue and criminal departments and to make applications to His Highness.

The form of address to be observed in making applications to the members of the family of the Nawab Nazim were defined by Regulation XVI of 1806.

Regulation XIX of 1825 prescribed the manner in which the Nawab Nazim was to sue or be sued in the Courts of Civil jurisdiction. The Agent to the Governor General, resident at His Highness's Durbar, was to institute and defend suits on behalf of His Highness, from whom no security was to be demanded and against whom no attachment was to issue.

Section 10 of Regulation XVI of 1793, Regulation XIX of 1805, Regulation XVI of 1806 and Regulation XIX of 1825 were repealed by Regulation XXVII of 1854. Henceforth, civil process, to be executed within the precints of the Killah of the Nawab Nazim, were to be transmitted to the Superintendent of Nizamut affairs but criminal process to be executed therein were at the discretion of the courts to be likewise transmitted or not. Section 5 of this Regulation authorized the Government of Bengal to define the limits of the Palace and from time to time to alter them.

Coming to more recent times, by Act XVII of 1873, the Nawab Nazim was exempted from the jurisdiction of the Civil Courts and he was declared incapable of contracting pecuniary obligations.

The public rights and priveleges of the Nawab Bahadur of Murshidabad were stamped with the authority of legistation by a short enactment in 1891, validating an Indenture between him and the Secretary of State for India in Council, which is known as the Murshidabad Act.

NAKKATITOLA.

At the junction of the Mobarak Manzil road with the main road is Nakkatitola, where leaning against a big tamarind tree, stands the well carved hornblende image of a Hindu goddess, with the nose mutilated, probably by Kalapahar, in Orissa, which was brought from there by some Hindu general of Ali Verdi Khan.

KOWARPARA.

Less than a quarter of a mile from Nakkatitola towards the south east, is Kowarpara, containing the temple of Radha Madhub, founded by Bangshibadan Gossami, in 1609 and maintained from the proceeds of lands granted under imperial firmans, which are still in the custody of the shebait. Murshed Kuli Khan also secured certain firmans and grants from the Emperor of Delhi for the support of the sheba.

It is said that one of the Nawabs once sent to the temple various kinds of cooked food on trays covered with embroidered Khanposhes. The shebait, who did not suspect any thing wrong and did not know what the contents of the trays were, admitted them into the temple and when they were uncovered in the presence of the bearers, the abominable food had vanished and in its place were found on the trays several kinds of sweet scented flowers. The bewildered bearers reported on oath the strange metamorphosis to the Nawab, who thenceforth began to pay to the temple the respect it deserved.

MOTI JHEEL.

About a couple of miles to the south of the Palace is the Moti Jheel or the Lake of Pearls. It is supposed to have been made out of an abandoned bed of the river Bhagirathee, in horse shoe shape, by Nawazesh Ahmed Khan, surnamed Shahamat Jang, the nephew and son-in-law of Ali Verdi Khan.

With materials brought from the ruins of Gour, Shahamat Jang built here a Sangidalan or stone hall, a stately pile ornamented with pillars of black marble; a mehalsara or harem and a mosque and

THE GRANT OF THE DEWANI.

FANCY PRESS.

several out-offices. He lived here with his wife, Ghasiti Begum, the daughter of Ali Verdi Khan. After his death she cantoned herself at Moti Jheel and distributed elephants and lacs of rupees to the troops of her deceased husband, expecting their support against Serajuddowla.

Moti Jheel was taken by Serajuddowla in 1756 from Ghasiti Begum, who was driven out or escaped and whose jewels were confiscated.

It was from here that Serajuddowla, in 1757, marched out for the battle field of Plassey.

Here, in 1758, Mir Jaffer built a Baraduary or house with twelve doors.

Major Adams after defeating Meer Kasem's troops at the mouth of the Ajai and at Cutwa, in 1763, and following the route, which six years before, Clive had pursued, found the remnants of the Nawab's defeated army well posted, their front covered by the Moti Jheel.

The day following, Adams escorted Meer Jaffer from here in a triumphant peagent into Murshidabad.

In 1765, Lord Clive stayed here for six days to negotiate with the Nawab for the transfer of the Dewani to the East India Company.

In April, 1766, Clive, who had returned to Calcutta after securing the Dewani, again came and stayed at Moti Jheel, and, on the 29th of that month, held here the first English Pooneah or the ceremony of commencing the revenue collections, sitting side by side with the Nawab. Clive sat as Dewan, while Najmuddowla sat as Nazim.

They received nazars from the assembled Zemindars. Clive, General Carnac, and Mr. Sykes accepted for themselves and for the East India Company the usual present of a Khillat or dress and an elephant to each.

At the Pooneah of 1767, which was held with peculiar pomp, Verelest sat on the right of the Nawab and Khillats of the value of Rs. 2,16,876 were distributed, among which were the following :—

Governor and Council . . .	Rs. 46,750
Nizamut	,, 38,800
Treasury	,, 22,634
Zemindar of Nuddea	,, 7,352
Rajah of Beerbhoom	,, 1,200
Rajah of Bishenpore	,, 734

In 1768, the Court of Directors ordered that the forms established by Lord Clive at the solemnity of Poonneah should in future be observed and when the Governor was not present, the Resident at the Durbar of Murshidabad should represent the king's Dewan. But the observance of the ceremony was prohibited in 1769.

In September, 1766, Clive again came and stayed at Moti Jheel.

On the 27th April, 1772, Samuel Middleton wrote to Warren Hastings, from Moti Jheel, that that morning he had caused Mahomed Reza Khan, the Naib Suba, and his Dewan, Amrit Singh, to be seized and proper guards to be placed upon their houses and effects.

LORD CLIVE.

WARREN HASTINGS.

MAZUMDAR'S MURSHIDABAD

FANCY PRESS.

Moti Jheel was the home of Warren Hastings when he became the Political Resident at the Durbar of the Nawab Nazim. (1771-73)

Sir John Shore, afterwards Lord Teinmouth, also lived here and admired its "cooing doves, whistling black birds and purling (pearly ?) streams."

Clive and Sykes finding it difficult and inconvenient to transact business from Cossimbazar, the Residency, had taken a loan of the Moti Jheel house from the Nawab Nazim, Najmuddowla.

In 1764, the allowance of the English Resident at the Court of the Nawab, who lived at Moti Jheel, was Rs. 1,000 for the expenses of his table and private servants, whether travelling with the Nawab or attending him at fixed places. The public servants of his establishment were as follow :—

1 Vakeel	20 Peons
2 Munshis	10 Mashalchies
4 Chobdars	12 Bearers
2 Jamadars	2 Chowri bearers

with a number of lascars and tent followers.

In 1785–86 the head quarters were removed from Moti Jheel to Madapore and thence subsequently to Berhampore.

Upto 1876 Moti Jheel was in charge of Government, when Captain Muir, the Agent to the Governor General at Murshidabad, retransferred it to the Nawab Nazim.

Moti Jheel is also known as the Company Bagh, from the fact of its having been in the occupation of the East India Company. It is now used as a pleasure garden. The new railway line runs past the bank of the Moti Jheel.

The only old building extant is the Musjed of Shahamat Jang, to which is attached a doorless building 65 feet long, 23 feet broad and 12 feet heigh, said to contain countless treasures. No body dares break open this masonry box, as labourers once employed for the purpose are said to have died of spitting blood on the spot.

In the mosque is kept a Koran, written in very large letters, said to have been caligraphed by Shahamut Jang himself.

The Baraduari of Meer Jaffer still exists, though in an altered and mutilated condition.

The Sangidalan and Mahalsara are gone, only the plinth of the former being visible. Some of its stone pillars and arches of hornblende lie behind the Nizamut Imambara and might with advantage be removed to the site of the Sangidalan.

The City gate of Moti Jheel, a large, broad, massive structure, is now a crumbling ruin.

The waters of the lake are no more "pearly", except at parts, the Jheel having been overgrown with weeds.

The Bhagirathee was much nearer to Moti Jheel in 1766 than it is now. The garden or park of Moti Jheel is almost surrounded by water and is connected with the city by a neck. At its apex is the site of the

SHAHAMAT JUNG'S MOSQUE AT MOTI JHEEL. FANCY PRESS.

Sangidalan. To the north of the neck, is an enclosed compound containing the mosque of Shahamut Jang, opposite to which, on the east bank, is a beautiful mosque at Raesbagh. The portion of the Jheel to the south of the neck contains a deep dug tank, known as Santi pukur, on the banks of which were the offices.

To the east of Shahamat Jang's mosque, is a small enclosure, within which are four tombs and to the east of which and outside it is one tomb. Of these five tombs, two are of marble, one of black stone, one of ordinary sand stone and the fifth is ordinary masonry.

The position of the tombs is as follows :—

I (Marble) Nawazesh Mahomed Khan, Shahamat Jang	I (Marble) Ekramuddowla, Shahamat Jang's adopted son.	I (Black Stone) Ekram's Tutor	I (Masonry) Ekram's Nurse
I (Stone) Shumshere Ali Khan (Shahamat Jang's General)			

It is said that at dead of night and on particular occasions, an aerial procession, visible to the fortunate few, starts from the tomb of Shahamat Jang at Moti Jheel and proceeds to the tomb of Mahabat Jang at Khoshbagh.

The central doorways of these two mosques situated on opposite banks of the river about three miles apart, and not visible from each other, are so placed that if a man starts from the one and travels in a line, perpendicular to the plane of the door of the one, he will enter straight into the doorway of the other, without any deviation.

The following couplet in Persian appears on the doorway of the mosque :—

"Dilpae tarikh ze sed ko safa
Goft uzoo Kurdut masjed ba pa,
1153."

Ekramuddowla was the younger brother of Serajuddowla and had been adopted in his cradle by his uncle, Nawazesh Mahomed Khan, who was childless. It was in the beginning of the rains in the year, 1159, H., that Ali Verdi Khan celebrated his nuptials with a daughter of Ataulla Khan, a general in his army, by his wife Rabia Begum, daughter of Ali Verdi Khan's brother. The nuptials were celebrated with great magnificence, and one thousand Khilluts were distributed among the relations and dependents of the Nazim. The festivities continued for a month and costly torras or victuals were sent all over the city.

Another daughter of Ataulla Khan had been betrothed to Serajuddowla, but she died before marriage and Ali Verdi Khan celebrated Serajuddowla's marriage with greater pomp with a daughter of Mirza Eraze Khan, grandson of Mustapha Kuli Khan, Prime Minister of Azem Sha, son of Aurengzebe ; when he was Nazim of Gujrat.

The garden known as Ataulla Khan situated on the present northern extremity of the city marks the site of that general's residence.

The view of Shahamat Jang's mosque from the opposite or Railway bank of the Moti Jheel has been marred by the recent construction of two unsightly corrugated iron sheds, for which the P. W. D. is responsible.

One of these sheds gives shelter to a stone, which has been removed from its original site in the vicinity, and which bears the following inscription, in memory of the son of Mr. Keating, who in 1774 was Superintendent of the Murshidabad Mint and in 1794 rose to be judge of the court of appeal :—

Here
Lyeth the Body
of
Ewan Keating who
was born on the 20th of
December 1779 and
Departed this life on
the 3rd of March 1785 aged
Five years Two months
and Eleven days.

The romantic garden of Moti Jheel has not unfrequently been used for Rooh ceremonies and is best suited for picnic parties. In these, the Murshidabad Kitchen, which produces the best kinds of dishes, which give pleasure to the palate, for whieh Murshidabad is so famous, has always held its own. In variety of preparation as well as in their excellence, the Murshidabad Kitchen stands unrivalled and the guest is rare who has tasted the productions of the local cullinary art and not admired their superiority. Of these the pollao stands pre-eminent.

It has many varieties. A good cook will make a seer of rice soak and absorb a seer of ghee, unless, which is always understood, he purloins a portion. This preparation of rice, ghee, onions, garlic and saffron (*crocus sativus*) is sought for with great avidity. The principal varieties being Akhni sada, Akhni tahedar, Ananas, Babuna, Falsa, Kowmla, Latafat, Mahi, Mitha, Morug mosallum, Quorma, Shapasand cabuli, Subud, Tooranj and Zurda. Of curries, the Quorma, Kalia and Subdeg are unrivalled. Of bread, the toonki, hawai, pareta, meethapareta, and nanpaw are inviting. Of milk-rice, the Shirbiringe is delicious. The nemush is a marvel, a tea-spoonful of milk being inflated into a large bubble, sweet and scented, which suits the *howai roti* or air-bread marvelously well. Of fish preparations, a whole big rohu will be dressed in tact, the bones all reduced to powdery softness, and different portions possessing different tastes, such as acid, sub-acid, sweet, saltish, chilly-hot and the like.

Of the extensive charities of Shahamat Jang in the shape of torras of dainty dishes and heavy purses, which he caused to be distributed daily throughout the city to the great relief of the poor and the needy, the Langerkhana establishment kept up by Government at Moti Jheel, where a number of old, lame, blind and decripid beggars receive their daily doles of rice at the mosque, or their monthly allowances at the Treasury, is a creditable though insignificant form, still preserved.

KERBELA.

To the south of the old gate of Moti Jheel, is the new Kerbella, where tazias or coffins are interred on the day of Ashra of the Moharram. The old Kerbella was to the west of this and nearly the whole of it has been cut away by the river. There is a building, of recent construction, at the new Kerbella, which is called the Baraduari, where the mourners pray or take rest.

AMANIGANJ.

About half a mile to the west of Moti Jheel, on the banks of an abandoned bed of the river, is Amaniganj, resorted to by Mahomedans for interment and by Hindus for cremation; so that if one says to another—"Go to Amaniganj"—that is sufficient to provoke him to commit a breach of the peace.

It was at Amaniganj that Ali Verdi Khan's troops were encamped before they marched under him against the Mahrattas, then causing disturbances in Orissa.

Nawab Nazir Sidi Darab Ali Khan, who rose subsequently to the rank of the chief eunuch of the Nizamut and who lived to see and serve four Nazims, namely Ali Jah, Wala Jah, Humayun Jah and Feredun Jah, built here what is known as the *Shubi Kerbella*, or imitation of the tomb of Imam Hossein at Kerbella in Arabia, not unoften mistaken, from its cupola, for a mosque. It faces west, unlike a mosque, which always faces east. When the work of construction was well nigh approaching completion, Darab Ali Khan rose one morning from a nocturnal dream to say that his death would happen as soon as the building would be completed. Hence, so long as Darab Ali Khan lived, one single mason used to work daily, as work was not to be stopped.

Towards the south of this building and almost adjoining it, lies buried, within a railed enclosure, Sadeq Ali Khan, the architect of the Nizamut Imambara, who, though illiterate, rose to be the Urz Begi or chief usherer of the Nawab Nazim, a post carrying great honors and emoluments. He died in 1850.

Close by is another walled enclosure, with the representation of a tomb, erected to commemorate the spot from which, after the interment of a *tazia* on the day of Ashra, issued forth blood. It is held in great reverence by Sheas.

In 1766, the river flowed below Amaniganj in a south easterly direction, till it reached Chuna Khali, after a bend near Neshedbagh, from which it took a south westerly course, flowing by Cossimbazar, Kalkapur and Saidabad.

BANAMALIPORE MOSQUE.

In 1756, an imperial firman was issued, granting mouza Adoni, appertaining to taluk Pergenah Lushkerpore, in Sircar Barangabad, now within the Collectorate jurisdiction of Rajshye, yielding a sum of Rs. 1,080 as *madadmash ba farzandan* of the mutwalli and other servants of the mosque at Banamalipore, founded by Dost Mahomed Khan, for its lighting, *farash* and Madrassa expenses. In the grant, there is a specification of the manner in which this amount, namely, Rs. 3 per day, is to be spent. The founder was an Afghan general of Ali Verdi Khan.

The second grant is dated fourteen years later, that is, 1770. The first grantee, namely Bedar Ali, having been found incompetent, was turned out and upon Dost Mahomed Khan's application, the new grant was made in the name of his nephew, Sheik Faqeerulla. By these documents, a valid appropriation has been judicially found to have been created.

(*Crossing over to the western bank of the river.*)

KHOSHBAGH.

Crossing over to the other side of the river, opposite Amaniganj, is Khoshbagh, a garden containing the cemetry of Ali Verdi Khan and his family. It consists of walled enclosures, the outer walls, which were loop holed for musketry and flanked by octagonal bastions, having in subsequent repairs undergone thorough change.

In the middle of the enclosures is the mausoleum, containing the tombs of Ali Verdi Khan, Serajuddowla and the principal members of their family. Ali Verdi Khan's mother and Serajuddowla's wife, Lutfunnissa Begum, who accompanied him in his flight, also lie buried here. The grand-father and the grand-son lie side by side. Government have of late put up marble tomb stones. The central and larger tomb is that of Ali Verdi Khan, while that to the east of it is the tomb of Serajuddowla.

The river once flowed very close to the enclosure and the pucca masonry ghat still exists. In 1766, the river flowed past towards the north and the east of Khoshbagh taking thence a straight easterly course towards Choona Khali. The present channel from Khoshbagh to Farrashdanga did not exist then.

In the outer enclosures there are numerous tombs with nothing to identify them.

Ali Verdi Khan had endowed the villages of Bhandardaha and Nawabganj, with a revenue collec-

SERAJUDDOWLA'S TOMB.

KUNTALINE PRESS, CALCUTTA.

tion of Rs. 305 per month, for the maintenance of the mausoleum. It is now kept up by Government and hence is in a proper state of preservation.

In the compound is a large mosque with a terrace in front.

The following is the position of the tombs, there being little to vouch for the correctness of the minor ones.

I	I	I	I
Ali Verdi's Daughter	Ali Verdi Khan	Serajuddowla	Merza Mehendi (?)
I	I	I	I
Ali Verdi's Daughter	Ali Verdi's Wife	Lutfunnissa	Mehendi's Wife (?)

BHATTAMATI.

About a mile to the west of the river, opposite Lalbagh, is Bhattamati, the seat of the junior branch of the Bangadhicaris of Dahapara, who settled there, when the emoluments of the office of Canongoe came to be divided between the two branches of the family, for the political purpose of creating rivalry and thereby lessening the power of either to abuse the trust imposed upon them. The remains of the family residence, temples, tanks, &c. still mark out the site, which is overgrown with jungle.

ROSHNIBAGH.

On the western bank of the river, opposite the Palace, is Roshnibagh, or the garden of light, the mausoleum of Shuja Khan, who died in 1739, after having erected his mausoleum and mosque. A very beautiful Koran, which claims to be in the handwriting of Ali and was procured at a cost of one lac of rupees, used to be kept in the mosque and has been removed for safe custody to the Nizamut Immambarah. The Persian distich on the slab of the mosque shews date 1156 H. The present building is in the place of the old and much larger building which has since been replaced.

On the banks of the river, near Roshnibagh, a bamboo structure used to be constructed for purposes of illumination on the occasion of the Bera.

North of the mausoleum is a temple of Siva with a stone bearing an inscription in the Nagri character as follows:—Sri Ganashaia nama. Sri Sambat 1876 Falgun badi 14 Ranga Natheswara Mahadeva sthapita Ranga Nath Pandita Maharashtra Munshi Adhicara Sadar Sircar Company Bahadur. Then follows in the Bengali chracter, Maha Falgun San 1226 Bangala.

The slab on the walls of the building containing the tomb reads thus:—

Ze Zilhej saddah roze e se shamba sal e rehlat dan
Ke Ferdousi burin jai e Shujauddowla ja ve dan
1101.

FARRABAGH.

A little to the north of Roshnibagh is Furrabagh, originally the garden house of Nazir Ahmed, a dis-

THE PALACE FROM ROSHNIBAGH.

FANCY PRESS.

traint officer under Murshed Kuli Khan. It was confiscated by Shuja Khan and converted by him into a pleasure garden, where he built a musjed and excavated a large tank. Nawab Ali Jah lived here in a Bunglow on the river bank, before he went on board a pinnace in which he died a few days after. The pillars of a gate and a sentry box are the only remains extant, besides underground plinths at various places. The large mosque was entirely cut away by the river, and some of the broken pieces of masonry, worn smooth by its action, are still visible in the water.

DAHAPARA.

To the south west of Farrabagh is Dahapara, said to be a form of Daccapara, from the fact of the settlement there of Dorpanaraen, the chief Canongoe, who migrated from Dacca to Murshidabad with many followers, and accompanied Murshed Kuli Khan to his new head quarters. The house of the Bangadhicaris, as the Canongoes were called, still exists. They are known as the Mahashais.

The Maharattas were entrenched at Dahapara before they looted Jagat Sett's house, in the absence of Ali Verdi Khan.

The founders of the family of the Mohashais were the brothers Bhagowan and Bangabenod of Khajoori near Cutwa, who received from Akbar a ferman appointing Bhagwan, Canongoe of Bengal, on condition of his retiring in favor of Bangabinod on the attainment of the latter's majority. Upon their death, the office of Canangoe devolped, in 1696, upon Hori Naraen, with the title of Bangadhicari. He was succeeded by Dorpanaraen, who subsequently fell out with Murshed Kuli Khan, having at the revenue settlement, refused to sign the assessment and collection papers prepared by the great Dewan, for submission to the Emperor of Delhi, except upon the satisfaction of his exorbitant demands. Murshed Kuli Khan obtained the signature of Raghunandan of Nattore, the Naib Canongoe, and repaired with them to Delhi, where the absence of Dorpanaraen's signature proved no obstacle to their approbation by the Emperor. On Murshed Kuli Khan's return to Murshidabad, Dorpanaraen's influence much declined.

His son, Sivanaraen, was appointed Canongoe. He was succeeded by his son, Lukshminaraen, who exercised curtailed powers and jurisdiction. On each succession a ferman used to be received on payment of large sums as nazar. Lukshminaraen died after the establishment of British ascendency in Bengal. His son, Surjanaraen, a minor, was charged by him to the custody of his Naib Canongoe, Ganga Govind Singh, who, it is said, obtained for himself the settlement of many of the minor's estates. The Perganas of Rookanpore and Shereshahabad only remained with the family. Lakshminaraen is said to have enjoyed a revenue of eighteen lacs. Surji Naraen succeeded to estates yielding Rs. 3,36,000. Some of his revenue free properties were resumed. Government offered him a stipend of Rs. 1,400 per month which he declined. Rookanpore with an area of 600 sq. miles and a revenue of Rs. 3,66,215, the richest Zemindari of equal dimensions in Bengal, had been assigned to Sivnaraen, probably in consideration of the reduction of the commission of two and a half per cent. on the revenues, when at the commencement of the eighteenth century, the emoluments of the office of Canongoe were divided between the two branches of the family, the junior of which lived at Bhattamati, to the south of Dahapara.

The records of the Canongoes consisted of the following papers :—

1. Dastur-ul-amul
2. Amul Dastur
3. Ferhest Dehat
4. Shahi Amdani
5. Awargy
6. Doul Takis bandobust
7. Jamabandi Khas
8. Jama Syer Chobootra Kotwali mai Chowkiat o guzarghat.
9. Jama Mahal Meer Bahari
10. Jama Pachowtra
11. Jama Mahal Budderky
12. Ism novisi Zemindaran
13. Hukikut baze Zemin
14. Jama Mokrary o istmurary.
15. Wasool Baki
16. Hukikut Rozedaran.

The settlements were based upon these papers supplied by the Canongoe, who was the registrar and the keeper of the imperial archives. The name and the remuneration of the office continued in Bengal even after the Decenniel settlement, and the Jamabandi prepared from the papers was not settled till long after the arrival of the first British resident at the Durbar of Murshidabad in July, 1765.

The titles of Bangadhicari and Rajah used to be enjoyed by the eldest member. The family title of Darpanaraen was Majumdar. Most of the fermans of the family have fallen into wrong hands. The ferman of 1679, which is still at Dahapara, describes the duties of the office.

The present representative of the family is Babu Protap Naraen Rai Mohashai, eking out his existence with the paltry income derivable from his office of Sub-Registrar, which Government kindly conferred upon him.

The following is a genealogical chart of the family :—

- Bhagawan
  - Hori Naraen
    - Darpa Naraen
      - Siv Naraen
        - Lakshmi Naraen
          - Surja Naraen
            - Chandra Naraen
              - Brojendra Naraen + Rani Lal Moni
                - Protap Naraen
                  - Dwijendra Naraen
              - Jogendra Naraen + Rani Bindubashini
- Bangabinod

THE MINT.

The site of the Mint at Murshidabad is one of considerable uncertainty. Some think that it was situated on the west bank of the river, opposite to Ichhaganj, and was thence removed to the site now occupied partly by the Nizamut Imambara, the ghat below which is known as the Mint Ghat. Considering how the Jagat Setts were connected with the coining of bullion in Murshidabad, the ghat and buildings known as the *Shamadhi* of Jagat Sett, near Dayabagh opposite to Ichhaganj, now cut away by the river, were perhaps constructed near the Mint.

The *Zurbe Murshidabad*, as the coinage was called, was a source of great gain to the Jagat Setts. The bullion was their monopoly and it brought a considerable amount as commission.

MANSURGANJ AND HEERA JHEEL.

About a mile to the north west of Furrabagh, opposite Jaffraganj, is the site of Mansurganj, where Serajuddowla, before he ascended the throne, constructed a palace at a convenient distance from family observation in view of securing indulgences in the most vicious pleasures, environed by an artificial canal, which he called the Heera Jheel or Lake of Diamonds.

When the building was nearly completed, Serajuddowla's grand-father, Ali Verdi Khan, who was fondly attached to his adopted successor, was invited to see it and when inspecting the building, he was locked up in one of the apartments most exposed to the view of the Nawab's officers and attendants, among whom were the Vakeels of some of the principal Zemindars. It was given out that he could be liberated only on the express stipulation that a tax was levied, to be devoted to the maintenance of this palace. Ali Verdi Khan agreed to permit Serajuddowla to establish a granary or market place, which brought in considerable *sair* revenue in the neighbourhood of the place, which was thenceforth called Mansurganj, or the storehouse of the victorious, in reference to one of the titles of Serajuddowla, as well as this artful trick of pleasantry, in which he is supposed to have outwitted the craft of more experienced age. The average amount of this *sair* revenue or abwab was Rs. 5,01,597. This imposition became known as the Nazarana Mansurganj.

The palace included the Emtazmahal, described as "big enough to accommodate three European monarchs." This was Serajuddowla's favorite residence. It was from here that Serajuddowla, only six hours before the arrival of Meer Jaffer from Plassey, fled, after having in the dead of night placed his favorite wife, Lutfunnissa Begum, in a covered carriage with as many valuable jewels as could be carried.

Meer Jaffer on his arrival at the city took up his residence at the Mansurganj palace on the 24th June, 1757.

Here, Meer Jaffer was waiting in state to receive Clive, to fetch whom he had sent his son, Miran. The Nawab's Durbar had assembled in the largest audience hall of the palace at Mansurganj. On the north was placed the auspicious throne and Clive, finding that he was hesitating to ascend, led Meer Jaffer by the hand and placed him on the Tukt Mobaruk and then, as the representative of the East India Company, presented Meer Jaffer with a nazar of gold mohars and congratulated him on his accession to the musnud of Bengal, Behar and Orissa. The rest of the assembly then presented nazars to Meer Jaffer. Clive, through his interpreter, informed the assembly that it was fortunate for the country that in the place of a tyrant, they had secured a good ruler.

It was here that Rajah Dullavram was confirmed and declared Dewan.

Walsh, who acted as Clive's private Secretary, Watts, the chief of Cossimbazar, Lushington, Ramchand, the writer, and Munshi Nabakissen, entered into the vaults of the palace and found stored there 176,000 in silver, 230,000 in gold, two chests of gold ignots, four chests of set jewels and two chests of loose stones and gems. This was in the outer treasury. The inner treasury of the palace contained eight millions sterling.

Ram Chand, who was a writer on sixty rupees a month, was, at the date of his death worth 720,000. Nobokissen whose salary was two hundred rupees a month, spent £90,000 at the sradh ceremony of his mother. The proportion that fell to the share of the English was £3,388,575, which represents only the sums which were *admitted* to have been received. Coin to the value of £800,000 was immediately placed on board barges and sent down to Calcutta.

The river has cut away the place entirely.

The place is a complete ruin, some broken walls and plinths only are visible.

The Jheel which has gone down into the river, was connected with it by pipes, some of which are still visible.

MORADBAGH.

At Moradbagh, near the Heera Jheel, was a palace where Clive, after his victorious entry into the city, put up. Meer Jaffer sent his son, Miran, to fetch Clive from here to the Mansurganj palace, where the Nawab was waiting in state to receive him.

Warren Hastings used to live here when he was resident at the Court of the Nawab.

Vansittart lived here when he came to depose Meer Jaffer and place Meer Kasem on the throne. His third interview with Meer Jaffer took place here. It was a long one and the next morning Meer Jaffer rose to find the palace of Mansurganj surrounded by English troops. Addressing Celd, who was standing at the gate of the Killah, Vansittart's letter in hand, Meer Jaffer said—"you have thought proper to break your engagements, I would not mine. Had I such designs, I could have raised twenty thousand men and fought you if I pleased. My son, the Chhota Nawab (meaning Miran) forwarned me of all this." Meer Jaffer passed the night in a boat near Moradbagh and then under an English guard proceeded to Calcutta.

It was from Moradbagh that under date the 14th February, 1787, Mr. Peter Speke, the resident at the Durbar, wrote to Mr. Edward Hay, the Secretary to the Government, a covering letter, forwarding many papers relating to Warren Hastings, which Mobarukuddowla desired him to send, one of which was a representation regarding the prosperity and splendour of Hasting's administration, bearing the seals of the following personages :—

1. Nawab Mobarukuddowla, Nazim.
2. Mani Begum } widows of Meer Jaffer.
3. Bubboo Begum }
4. Khyrannissa Begum } sisters of Meer Jaffer.
5. Nafisunnissa Begum }
6. Mir Murtaza } sons of Miran.
7. Fatteh Ali Khan }
8. Sultan Mirza Daood, son of Sha Suliman, King of Persia, and son-in-law of Miran.

9. Ghazanfer Jang, son of Sultan Mirza Daood, and son-in-law of Mobarukuddowla.
10. Ghalib Jang, son of Ihtramuddowla, brother of Meer Jaffer.
11. Syud Baker Ali Khan, husband of Meer Jaffer's sister.
12. Syud Mahomed Hossein, eldest brother of Khan Khanan Bahadur Mozaffer Jang.

There are no traces of the palace left.

(*Crossing over to the eastern bank of the river.*)

NESHADBAGH.

About three miles to the south-east of the Palace and about a mile to the east of the old river bed, called Bansbarijheel, is Neshadbagh, the residence of Mahomed Reza Khan, the Naib-Dewan and Naib Suba. The Court of Directors of the East India Company in 1768 expressed their approbation of his services and allowed him a salary of nine lacs annually. Under Warren Hasting's orders, however, Mahomed Reza Khan was cought at Neshadbagh by Anderson, assistant to Mr. Middleton, the resident at Murshidabad, and then deported to Calcutta, for embezzlement and mismanagement.

It was at Neshadbagh that Mahomed Reza Khan entertained the Europeans of the station on the occasion of the recovery of King George III. It was in 1789. Mahomed Reza Khan had heard that the Governor General would give an entertainment in consequence of the King's recovery and as he was a general well-wisher of the English, he very much rejoiced at such agreeable news and intended to invite the English gentlemen at his house on the same day that the entertainment was given at Calcutta, but as he thought they would be enjoying themselves and giving entertainments amongst each other, he requested the company of all the English gentlemen on the 12th August, 1789. The company began to assemble at 8 o'clock and at 9 His Highness the Nawab Mobarakuddowla, with his son and the principal inhabitants of the city of Murshidabad, together with most of the English gentlemen having arrived, the illuminations began and the entertainment was conducted with great propriety. Opposite to the east front of the Nawab's large upper roomed house at Neshadbagh, there was a most beautiful illumination, representing a building which continued to burn with undiminished splendour till near 2 o'clock in the morning. In the intermediate space, there was a little temple with these words written upon it—"Long Live George III." The avenue leading to the house was hung with variegated lamps and the edge of the tank, situated to the south of the Nawab's lower roomed house, was also illuminated. The supper was placed upon the table at twelve o'clock and was a very elegant one.

The Neshadbagh house, where this entertainment was held, although seven years old, had never before been used.

The tank, which is one of the largest and well stocked with large fish, still exists but there are few traces of the buildings.

The office of Naib-Dewan was abolished in 1772 and the Calcutta Council of five, including the Governor, adopted a plan under which the internal Govenment underwent great changes. The Khalsa or exchequer and the treasury were removed from Murshidabad to Calcutta.

The family of Mahomed Reza Khan is now known as the Chitpore Family of which the following is a genealogy :—

Descended from Huzrut Imam Reza
|
Syud Abu Torab
|
Hakim Syud Hadi Ali Khan,
(who came from Persia to Delhi and was sent to Murshidabad for the treatment of Nawab Ali Verdi Khan)
|

Mahomed Reza Khan, Deputy Governor of Dacca, Naib Subah and Naib Dewan under the East India Company.	Syud Ahmed Ali Khan, Mir Saman of the Nizamut	Syud Mahomed Hossein Khan who wrote many medical books which are still considered as good authority.
	Syud Mahomed Ali, Mir Saman	

|
Syud Mahomed Reza,
(the Nizamut astrologer, who had, on the day of Nowroze, that is, many months before, predicted the Great Earthquake of June, 1897, and lived, from many days before the date of thecatastrophe, in a straw hut, away from his brick-built house)
|
Syud Ali Reza
|
Syud Zeki Reza
(the present Librarian of the Palace)

SARGACHHI AND CHAMPAPUKUR.

The double row of tall deodars, 480 in all, near the Bahramganj Dak stables, leads to Champapukur, a summer residence of the Nawabs. There was a beautiful bunglow in the centre of a beautiful oval shaped tank. Nawab Ali Jah used to live here frequently. To Champapukur he returned from Monghyr and it was from Champapukur that he went to Furrabagh a few days before his death.

The encircling waters exist but the bunglow is gone.

CHUNA KHALI.

About four miles to the south of the Palace is Chuna Khali, which was very thickly populated, but is now overgrown with jungle. The place is noted for good mangoes. The manufacture of what was known as Chuna Khali paper is now an extinct art.

Brindaban, a Hindu landholder, lived in the vicinity of Chuna Khali. Being displeased with a Mahomedan *faqir* on account of his importunities, he turned him away from his house. The mortified *faqir* collected a few bricks and stacked them, obstructing Brindaban's passage. This he called his Musjed and at the appointed hours, he shouted forth the *azan*, to the annoyance of the Hindu Zemindar, who was so much enraged as to throw away the bricks, with the object of sending away the *faqir*.

The offended Mahomedan mendicant complained to Nawab Murshed Kuli Khan, and Kazi Mahamed Sharaf passed upon Brindaban the sentence of death. Murshed Kuli Khan would not sanction the infliction of the extreme penalty of the law and in order to save the life of the Hindu, asked the Kazi whether any less severe punishment would not meet the ends of justice. The Kazi was inexorable. Neither Murshed Kuli Khan's endeavours, nor the intervention of Prince Azemoshan availed any thing, for the Emperor, to whom a reference had been made, exclaimed *Kazi Sharaf, Khoda ki taraf*, upholding the verdict of the Kazi saying Kazi Sharaf was on the side of God.

MUSNUD AULIA.

At Chuna Khali is the shrine of Musnud Aulia. There is a stone lying on the ground with an inscription in Toghra or the old Arabic character, dated the 2nd Moharram, 896, or 15th November, 1490, containing the name of Abul Mozaffer, Feroze Sultan, one of the kings of Gour.

There is another stone bearing the following inscription :—

In Kabr Sultan Mahomed Waledeh Fateh Mahomed ibn ul Huddad Multani Fittarikh huftam Rabi ul awal 1153 Hijratan Nawavi.

The mosque bears date 1188 H.

SANNYASIDANGA.

Sannyasidanga is situated on the west bank of the old bed of the river. It was the residence of Chain Rai, a dewan of Ali Verdi Khan. The remains of an old temple are visible.

BAHARAMGANJ.

The Dak stables or relay house at Baharamganj, situated on the east bank of the abandoned bed of the river Bhagirathee, marks the site of a market place which was founded by Baharam Jang, brother of Dilawar Jang and son of Mahomed Reza Khan. An old temple and a pucca ghat still exist.

COSSIMBAZAR.

The suburban town of Cossimbazar is the site of the first English factory, founded about the year 1652. It was the largest silk emporium of the East India Company. Cossimbazar was then situated on the left or western bank of the river of that name. Towards the beginning of the nineteenth century, the Cossimbazar river, as the Bhagirathee was then called, abandoned its old and circuitous course and took a straight cut, thus leaving Cossimbazar far off inland.

Cossimbazar is mentioned in a letter, dated 1666, written by the French traveller, Tavernier. It was a healthy station, for one finds Mr. McGuire, a servant of the Company at Calcutta, applying to the Council for going to Cossimbazar for the "recovery of his health". It was a place of great trade, the most vendible commodities being gold, silver, silk and muslin.

The French and the Dutch also carried on trade and established their factories here. The town was about two miles long with narrow streets. Its population was about one lac and the brick-built houses were so thickly situated that one could make a circuit of the whole town by jumping from one roof to another. All these houses together with the factories have disappeared and the only traces of this once populous town are left in the remnants of the residency in the shape of a small mound and the English and Dutch cemeteries, besides the house of Kantoo Babu, the Satighat and a few temples.

COSSIMBAZAR RAJBARI.

The founder of the Cossimbazar house was Kali Nath Nadi of Shijla in Burdwan, who came and settled at Sripur, near Cossimbazar. His grand-son, Radha Krishna Nandi, kept a shop where he sold silks, kites and betel-nuts. His son, Krishna Kanta Nandi, better known as Kantoo Babu, became a favorite of Warren Hastings, who placed him in charge of the supervision of several lucrative Zemindaries, on his appointment as Governor General in

1772. In his march against Cheyt Singh of Benares, Kantoo Babu accompanied Warren Hastings, who granted him a jaigire in Ghazipur and obtained for his son, Lokenath, the title of Maharajah from the Nawab Nazim of Bengal, who was then the fountain of honor. Kantoo Babu visited Jagannath and, on his return, died in 1778.

Lokenath succeeded to the vast estates left by his father. He died in 1804, having been afflicted with an incurable disease.

Harinath, his son, a child aged one year, succeeded him. During his minority, his estates were managed by the Court of Wards. Towards the construction of the Hindu College in Calcutta, Hari Nath, on the attainment of his majority, contributed a large sum. Lord Amherst conferred upon him the title of Rajah Bahadur. He died in 1832, leaving his widow, Rani Horosundari, still living at Benares, a minor son, named Krishna Nath, and a daughter, who was married to Babu Nobeen Chandra Nandi, the father of the present proprietor of the Cossimbazar Raj.

Krishna Nath received English education and mixed freely in English society. Lord Auckland conferred up him the little of Rajah Bahadur. Extravant beyond bounds, he soon spent away the large accummulations of his minority. The sum of forty one lacs disappeared in four years. But education was always near to his heart. On the death of David

Hare, whose statue adorns the grounds of the Presidency College of Calcutta, he convened a memorial meeting and contributed the largest sum. Pleased with his vocal music, Krishna Nath remitted one lac of rupees due from Nabakrishna Banerji of Meherpur, on account of arrears of rent. Another lac he gave to Rajah Digambar Mitter, for an announcement had appeared in a newspaper that Krishna Nath had made such a gift, when none were in contemplation.

He executed a will devising that Government should take possession of his properties and apply the same to the establishment of a College to be called the Krishna Nath University of Banjetia. In that will, a monthly allowance of Rs. 1,500 only was provided for his widow. To his private servant, Keshav Chandra Sircar, he bequeathed three lacs of rupees, besides several houses, jewels &c. Provision was also made for the supply of daily food to the blind, the lame and the crippled. To this will, three codicils were discovered and in the second one occurred the following passage—"I part with the desire of life solely from the fear of being disgraced, as I am not concerned in the matter of Gopal's case nor did I beat or maltreat him. This I solemnly avow, it is only on account of the Deputy Magistrate, Chander Mohan Chatterjee, that such excessive measures have been adopted towards me. I therefore write this letter that no one else may incur blame on account of my parting with my own life."

This will formed the subject of litigation in the Supreme Court, the litigants being the East India Company, the widow, Mr. C. G. Strettel and Keshav Chandra Sircar. The Company and Keshav claimed under the will, while the widow denied its validity. The will was dated the 30th October, 1844. The Court held that the mind of the Rajah, a prey to anguish and fear, had become unsettled and weakened at the time of the execution of the instrument, the day after which he shot himself at Calcutta, whither he had fled from Cossimbazar to avoid molestation.

The widow in whose favor the litigation ended was no other than Rani Surnomoi of world-wide reputation. Called to the charge of extensive estates, young as she was, she found them in chaos and confussion. The prudent and unselfish management of her Dewan, Rai Rajib Lochan Rai Bahadur, coupled with her own ever-ready support, soon improved the state of affairs.

Born in 1828, Surnomoi was a widow at sixteen, with two young daughters. Her whole life was one of charity. The most munificent lady of her times, she was a devout and pious Hindu, ever ready to devote her vast resources to works of public utility and practical benevolence. The alleviation of human suffering in every form shared her bounty. She took particular delight in feeding and clothing the poor. The daily distribution of doles of rice to thousands of beggars, who beseiged her house every morning, was an affair of stupendous proportions. In 1871 the title of Maharani was conferred upon her and the title of Maharajah was to be conferred upon her successor. The Imperial Order of the Crown of India was conferred upon Maharani Surnomoi in 1878. On the 25th August 1897, she expired on the banks of the Bhagirathee at her residence at Saidabad, whither she had been removed from Cossimbazar. Her cremation which was attended by sorrowing crowds drawn from all classes, took place amidst sighs and lamentations. On that memorable day every one thought that he had suffered a personal bereavement.

The heir-at-law was her mother-in-law, Rani Horosundari, but preferring her life of retirement, she executed a release in favor of her husband's sister Gooind Sundari's son, Babu Manindra Chandra Nandi, who assumed the title of Maharajah, which received Government recognition in May, 1898. On his assumption of the charge of the Raj, the late Maharani's able Manager, Rai Srinath Pal Bahadur, left service.

Maharajah Manindra Chandra Nandi was returned by the Zemindars of Bengal to represent them in the Bengal Council. Of unostentatious habits and genial temperament, kindly disposed towards his numerous relatives, mixing freely with his subordinates, accepting hospitality at the humblest cottage, generously prone to do acts of benevolence, extending his co-operation and support to popular movements, Maharajah

MAHARAJAH MANINDRA CHANDRA NANDI.

MAJUMDAR'S MURSHIDABAD.

FANCY PRESS.

Manindra Chandra Nandi, with the difficulties that attend the maintenance untarnished of the famous name of his illustrious predecessor, is well spoken of by all who come in contact with him.

The following is a genealogy of the Cossimbazar Raj :—

Kali Nandi

- Son
  - Radha Krishna Nandi
    - Krishna Kanta Nandi alias Kantoo Babu
      - Maharajah Loke Nath Rai Bahadur
        - Kumar Hori Nath + Rani Horo Sundari
          - Rajah Krishna Nath Bahadur + Maharani Surnomoi
          - Govind Sundari + Nobeen Chandra Nandi
            - Maharaja Monindra Chandra Nandi
              - Maharaj-Kumar Mohim Chandra Nandi
- Son

The stone pillars and arches of Cheyt Singh's house which were brought by Kantoo Babu were fitted up at Cossimbazar and may still be seen inside the Rajbari. It is said that Kantoo Babu gave shelter to Warren Hastings when Serajuddowla ordered his arrest.

THE TEMPLE OF NEMINATH.

The temple of Neminath at Cossimbazar is the oldest Jaina temple in Murshidabad, containing the images of all the saints of the Jainas. It is on the south-western bank of the Cassimbazar river and is resorted to by large numbers of Jaina pilgrims. During the rains, the temple can be reached in boats which pass down the old bed of the river under the bridge at Farashdanga. At the back of the temple is the Modhugereh, or Honey pit, said to contain countless treasures concealed by the Jainas during the Mahratta disturbances.

BRITISH FACTORY AT COSSIMBAZAR.

As early as 1610, the East India Company sent their factors to Cossimbazar and in 1658, constructed a fortified factory. This was an irregular square with solid bastions, each mounting ten guns, mostly nine and six pounders, with a saluting battery on the curtain to the river side of twenty four guns, from two to four pounds. The garrison in 1757, when Captain Grant left it, consisted of fifty military under a sergeant.

The duties of the British Chief at this factory had, long before the acquisition of the Dewani, been as

OLD ENGLISH RESIDENCY AT COSSIMBAZAR.

KUNTALINE PRESS, CALCUTTA.

much diplomatic as commercial, and negotiations with the Nawab were carried on through him.

At this factory, Warren Hastings spent his early years (1752-57), making bargains for stuffs with native brokers. Here he distinguished himself by his sympathy with the natives and here he acquired his knowledge of Persian.

It was here that Warren Hastings married the widow of Captain John Buchanon, who bore him two children and who died here in 1759 and was buried in the cemetry close by, just opposite to the site of the old factory, now popularly known as the British Residency.

Serajuddowla seized the factory, made Warren Hastings a prisoner and sent him to Murshidabad.

All traces of the factory and the residence of the agent or Chief have disappeared, except a small mound containing a portion of the foundations, to which of late a few steps have been added.

OLD ENGLISH CEMETRY AT COSSIMBAZAR.

The cemetry belonged to the early English residents of Cossimbazar and contains the tombs of several persons who died between 1735 and 1800.

Mrs. Hastings lies buried here. The monument over her grave bears the following inscription :—

In memory of
Mrs. Warren Hastings,
and her daughter,
Elizabeth,
who died 11th July, 1759
In the 2 year of her age.

This monument was erected
by her husband
Warren Hastings, Esquire,
In due regard
of her memory.
Restored by Government
of Bengal, 1863.

The cemetry contains the tombs, among others, of the following persons :—

Anstruther (1735), Rose Grant (1775), A. Downie (1781), Captain Hartie (1782), Captain Clerk (1783), Campbell (1784), Charles Crommelin (1788), John Peach (1790). &c.

RAJAH A. N. ROY'S RESIDENCE,

Cossimbazar is also the residence of Rajah Ashutosh Nath Rai, who traces his descent from Daksha, one of the five Brahmins, learned in the Vedas, who

RAJAH A. N. RAI.

MAJUMDAR'S MURSHIDABAD. FANCY PRESS.

were brought from Kanouj by Adisur, King of Bengal, for the performances of religious rites. One of his ancestors, namely Jai Gopal Chattopadhya, obtained in the latter part of the seventeenth century, the title of Rai, which has since been held in the family, for services rendered to the Mahomedan rulers of Bengal. The first of the family, (which for centuries has retained its rank as one of high class Kulins), to settle at Cossimbazar was Babu Dina Bandhu Rai, who secured a good appointment in the silk factory of the East India Company.

His second son, Babu Jagabandhu Rai, began life as a vernacular writer in the same factory, but subsequently served in the salt and the revenue department at Midnapore, becoming ultimately the Dewan or Sheristadar of the Maimensingh Collectorate.

His son, Nrishinga Babu, was involved in two heavy law suits, the one instituted by Rajah Krishnanath Nandi of Cossimbazar for damages laid at three crores of rupees, while the other was brought by his cousin, Bhubaneswari Devi. He won both the cases and left his wealth to his two sons, Babu Nabakrishna and Babu Rajkrishna, both of whom made good use of their money. The death of Nabakrishna, who was childless, left Rajkrishna the sole owner of the family properties, which, on his death, devoled upon his only son, Babu Annada Prosad, whose minority ushered in the Court of Wards to manage his estates. Government bestowed on him the title of Rai Bahadur in recognition of his acts of munificence. An official conference at Calcutta in connection with the proposal of bestowing upon him the title of Rajah Bahadur took him to the metropolis, where to the sorrow of a large circle of friends and admirers, he died on the 20th February, 1880, before that honor could be conferred upon him. To his liberality the Calcutta Zoological Gardens owed a beautiful house, which has since been removed.

The Court of Wards again stepped in to manage the estate, which devoled upon his minor son, Babu Ashutosh Nath Rai, whose mother, Rani Arnakali Devi, took charge of his person.

The unostentatious charities of this pious lady, her benevolent disposition and her sense of the wants of her sex have excited general admiration. She has spent over half a lac for the Sanskrit Tol at Berhampore and it is her sole contribution that supports that useful institution. The Zenana Hospital at Berhampore, now amalgamated with the Berhampore Charitable Hospital, is her gift.

On the 29th January, 1893, she celebrated the marriage of her son, with a grand daughter of the late Mr. Justice Anukul Chandra Mookerjee.

Babu Ashutosh Nath, who was born on the 7th September, 1876, attained his majority in September, 1897, when he assumed charge of his vast Zemindaries. Ever since, he has evinced a charitable disposition, consonant with the traditions of his family. On hear-

AFTER RAJA A. N. ROY'S INSTALLATION.

MAJUMDAR'S MURSHIDABAD. FANCY PRESS.

ing from Sir Alexander Mackenzie that the Dufferin Hospital Building in Amherst Street badly needed funds, young Ashutosh Nath gave a donation of a lac of rupees. In May 1898, the title of Rajah was conferred upon him in a Durbar held at his residence at Cossimbazar, presided over by the Hon'ble Mr. Buckland.

He maintains at his sole cost four charitable dispensaries and two English schools. Since the attainment of his majority he has spent more than another lac in charities. As one of the representatives from the province of Bengal, he was invited to the Coronation Durbar at Delhi and was awarded a Durbar Medal.

Rajah Ashutosh Nath Rai is a keen sportsman and for the destruction of wild and dangerous animals, which fall easy victims to the charms of his arms, he spends not a small portion of his time, sometimes travelling for the purpose far beyond his district.

The management of his affairs, over which he exercises regular supervision, is in the hands of his faithful manager, Babu Sat Kori Mukerjee, who in the discharge of his duties combines experience with competency and honesty.

THE DUTCH CEMETRY AT KALKAPUR.

A little to the west of the English cemetry is Kalkapur, where lies the old Dutch cemetry, containing forty three tombs, of which only a few bear inscriptions, dating from 1721 to 1792.

The Dutch fortifications at Kalkapur were taken possession of by a party of the East India Company's troops in 1781, by order of Warren Hastings.

BISTUPUR TEMPLE.

The temple of Kali, situated about a mile to the south of Cossimbazar, was built by Krishnanand Hota, the gomasta of the East India Company. It is situated on the banks of the old bed of the Cossimbazar river. Every Tuesday and Saturday a large number of devotees attends to offer puja.

BYASPUR TEMPLE.

The temple of exquisite workmanship, at Byaspur, near Cossimbazar, was built by the ancestors of Pandit Krishna Nath Nyapanchanon. The image is of Siva.

HOTAR SANKO.

This bridge or culvert over the Bistupur Beel, supposed to be the old bed of the river Bhagirathee, then known as the Cossimbazar river, connecting Cossimbazar with Saidabad, was built by Krishnanand Hota, who was the East India Company's gomasta at Cossimbazar.

The Calcutta Board wrote to the Directors of the Company in England under date the 21st December, 1758.—"Gentlemen at Cossimbazar acquaint us that upon examining the accounts of Kussendah, the Company's Gomasta, they had found great reason to suspect him guilty of several frauds in the management of of the investments, that they had already detected him in giving in false accounts for the year 1756 in which he had overcharged Rs. 8,427, in the real cost of the goods provided by him."

KUNJAGHATA RAJBARI.

The importance of the Kunjaghata family is enhanced by reason of its connection with Maharajah Nanda Kumar of historical notoriety. The chief objects of interest at the Rajbari are several firmans and an original painting of Gouranga and his comrades, said to have been prepared for Maharajah Nanda Kumar.

Nanda Ram received the title of Lala Rai from the Emperor of Delhi, during the rule of Saista Khan, King of Bengal, with the privelege of keeping two thousand horse and three thousand infantry.

His son Satrujit Rai, made considerable additions to the family property. Jagat Chand, his son, was Darogah or Superintendent under Mani Begum, the guardian of her step-son, the Nawab Nazim. He received the title of Rai and the privelege of keeping five hundred cavalry and an equal number of infantry.

Like Nandaram, Padma Lal Rai, was the head of another family of Kulin Brahmins. His son, Nanda Kumar, was Fouzedar of Hooghly, when Serajuddowla was Nawab Nazim. He served the Nizamut in various capacities from his earliest days. He was a favorite of Clive and was nicknamed the Black Colonel. As he was intriguing, aspiring and unprincipled, his life was not free from adverse vissicitudes. In 1764 the Emperor Sha Alum conferred upon him the title of Maharajah. After many years of a most eventful life, on the 6th March, 1775, a charge of forgery was laid against him, then aged seventy, and a warrant was issued for his arrest. One Bolaki Das, a banker at Murshidabad, had executed in his favour a bond for Rs. 70,000, upon payment of which by his executors after his death in 1769, Nanda Kumar had torn off the top of the bond in token of entire satisfaction. The deed alleged to be forged was an acknowledgment of this paid off debt.

Nanda Kumar was confined in the common Jail, where he could not eat or drink without losing his caste. Pandits were sent to persuade him that he could be purified by penance. But these did not avail. At last, in a tent pitched on the roof of the Jail, he partook of sweet-meats. Messages of sympathy poured in from many Europeans.

His trial before the Supreme Court began on the 8th June, 1775, before a Jury composed of twelve Englishmen. The Counsel to defend him was Farrer. The prisoner pleaded not guilty. On being asked by whom he would like to be tried, he answered, by God and his peers. The trial went on for eight days, and the Judges and the jurors remained in the Court house during all this time. At four in the morning of the 16th, the verdict of guilty was given and sentence of death was passed. Saturday the 5th August was fixed for the execution. Several petitions were made for time to appeal to the King of England. One of these was from Nanda Kumar himself and another was from the Nawab Nazim. The Judges rejected them. Only a few hours before the appointed time, Nanda Kumar took leave of his son-in-law. He passed the interval in prayer and meditation, never for a moment losing courage. The sight of the gallows caused him no agitation. He himself gave the signal and in an instant it was over. No body thought that a Brahmin and a Maharajah would be hanged. On that memorable day no Brahmin cooked his food on the Calcutta side of the river.

Nanda Kumar left a son named Gooroodas, who became Dewan of the Nawab Nazim, and a daughter named Sumani, whom he had married to Jagat Chand. The issue of this marriage was a son named Mahanand, who inherited the property and the dignity of his father and obtained the title of Rajah. The family property of Goaljan, situated on the west bank of the river, opposite to Kunjaghata, was acquired by him as a Jaigire from the East India Company.

His son, Rajah Bijoy Krishna, became involed and was compelled to sell some of the family property. Krishna Chandra and after him his son, Kumar Durga Nath next represented the house. The latter left a son, Kumar Devendra Nath, who was born in 1874, and now represents the house of Kunjaghata.

The original residence of Nanda Kumar was at Bhadurihat or Badrihat in the *Rarh*. On the east bank of the Bhagirathee, he occupied a house, which stood on the site of the Nawab Bahadur's building on the Shanagore Ghat. He may have lived occasionally at Kunjaghata after his marriage with Sumani.

```
                                   Mathura
                                      |
                                   Daughter + Ram Gopal Rai
                                                 |
                                   Chandi Charan Rai
                                                 |
Lala Nanda Ram Rai                     Padmalal Rai
        |                                        |
  Satrujit Rai                     Maharajah Nanda Kumar
        |                                        |
        |                  +---------------------+--------------+
        |                  |                                    |
Jagatchand + Sumani                                    Rajah Gooroodas
              |
     Rajah Mahananda
              |
     Rajah Bijoy Krishna
              |
     Krishna Chandra
              |
     Kumar Durga Nath
              |
Kumar Devendra Nath Rai
```

ARMENIAN CHURCH.

The Armenian Church, at Saidabad, was built in 1758, at a cost of two lacs and thirty six thousand rupees. The last tomb here is of Varden. To the east is the site of the Church built in 1665.

FARASHDANGA.

The Berhampore water works pumping station marks the site occupied by the French factory at Cossimbazar. The place is called Farashdanga, much of which has been cut away.

TEMPLE OF DOYAMOI AT SAIDABAD.

The temple of Doyamoi Kali at Saidabad was built by Krishnananda Hota in 1752.

Saidabad was the residence of Kasi Singh, a very wealthy grocer, who from his shop there supplied provisions to the Cossimbazar Raj during the great litigation in which Surnomoi was involved, when the fate of the Cossimbazar Raj was trembling in the balance and he acted on the more strength of his conviction that the Rani would succeed and pay him his prices.

Saidabad is now the residence of Babu Boikunt Nath Sen, the leader of the Berhampore Bar, the feeder of the Congress, the supporter of national movements, the pillar of many estates, and the hope of aggrived, poor and persecuted litigants.

The site of Seta Khan's Bazar, which was a very thickly populated locality, was in the neighbourhood of Saidabad.

MADAPUR.

About three miles to the east of Cossimbazar is Madapur, where Clive encamped on the 25th June, 1757, before his entry into Murshidabad, after the victory at Plassey.

It was the head quarters of the English agent for some time, before removal to Berhampore.

The large building used as the Jail remains unutilized.

BERHAMPORE CEMETRY.

Over a mile to the south of Cossimbazar, lies the English Cemetry at Berhampore, having an enclosure, the northern walls of which, on either side of the entrance gate, are studded with tablets commemorative of the tombs of military men and their family. In the enclosure are several monuments over the tombs, of which there are many and among which are the following :—(1) Captain James Skinner, 1773; (2) Captain John Friend, 1787; (3) Frederick W. S. Griffiths, 1791; (4) Daniel Robinson Leckie, who was

Registrar of the Dewani Adalat of City Murshidabad and died in 1792; (5) Neil Rainy, 1793; (6) Caroline Brown, 1798; (7) John Wilson, 1803; (8) Captain Lambert, 1805; (9) Adam Frere, 1811; (10) Col. Mitchel, 1833; (11) Colin Shakespere, 1835; (12) George Thomas, the Irish Adventurer of Rajputana; (13) Creighton, the explorer of Gour; &c.

Adjoining to the Cemetry is the Berhampore Race Course and Parade Grounds.

To the east of the Cemetry lie the tombs of the Burma State pensioners who died at Berhampore.

GRANT HALL.

The town hall of Berhampore, founded in honor of Sir John Peter Grant, the Lieutenant Governor of Bengal, is vested in Trustees, one of whom is Babu Dina Nath Gangooly, the veteran Vakil of the Berhampore Bar, whose fearless advocacy, unassuming manners, readiness to succor distress, sympathy with benevolent movements, sincerety of purpose, straight-forwardness, support of female education, magnanimous heart and indomitable energy have won for him the esteem of his colleagues and the admiration of the public.

The house, which was converted into the Grant Hall, belonged originally to Mr. J. Marion, late Superintendent of the Palace.

BERHAMPORE CANTONMENTS.

The barracks round the Square at Berhampore, which is a lawn of thirty five acres, and which is one of the most beautiful in Bengal, were erected in 1757, after the destruction of the factory house and the dismantling of the fortifications at Cossimbazar. Mr. John Brohier, who was deputed for the purpose, arrived at Cossimbazar on the 5th October, 1757, and reported that the principal part of the factory at Cossimbazar had been burnt down and that the fortifications of the factory were in capable of being repaired effectually. He suggested the construction, by removing huts and levelling ground, of a new fort, on a clear spot, which could be obtained from the Nawab, by erecting a pentagon and having an esplanade of seven hundred yards round. He also submitted the plan of a citadel and fortifications, with which he considered it necessary to enclose the place. According to his estimate, twelve thousand tank diggers and five thousand coolies were required to ram the ground, clear away rubbish, fill up tanks, bring in brush wood, serve brick layers and do other things.

The Board of Directors of the East India Company, being of opinion that a fortified place, near the capital of the subaship, capable of resisting any force that the native government could bring against it, would be the means of enforcing their influence at the Durbar and checking any designs that the Nawab's

Dutch Cemetry.

Armenian Church.

Lady Hasting's Tomb.

English Cemetry.

Berhampore Cantonments.

Site of old English Residency.

government might in future conceive against them, wrote to Mr. Manningham, then at Murshidabad, to obtain a grant from Meer Jaffer of the Berhampore plain and a perwana to build a factory and fortify it. They heard from Mr. Scrafton that a sanad had been sealed for four hundred bighas of land in Berhampore but work was deferred till the citadel at Calcutta was finished or, at least, till Captain Brohier was in a position to be sent to Cossimbazar to supervise the work. The plan of a fort was subsequently abandoned, the importance of Murshidabad sinking with the rise of Calcutta. The construction of the Barracks, however, was completed in 1767, at a cost of £ 302, 270.

The cantonments of Berhampore will always be remembered as the scene of the first overt act of the Indian mutiny of 1857. They were vacated on account of the malarial condition of Berhampore, which now, however, is a healthy station.

The European translator of the Sier-ul-Mutaqherin thus describes the Cantonment of Berhampore—"There is an army of Europeans and natives cantoned in the finest and healthiest boracks that any nation can boast of. They form a regular elegant town. The army consists of general in a regiment or two of Europeans, seven or eight regiments or battalions of sepahees and a train of Artillery, with fifteen or twenty field pieces." (1786)

KRISHNA NATH COLLEGE.

In November, 1853, a College was opened at Berhampore and located in Barrack No. 10. The present beautiful building, situated to the south of the Cantonments, was erected with public subscriptions, the foundation stone being laid on the 29th July, 1863, by Sir Cecil Beadon, the Lieutenant Governor of Bengal. It was completed in 1869, when the classes were removed there from the barracks.

As a Government Institution it was known as the Berhampore College. On the proposal of Government to abolish it, the late Maharani Surnomoi undertook to bear the cost of maintenance, the management being vested in a Board of Trustees. Of late, landed property has been endowed by Maharajah Manindra Chandra Nandi of Cossimbazar and the name of the Institution has been changed to Krishna Nath College, in memory of the late Maharani's husband, who, by his will, subsequently declared void, had bequeathed his properties for the establishment of a University at Banjetea.

CHOA.

The village of Choa, situated in the eastern parts of Murshidabad District, a few miles beyond the Vanderdah, celebrated for its now extinct pearl fishery, is the seat of a branch of the illustrious

Sarvadhikari family of Bengal, which claims for its founder Sureswar, posted by the Emperor of Delhi to Orissa as Dewan. The grant of the Jaigire of Raghunathpur, yielding a revenue of two lacs annually followed from Delhi to support the title of Sarvadhikari (literally, possessor of all) which Mahammad Toghluk, the Pathan King, conferred upon him. His younger brother, Ishaneswar, held high office at the imperial Court. Rajah Janakiram and his son, Rajah Mohendra Narayan, held responsible posts in the Nawab's cabinet during the rule of Ali Verdi Khan and Serajuddowla. Rajah Bhubon Mohun and Rajah Rajkisore served the East India Company as Dewans. Later on, Rajah Sita Nath was one of the Dewans of the Nawab Nazim of Bengal, during the middle of the last century.

The most prominent member of the family resident at Choa is Rajah Rajkisore's great grand son, Babu Sris Chandra Sarvadhikari, whose steadfast devotion to public duties and single minded advocacy of his country's cause have won for him the admiration of all classes of the community. His platform speeches, dealing with a great variety of topics, couched in what has been declared by competent authority as excellent English, bearing ample evidence of his experience of the country, have been published by public subscription under the authority of Rajah Peary Mohun Mukherjee and others, an honor which has seldom fallen to the lot of many Indian speakers, and a compliment which this scion of an ancient family may well be proud of.

FARIDPUR.

Near Plassey, is Faridpur, containing the tomb of Serajuddowla's general, Mir Madan, killed in the battle of Plassey, as also the tomb of Baba Farid, a faqueer, from whom it derived its name.

DADPUR.

A little to the north of Palssey is Dadpur where Clive encamped after the battle and met Meer Jaffer the next day, embracing him as Nawab Nazim of Bengal, Behar and Orissa.

MANKAR.

In 1744 Ali Verdi Khan encamped at Mankar, near Plassey, and invited the Mahratta general, Bhashkar, to make peace.

Here, in 1757, Serajuddowla halted before he marched down to Plassey.

PLASSEY.

Plassey is situated on the left bank of the Bhagirathee and is about thirty five miles south of

Murshidabad City. It is now within the jurisdiction of the Collectorate of Nuddea and should certainly be transferred to Murshidabad.

The historical mango grove, which formed the bivouac of the English forces, was eight hundred yards long and three hundred yards broad and was surrounded by an earthen bank and ditch. It was planted with trees and diagonal to the river. The last of the trees fell some years ago. Spoons and other things made of the wood were sold as souvenirs and fetched high prices.

Just beyond the grove stood a hunting box belonging to the Nawab, surrounded by a masonry wall.

The major portion of the field of battle has been cut away by the river.

A monument has been erected bearing the following inscription :—

PLASSEY.

ERECTED BY THE BENGAL GOVERNMENT, 1883.

At Plassey the army of Serajuddowla lay encamped under Dullavram and Meer Jaffer. Clive and the Calcutta Council took this as a sign of hostility. At Clive's request, Serajuddowla recalled his troops to Murshidabad. On the 13th June, 1757 Clive marched from Chandernagore and asked the Nawab's agents in his camp to intimate to him that Clive was marching on Murshidabad. On the same date, Watts, the English agent at Cossimbazar, under instructions previously received, left it with his subordinates, and reached Clive's camp in safety. Serajuddowla being apprised of this, ordered his army to take up its former position at Plassey. On the 21st June, the Nawab's troops reached Plassey. Clive had arrived at Palti on the 16th, whence he dispatched the next day a force of two hundred Europeans and five hundred Sepoys, with a field gun and a small howitzer, under Major Eyre Coote, to take possession of Cutwa, a fort, where the Nawab had kept large supplies of grain and military stores. Clive arrived there the same evening with the rest of the army. He hesitated whether it would be prudent to march against the forces of the Nawab, which were reported to be overwhelming. He summoned a council of war. The question put to them was whether the English army should at once cross over to the island of Cossimbazar, and at all risks attack the Nawab. Coote voted for immediate action. Clive was against immediate advance. The decision of the majority was not to fight. In this predicament, Clive retired to meditate. Through exhaustion, he fell asleep but after an hour rose, determined to fight. Immediate orders were given to the army to cross the river. His tiny force consisted of nine hundred and fifty European infantry, one hundred European artillery, fifty English sailors and a little over two thousand native troops. Eight six-pounders and two small howitzers composed the artillery train.

At day break this little force began to cross in the boats which had accompanied it from Chandernagore. In about ten hours' time, it was securely planted on the east bank of the river, without meeting any opposition, fifteen miles south of Plassey. Marching almost immediately, they reached the village of Plassey in about six hours. On the morning of the memorable 23rd June, 1757, they halted and bivouacked in a large mangoe grove. From there, the sound of martial music of the Nawab's Camp reached their ears. It was only a mile off. The Nawab's force consisted of thirty-five thousand infantry, fifteen thousand cavalry and fifty-three field pieces, with fifty Frenchmen under M. St. Frais, occupying a strong position covered by intrenched works. The Nawab's army left at day break, to take up their position under the commands of Mir Madan, Mohan Lal, Dullavram, Yar Lutf Khan and Meer Jaffer.

The movements of the army were being watched by Clive from the Nawab's hunting box, which had been taken possession of, the night previous. The English army, under his direction, took up its position. Three hours of continued fighting produced little effect. The English were advantageously protected by the earthen bank of the grove, not stronger than the mud walls that surround the mangoe gardens or protect the mulbery plantations of to-day.

Then an unforeseen circumstance ensued, which damped and destroyed the Nawab's unprotected ammunition. From the heavy rain which fell for one full hour the powder of the English did not suffer, being well protected, that of the Nawab becoming useless.

When the fighting was resumed, the Nawab's General, Mir Madan was wounded and died shortly after. The Nawab lost courage and leaving his army in charge of his other generals, he left for Murshidabad on a camel, escorted by two thousand horsemen.

His generals slackened fire but Frais persisted on, till abandoned by his comrades he had no alternative but to retire. The victory of Plassey was complete by five in the afternoon of the 23rd June. Intimation of the defeat of his army reached Serajuddowla at Murshidabad, which he quitted to join the French believed to be advancing from Patna.*

A DIARY : PLASSEY AND AFTER.

June 23,
1757.

1 A. M. The English reached Plassey.

6 A. M. The Nawab's army marched out of the intrenchments.

8 A. M. The first shot fired by the Nawab's Artillery.

8½ A. M. The English army retired into the mangoe grove, having last 10 Europeans and 20 sepoys.

---

* *Milleson's Decisive Battles.*

THE BATTLE OF PLASSEY.

MAJUMDAR'S MURSHIDABAD. FANCY PRESS.

11 A. M. Clive consulted his officers about continuing the cannonade all day and attacking the Nawab's camp at night.

12 Noon. A heavy shower damaged the Nawab's powder, that of the English being protected by paulins. Information reached the Nawab that Meer Madan had been mortally wounded.

1 P. M. The Nawab sent for Meer Jaffer, exhorted him to fight and placing his *turban* before him, said, Meer Jaffer, that *turban* you must defend.

1½ P. M. Dullavram counselled the Nawab to return to the capital.

2 P. M. The Nawab ordered his army to retire into the intrenchments.

2½ P. M. The Nawab's artillery ceased cannonading but Sinfray stuck to his position at the tank.

Major Kilpatrick advanced towards the tank, with two field pieces without Clive's orders.

Clive, who had, from fatigue, fallen asleep in the Nawab's hunting box, being informed, hurried up and reprimanded Kilpatrick.

Clive sent Kilpatrick back to bring up the whole army.

Meer Jaffer's friendly troops, being mistaken for the enemy, Clive detached three platoons to oppose them, when they were advancing to join him.

THE FLIGHT OF SERAJUDDOWLA.

The death of Mir Madan and the inactivity of his other general's had so disheartened Serajuddowla and the idea that the English would storm his camp so demoralized him, that, mounting a swift camel, and escorted by two thousand horsemen, the Nawab, hurried towards the capital, which caused great panic and confusion, resulting in the flight of his army in all directions.

5 P. M. The whole of the English army entered the Nawab's deserted camp, *at the exact hour at which, one year before, Serajuddowla, with Meer Jaffer, had entered Fort William.*

6 P. M. Clive sent forward a detachment under Major Coote to observe if the Nawab's army rallied and intimated Meer Jaffer to meet him at Dadpur the next morning

8 P. M. The English army arrived at Dadpur.

12 P. M. Serajuddowla arrived at Murshidabad.

June 24.

5 A. M. Clive deputed Scrafton and Omar Beg to conduct Meer Jaffer to Dadpur.

On Meer Jaffer's arrival at Dadpur, Clive saluted him as Nawab Nazim of Bengal, Behar and Orissa.

7 P. M. Meer Jaffer arrived at Murshidabad.

10 P. M. Serajuddowla escaped and left the capital.

12 P. M. Meer Jaffer got information of Serajud-dowlas' flight, and sent out parties for his arrest.

June 25.

11 A. M. Mohon Lall and others were seized.

12 Noon. The English army arrived at Madapur.

3 P. M. Watts and Walsh, being deputed by Clive, arrived at the city and visited Meer Jaffer.

June 26. Watts and Walsh visited Jagat Sett and there met Meer Jaffer and Dullavram.

June 27. Clive waited at Cossimbazar, having been informed by Jagat Sett, through Ranjit Rai, that there was a plot to assassinate Clive on his arrival at the city.

June 29.

8 A. M. Clive entered Murshidabad, escorted by 200 of the battalion and 300 Sepoys.

Clive placed Meer Jaffer on the Masnad of Murshidabad.

July 2. News reached Murshidabad that Serajud-dowla, while cooking some food for his infant daughter in a deserted garden on the bank of the river opposite to Rajmahal, had been discovered by a *faqir*, whose ears he had caused to be cut and on receiving intimation from Sha Dana, for that was the name of the *faqir*, Mir Kasem Khan and Mir Daud crossed over to the garden and seized Serajuddowla. Mir Kasem Khan stripped his favorite wife, Lutfunnissa, his companion in prosperity and adversity, of her jewels, while Mir Daud stripped the other ladies of theirs. These were valued at crores.

Serajuddowla was rowed down with insolence and indignity to Murshidabad which was reached full eight days after his flight.

He was taken to the presence of Meer Jaffer, when Miran insisted on his being put to death immediately. Meer Jaffer consulted his courtiers. There was difference of opinion. Meer Jaffer expressed none. Miran, seeing Meer Jaffer was unwilling to assent, advised him to go to rest, assuring him he would take care of the prisoner. Meer Jaff retired into the Zenana with the desire, knowledge and assurance that Serajuddowla would be spared (*Macferlane*) and the assembly dispersed.

Serajuddowla's Tragic End.

Serajuddowla, whose supplications for life were all futile, was then confined in a cell :—

> "The desolator desolate,
> The victor o'er-thrown,
> The arbiter of others' wishes,
> Now a supplicant for his own."

The boisterous entrance into it of some ruffians struck terror in him and he more than suspected their design. He recovered from his agony and asked for water to perform ablutions to say his prayers.

A pitcher was close at hand and it was thrown over his head. He prostrated himself and asked forgiveness of God.

While in this humble posture, Mahamdi Beg, who had been nourished by Serajuddowla's grand-father, struck him with his knife. This was only three hours after Serajuddowla's arrival at Murshidabad.

His mangled remains were placed upon an elephant and paraded through the streets of the city.

The elephant stopped at the place where Hossien Kuli Khan and his blind brother had been slaughtered by Serajuddowla; and a few drops of blood fell from the mutilated body.

The elephant approached the house of Amena Begum, his mother. Distracted, she rushed out of her purdah, clasped the mangled remains to her bosom and kissed in tenderness the disfigured face, once the most handsome. She fell down, yelling in grief.

The elephant proceeded on and when the remains were placed at the masouleum, the tomb of Ali Verdi Khan rent in two and his heart's blood gushed out.

At Khoshbag, three miles south of Mansurganj, the grand-father and his adopted pet are lying side by side. Miran, the author of this murder, the murder of a youth, who was a sovereign at nineteen, was struck dead by lightning and lies entombed at a safe distance at Rajmahal, opposite to the place of Serajuddowla's seizure.

As the solitary visitor stands by the side of Serajuddowla's tomb at Khoshbag, a feeling of awe suddenly overtakes him, and he asks in his mind—should Serajuddowla, the embodiment of oppression, rise !

Crossing over to the western bank of the river.

SAKTIPUR.

On the west bank of the Bhagirathee, opposite to Dadpur, is Saktipur, containing the temple of Kapileswar Siva, built by Jairam, in the seventeenth century. It is about thirty feet square and sixty feet high. The remains of an earlier stone temple lie scattered about.

RANGAMATI.

Known also as Karnafala and reputed to have been the residence of Karna and the capital of the kingdom of Karna Subarna. The Gupta Kings lived here. Several Rabi Gupta coins were discovered in the locality.

The Chinese traveller, Hiuen Tsiang visited this place in the second century, A. D. The major portion of the Hindu capital is now in the midst of the river. Several old elevated places, such as Rakhashidanga and Rajbaridanga, are still extant. Broken Hindu images are found all over the place.

Rangamati is now included in Pergana Fattehsingh, the Zemindari of the Nawab Bahadur of Murshidabad. Its yellow or reddish clay, its cliffs and high bluffs, its elevated ground and undulations as also its romantic associations, make Rangamati a most interesting place in Murshidabad.

FATTEHSINGH.

Tradition ascribes the rule of a rajah of the Hari caste named Fatteh Singh over the tract of the country now known as Fattehsingh. The capital of this kingdom was Fattehpoor or the city of victory, six miles to the south-west of the town of Kandi.

Another tradition says that Fatteh Singh and Beer Singh, two brothers came from the north-west and subjugated the tracts of the country known respectively as Fattehsingh and Beerbhoom, while a third tradition ascribes the name of Fattehsingh to Fatteh Sha, the Pathan King of Bengal.

Fattehsingh was comprised in Sircar Sharifabad, which finds mention in the Ain Akbari. The revenue of the Perganah is stated to have been Rs. 52,411-8-0. The Perganah was then bounded by the Bhagirathee on the east, the Dwarka on the north, the Mourakshi on the west and the Ajai on the south. There has been little variation in the limits of the Perganah, which now comprises most of the villages in the thanas of Kandi, Bharatpore, Gokurna, Khargram, etc. Some of its villages lie in Burdwan. The present perganahs of Gopinathpore, Radhaballovpore, Kantanagar and Mooniadihi which formerly appertained to Fatteh Singh, have now been separated from it.

At the revenue settlement effected by Murshid Kuli Khan, Ananda Chandra, a member of the Jamo Bagdanga family took a settlement of Fattehsingh for a revenue of one lac and eight thousand rupees. In 1126, B. S., Surja Naraen obtained a settlement from the Nizamut in his own name. From that year to 1151 B. S., Fattehsingh continued in the hands of the descendants of Rajeswari, wife of Surja Moni, when it was recovered by Nilkanta. Parvati, the widow of Hori Prosad, next wrested it from his hands, through the help of Kantoo Babu of Cossimbazar, and it remained in her possession till 1175 B. S., when the property was divided into halves, the Nawab making over a moity each to Nilkanta and Parvati. As rewards for their labors as mediators, Ganga Govind Singh and Kantoo Babu received certain portions of Fattehsing, which came thence forward to be known as Radhaballavpore and Kantanagar. The rest of the Parganah in two equal shares continued in the hands of Nilkanta, living at Jamo and Parvati living at Bagdanga each moity being registered as a separate Towzi.

The Bagdanga family got involved in debts, which, originally incurred from Rajah Udwant Singh of Nashipore, increased in course of time to an amount beyond the power of the proprietors to repay. The result was that half the Perganah of Fattehsingh, which had been hypothecated, was sold away by public auction, by the Civil Court, and was purchased by the Nawab Bahadur of Murshidabad, who is its present proprietor.

Perganah Fattehsingh is the home of many old and respectable Mahomedan families, the founders of which came to India from Persia and Arabia with the Mahomedan conquerors. They are al. Sheiks and Syuds of the Sunni sect. It is also the seat of many old Uttarrarhi Kyastha families of note.

JAMO AND BAGDANGA.

Few Zemindars of Bengal can claim the antiquity which belongs to the family of Sabita Rai, who migrated from the banks of the Narbada, and came to Bengal with Man Singh in 1589. The present Zemindars of Jamo are direct descendants of Sabita Rai, while the Zemindars of Bagdanga are connected with him through Rajeswari, seventh in descent from him.

The family possesses an old Sanskrit manuscript, in which are recorded various acts of prowess, benevolence and charity, performed by various members. Jairam, a great grand-son of Sabita Rai, built the temple of Kapileswar, for the sheba of which he made elaborate arrangements. His brother, Bhim Rai, performed the worship of twelve lacs of Sivas. His son Santosh, known also as Jadunandan, outwitted him by worshipping double that number. In 1126 B. S, Surja Moni, the husband of Rajeswari, the seventh in descent from the founder of the family, obtained from the Nawab Nazim, a settlement of the main family property in his own name. Baidyanath, his brother-in-law, did not prefer any objection. Surja Naraen incurred the displeasure of the Nawab and was in consequence put into jail, where he expired, and his properties were confiscated. Nilkanta, the son of Baidyanath, recovered them on payment of all arrears of revenue and nazars to the Nawab. He obtained from Serajuddowla the title of Rajah, the sanad of which is still in the possession of the family at Jamo.

Parvati, the widow of Hori Proshad, wrested the properties from the hands of Nilkanta, who was imprisoned at Murshidabad and set at liberty in 1175 B. S. At the intercession of Dewan Ganga Govind Singh and Kantoo Babu, the family properties were divided into halves, each of the two branches of the family getting a moity. The mediators got a portion each as reward for their labours. This was about the time when the great Bengal famine took place in 1176 B. S. Litigation ensued and both branches got involved in debts, which were so full of disaster to the Bagdanga branch. The bulk of the property was mortgaged with Rajah Udwant Singh of Nashipore and for the debts which went on increasing continually, the properties passed away from the family. The original debt was incurred by Paramananda, known as Paban Babu of Bagdanga. He died in 1227 B. S., leaving to his childless widow the legacy of a heavy debt. She adopted Mohananda, whose efforts succeeded in recovering the properties, though encumbered, from the hands of the creditor. He married his daughter to Narendra Naraen of Jamo and thus succeeded in reconciling the two branches of the family, which had suffered so much from discension.

Rajah Mahananda died in 1270 B. S., leaving behind him three sons, five daughters and a widow named Rani Muktakeshi, a lady who has experienced great vicissitudes and to whom the Nawab Bahadur of Murshidabad has given the means of sustenance by granting in perpetuity eight mouzas from his Zemindari. Her third daughter married the son of Rajah Jogendro Naraen Rai of Lalgola.

Of the members of the Jamo branch of the family, Rajah Norendra Naraen was an embodiment of many good qualities. His sons, the present proprietors, have kept alive the reputation of the house, no insincere friend of which has been Babu Ramendra Sundar Trivedi, their great grand-father's sister, Doyamoi's great grand-son.

The following is a genealogy of the family :—

- **Basanta Rai**
  - **Kamala**
  - **SABITA RAI**
    - **Dharik**
      - **Gangan**
        - **Rai Sen**
          - **Devi Rai**
            - **Udai Chandra**
              - Kissen Ram
                - JAMO BRANCH
                  - Baidyanath
                    - Nilkantha
                      - Lakhi Naraen + Ram Mani
                        - Kali Naraen
                          - Mahindra Naraen
                            - **Dakhayani** + Norendra Naraen + Bhabatarini
                              - (by Dakhayani) **Devendra Naraen**
                              - (by Dakhayani) Dwijendra Naraen
                              - (by Bhabatarini) Purnendu Naraen
                              - (by Bhabatarini) Sharadendu Naraen
                              - (by Bhabatarini) Baradendu Naraen
                        - Doya Moi —— + Bala Bhadra Tribedi
                          - Kristo Sundar
                            - Govind Sundar
                              - Ramendra Sundar Tribedi
                - BAGHDANGA BRANCH
                  - Rajeswari + Surja Moni
                    - Hori Prashad
                      - Kali Sanker
                        - Paramananda
                          - Mahananda + Muktakeshi
                            - Jogindra Naraen
                            - Upendra Naraen
                              - Manabendra Naraen
                              - Kantindra Naraen
                              - Pandit nor)
                            - Jagadindra Naraen
  - **Ajaee**

KANDI.

Kandi is the head-quarters station of the sub-division of that name, once the residence of Ganga Govind Singh, the Dewan of Warren Hastings.

Hara Krishna Singh was the first of the family to settle at Kandi. On account of the Mahratta disturbances, he migrated to the opposite bank of the river and selected the village of Boalia, having obtained a grant of the land from the Nawab.

His second son, Gouranga Singh Majumdar, became assistant Canongoe under the Bangadhikaris. In 1178 B. S., he obtained a Sanad from the Emperor Sha Alum and endowed the lands covered by it to the family diety, Radhaballavji. It is said that he built at Kandi a house with parapets and cornices which resembled those of Serajuddowla's palace, the news of which so enraged the Nawab that the edifice had to be pulled down.

Gouranga, being childless, adopted Radhakanta, his younger brother's son, a revenue officer of rank under Ali Verdi Khan and Serajuddowla, who was subsequently appointed by Clive as assistant to Mahomed Reza Khan, the Naib Dewan and Naib Suba and Dullavram, in the administration of Revenue.

His natural and younger brother, Ganga Govind Singh, became Dewan of Warren Hastings who placed great confidence in him, which in a great measure fecilitated Ganga Govind's amassing great wealth and receiving presents to the tune of several lacs. After the aboliton of the Provincial Councils, Hastings appointed him Dewan of Revenue and Naib Canongoe and his son, Prankrishna, Naib Dewan of the Committee. Lord Cornwallis appointed Ganga Govind Jamanovis to effect the Permanent Settlement. Ganga Govind spent twenty lacs at the Sradh of his mother.

His uncle, Radhakanta, took Prankrishna in adoption, whose son, Krishna Chandra, became so well known as Lala Babu, a name which was given to him by his grand father, Ganga Govind. Lala Babu distinguished himself by his devotion, piety and self abnegation. Leaving behind his vast properties, he retired to Brindaban and died at Gobardhan. His widow, the celebrated Rani Kattayani, who belonged to the Roshora family, spent sixteen lacs in charity. She performed the ceremony of Anna Meru, or the mountain of rice, which with valuable presents was distributed to deserving people.

Her son, Sri Naraen Singh, married three wives. The first wife adopted Hori Mohan Ghosh, Rani Kattayani's brother's son, who assumed the name of Protap Naraen Singh. Protap contributed Rs. 50,000 for the construction of the Calcutta Fever Hospital. The title of Rajah Bahadur was conferred upon him by a Sanad, dated the 20th April, 1854. The school at Kandi was established by him in 1859. He was appointed one of the four non-official members of the Bengal Legislative Council and the order of the C.S.I. was conferred upon him. He died in 1866.

The second widow of Sri Naraen adopted Ram Mohan Ghosh, the natural and younger brother of Protap Chandra, who assumed the name of Isvar Chandra Singh.

The family gods are maintained at Kandi but the members removed to Calcutta, where they are known as the Paikpara Rajahs.

The following is the genealogy of the Kandi family :—

- Horo Krishna Singh
  - Muralidhar
    - Naraen Singh
    - Gouranga Singh
      - *adopted* Radhakanta*
    - Behari Singh
      - Dindayal
      - Radhakanta*
      - Radhacharan
      - Ganga Govind
        - Prankrishna
          - Krishna Chandra *alias* Lala Babu *married* Rani Kattayani
            - Senior Widow + Sri Naraen Singh + Junior Widow
              - (Senior Widow) *adopted* Protap Chandra
                - Giris Chandra
                - Purna Chandra
                - Kanti Chandra
                - Sarat Chandra
              - (Junior Widow) *adopted* Isvar Chandra
                - Indra Chandra *married* Rani Mrinalini

SONARUNDI.

Jagamohan Dalal, belonging to the caste of weavers, lived in the village of Sonarundi, near Kandi. His son, Nittyananda, who was born in 1752, with the help of his superior knowledge of Persian and Arabic, succeeded in introducing himself to the Emperor Sha Alum, who conferred upon him the title of Daneshband and appointed him Mir Munshi at Delhi. He was next accorded the priveleges of Haft Hazari and of keeping five guns and the title of Maharajah, Amir-ul-Mulk, Azmut-ud-dowla, Safdar Jang. He started the Daneshabda or era after his name and constructed several works of public utility in his native village.

On his death in 1821, he was succeeded by his son, Jagadindra Banwarilal, who received from Lord William Bentinck the title of Maharajah Bahadur. It is said that at his investiture he failed to oil the palm of the Arezbegi or Chief Usherer and herald of the Nawab Nazim's Court, and was in consequence announced as Maharajah so and so, Makoo Jang, Makoo meaning the shuttle of the weaver. Towards the cost of the Burmah war, Jagadindra contributed three lacs of rupees and he gave half a lac for the construction of the Strand Road of Calcutta.

His younger brother Jagadindra Banwarigovinda also received the title of Maharajah from Lord Canning.

Banwari has been a favorite name with the family. The village is called Banwariabad; the family diety, the image of Krishna, is called Banwari Deb, and Banwarilal, Banwarigovind, Banwarikishore, Banwaridoyal, Banwariananda, Banwarimukunda and Banwaribirendra have formed parts of the names of several members of the family, once so famous for its opulence.

TALIBPUR.

About three hundred years ago Moulana Fussi come from Upper India and settled at Talibpur, situated near Kandi. He received from the Emperor Jehangir a Sanad of rent free lands, still in the possession of his descendants. He was a great Persian and Arabic scholar and died at the age of eighty.

His only son, Moulvi Din Mahammed, is still remembered in the work of public utility left by him, namely the embankment from Tenga to Babla, which bore his name.

The embankment runnning parallel to the Din Mahommed Bund was raised by his son, Pir Mahommed.

One of his sons, Golam Rasool, became famous as a Persian and Arabic scholar.

Of the two sons of Golam Rasool, the elder, namely Moulana Golam Batul became a successful practitioner at the bar of the late Sudder Dewani Adalat. He constructed a large house, excavated many tanks, built musjeds, and maintained a mosaffer khana or traveller's rest house. The vast estate left by him devolved upon his only son, Munshi Newaz Hossein.

The younger son of Maulana Golam Rasool, namely Moulvi Golam Subdar, followed his brother's profession and became an eminent practitioner of the Saddar Dewani Adalat. His eloquence and verbosity gained for him the surname of "Totia Bung" or the parrot of Bengal. His earnings were devoted to works of utility and benevolence. He died at the age of sixty-nine, leaving behind him three sons and a considerably larger estate than he had inherited.

Munshi Newaz Hossein married the daughter of Golam Subdar. For his personal beauty he was called "Babu Meah." His deligence and knowledge of zemindari affairs helped him in increasing the family properties, the whole of which he endowed for the maintenance of a mosque, a rest house, a free school and a Charitable Dispensary at Talibpur.

Munshi Zillar Rahaman, popularly known as Rajah Meah, has well maintained the reputation of the family. As manager of his vast zemindaries, he has, by diligence and assiduity, brought about peace and prosperity among his tenantry. As a devout Mussulman, he is punctual in the performance of religious observances. As a public spirited zemindar, his purse is always open to works of public utility. Among these the Charitable Dispensary, the poor house, the free Madrassa, the Zenana Hospital and the large tanks at Talibpur bear ample testimony of his genorosity. His contributions have been as frequent as they have been large. As an examplary landlord he has proclaimed to his tenants that he charges no interest upon arreas of rent.

SALAR.

The village of Salar near Kandi is noted as the monastery of Sha Rostum, whose descendants still reside there, foremost among them being Khondkar Fazl Rubbee, Khan Bahadur, who has the honor of tracing his descent from Caliph Abu Bakr, through his son, Mahomed, the Governor of Egypt.

Rostum, popularly known as Sha Rostum, the son of Khawja Mahomed Shariff, the thirteenth in descent from Abu Bakr, who migrated to Khorasan, was the first of the family to come to India. Upon his death the Emperor Sha Alum in 1762, granted certain lands for the maintenance of the mosque, monastery and shrine of Sha Rostum. More than two hundred years ago, Nawab Shaista Khan granted for the house and monastery of the aneestors of Khondkar Fazl Rubbee, Khan Bahadur, some lands upon which the house of the Khan Bahadur still stands. Thirty-three years later, Murshed Kuli Khan, the Nazim, granted to his ancestors by a ferman, dated 1131 H. one hundred and fifty bighas of land in mouza Dhaoa.

Sha Zeaduddeen and Sha Serajuddeen, the son and the grandson of Sha Rostum, were persons of eminence, the latter holding the office of Kazi-ul-Kazzut or Chief Justice of Gour under Sultan Gaesuddeen, the King of Bengal. (669—775 H.)

The first of the family who obtained the title of Khondkar (spiritual teacher and leader) was Sha Azizulla. Of his descendants, Mufti Moez was the first to accept service under the British Government. He acted latterly as tutor to Humayun Jah.

A member of this family, namely Seraj-ul-Huq, was the first Moulvi of the Civil Court of Murshidabad. Another member, Moulvi Mohsen, held service in the Nizamut.

Thirty-first in descent from Abu Bakr and sixteenth from Sha Rostum is Khondkar Fazl Rubbee, born in 1848. He entered the service of the Nizamut and travelled with the late Nawab Nazim in Europe, returning in 1874 to Murshidabad, where his services were in great requisition.

A man of examplary fortitude, straight forward, honest and zealous, conspicuously successful in the discharge of duties, a great helpmate in times of difficulty and stress, having the courage of his convictions and a thorough grasp of all questions of state or management, however intricate, paying, in the discharge of his onerous duties attention to the minutest details and a great supporter of public benevolent movements, Khondkar Fazl Rubbee commands not only the confidence of his employer but also the respect of the public. Sir Alexander Mackenzie, the Lieutenant Governor of Bengal, in handing him Lord Elgin's Sanad conferring on him the title of Khan Bahadur said—"Khondkar Fazl Rubbee, Dewan, of my old friend, the Nawab of Murshidabad, is distinguished not only by his social position but also by his historical work Origin of the Mussulmans of Bengal."

"In recognition of his services as Dewan of His Highness the Nawab Bahadur of Murshidabad," Khondkar Fazl Rubbee, Khan Bahadur, was honored with a certificate presented to him in the name of His Most Gracious Majesty King Edward VII, Emperor of India.

In history and ethnology the Khan Bahadur takes particular delight. His work, "Origin of the Mussulmans of Bengal," has been well spoken of. He is the author of many valuable manuscripts, the result of great labor and research.

He is kind and hospitable beyond bounds. Like Lord Cornwallis, Dewan Fazl Rubbee, Khan Bahadur, is serene in all straits.

The village of Salar is also the residence of Moulvi Chowdhuri Karamutulla, whose ancestor, Gholam Mahmood, was employed as an agent of the Dutch factory at Chinsurah, at the Court of the Nazim.

Khan Bahadur Fazl Rubbee has in his possession the following old Sanads and fermans :—

1. Sanad from Shaista Khan, dated 1098 H., containing the grant to his ancestors of the land on which his house stands.

2. Sanad from Murshed Kuli Khan, dated 1131 H., granting to his ancestors 150 Bighas of land in Mouza Dhaoa.

3. Ferman of Sha Alum granting seventy thousand dams, (forty dams going to the rupee) to be paid out of Perganah Zafur-o-jal for the expenses of the Musjed, monastery and Durga of his ancestor, Sha Rostum. This is dated the 1st Jamadi-ul-Sani, in the fifth year of the Emperor's reign, corresponding to 1762 A. D.

SHERPUR ATAI.

Sherpur Atai in the Kandi Sub-Division is the place where, in 1600, Man Singh fought the Afghans and defeated Osman, the son of Kutloo Khan, the Afghan Chief. The annual fair in honor of Dada Pir is held close by.

SAGAR DIGHI.

The large tank south of the railway station of that name was excavated by King Mahipal in the eighth century. It is more than a mile in length.

On an eminence close by is the tomb of a faqueer said to have possessed supernatural powers.

MAHIPAL.

A little to the north of the railway station of Barela is Mahipal, the capital of Rajah Mahipal of the Pal Kings of Bengal. The place is twelve centuries old. Captain Layard who visited the place found a stone image in a tank close by which may still be seen at the Calcutta Museum.

EK ANA CHANDPARA.

A little to the east of Sheik Dighi, on the road to Jangipore, is Ekana Chandpara, where Hossien Sha, the celebrated King of Gour, used to live in his boyhood, and where he served a Brahmin of the name of Subudhi Rai. When Hossien Khan obtained the throne of Gour, he granted this village to the Brahmin as a Jaigire upon payment of a nominal revenue of one anna only. Hence the name of the village.

Hossien Sha Badsha, as Syud Sharif Makki, the King of Gour, was known, came with his brother and his father from Termiz and settled at Chandpore. After marrying the daughter of the Kazi, he introduced himself into the court of Sidi Badr, known as Sultan Mozaffer Sha (1495-1498 A. D.) and after the assassination of that Abyssinian, the nobles of the Court elevated him to the throne of Bengal.

SHEIK DIGHI.

About five miles north of the Bokhara station is Sheik Dighi, a large tank excavated in 1514 by Syud Sharif Makki Sultan Alauddeen, known as Hossien Sha, the Pathan King of Gour. On the west bank lies buried Faqueer Abu Syud. The tank and the village, known as Sheik Dighi, are now the property of the Nawab Bahadur of Murshidabad.

GIRIA.

Five miles north east of Jangipore and thirty seven miles from Murshidabad is Giria, spelt also Gheria, the scene of action in 1763.

After his reverses at Catwa, Mir Kasem, resolved to fight his decisive battle, caused his army to assemble at Suti. The position was strong naturally and artificially. The whole front was covered by intrenchments. The village of Giria lay about a mile from the scene of action. Here the English were repulsed in August, 1763.

Giria had been the scene of another battle in 1740, when Ali Verdi Khan defeated Serferaz Khan.

The two battles were, however, fought on different sides of the river.

UDUANALA.

The small stream known as the Uduanala, or Udhuanala, gave its name to a strong pass leading into the hill tracts of Rajmehal.

Mir Kasem had fortified this pass and made it impregnable and a position of great advantage. The ramparts of the intrenchments were sixty feet high and ten feet broad. These were surmounted by a parapet, eighteen feet high and seven feet thick; and along the entire front was caused to be dug a ditch, sixty feet wide and twelve feet deep. Batteries were erected at convenient intervals and upon them more than a hundred pieces of cannon were mounted. (Malleson's Decisive Battles).

Mir Kasem was betrayed by a deserter, who, creeping out of the defensive position on the night of the 4th September, 1763, made his way to the English camps. The fort was stormed, Mir Kasem's brigades under Sumru and Markar seeking safety in flight.

BHAGAWANGOLA.

Till the early part of last century, Bhagawangola was a very busy emporium for inland navigation. It was the chief granary of the capital. The site has changed frequently by reason of the encroachment of the river. Here in 1757, Serajuddowla took boat in his flight from Murshidabad after the battle of Plassey. The search parties sent out from Murshidabad seized here the Nawab's women and baggage.

LALGOLA.

Lalgola is the residence of Rajah Jogendra Naraen Rai.

GYSABAD.

Four miles north of Azimganj is Gysabad, founded by Gyasuddeen I, King of Gour (1367—1373) and built with materials brought from Mahipal. Stone images, coin and slabs bearing inscriptions in the Pali character, found at Gysabad, have been sent to the Calcutta Museum. There is a Hindu temple belonging to the Nashipore raj where a fair is held annually.

SADEQBAGH.

About six miles north of the Palace, on the east bank of the Bhagirathee is Sadeqbagh, where Clive halted on the 23rd April, 1766, on his way to Lucknow.

The Akhra of Mahant Mastaram Aulia, at Sadeqbagh, was founded in 1646 and is maintained from the proceeds of imperial grants of land, which were supplemented by the Nawabs. Whenever a succession to the Mahantship opened out, the Nawab Nazim used to go to the Akhra and put on the forehead of the installed successor the *tica* or dot of confirmation and recognition.

Mastaram Babaji was a man of great occult practices. He could walk over the water of the Bhagirathee with his wooden sandals on. He lived to see the battle of Plassey and was instrumental in saving Tara, the widowed daughter of Rani Bhowani, from the evil designs of Serajuddowla. Two stories are current in this connection. The one is that when Serajuddowla arrived at Barnagore, he found a funeral pyre burning, which had been previously arranged as an indication that it was Tara who was being cremated, so that the Nawab returned disappointed. The other version is that Serajuddowla, when he approached Tara, found her afflicted with small pox and came away in annoyance. Needless to say that she recovered her usual health as soon as the Nawab had left the precints of Rani Bhowani's house. Her miraculous affliction and her miraculous cure were attributed to the occult powers of Mastaram Babaji.

Ahirin Goalin sat weeping on the banks of the river, unable for want of a ferry boat to cross over to the opposite side. If she did not return home the same evening, she would lose her caste and her reputation. Mastaram asked her to close her eyes and follow him. In an instant she opened her eyes and found herself set on the other side of the river, without the help of a conveyance.

Mastaram's bamboo sonta or sceptre is still preserved in the Akhra. Preserved also is a piece of stone, which he seized, while it was engaged with all the vigor of life, to errode the banks of the Bhagirathee, endangering the Akrah itself.

BARNAGAR.

Opposite to Sadeqbagh, on the west bank of the river, about a couple of miles from the Azimganj Railway Station, is Barnagar, formerly the residence of Rai Udai Naraen of Rajshye. Here lived, on the banks of the sacred Bhagirathee, the famous Rani Bhowani, who spent enormous sums of money in founding endowments and charitable institutions and gave away rent free lands to numerous Brahmins. She was a most talented lady, possessing extraordinary business habits. Her piety and devotion were unparalled and her good name as a pious, devout, liberal and actively benevolent lady has become a household word in Bengal.

The revenue paid by her to the Nazim was seventy lacs and the rents collected by her were more than a crore and a half.

RANI BHOWANI'S TEMPLE.

BHUWANESWAR TEMPLE.

MAJUMDAR'S MURSHIDABAD.

FANCY PRESS.

In the early widowhood of her daughter, Tara, she experienced a great misfortune. On the occasion of her marriage, Rani Bhowani had consulted the best Pandits and astrologers of Benares, Mithila, the Deccan &c. They fixed a most auspicious day, when Tara's marriage took place. But her husband died shorty after. When the dicision of the learned men were reviewed, it was found that they had omitted to notice the Saptashalaka, which took away from the day its auspicious character and made it a most evil day for the performance of marriage.

The temples of Bhubaneswar Siva and Rajrajeswari built by Rani Bhowani and of Gopal built by Tara, still exist, the workmanship being excellent.

Her son, Rajah Ram Krishna, was a devout Sakta. He conducted his meditations on a seat placed over five human skulls under a Bel tree, which still exists. He excavated a canal from Barnagore to Kriteswari, to come by boat to that temple, of which he was a frequent visitor, and which was a favorite place for his practices.

Ram Krishna became so estranged from temporal matters that, for want of attention, most of the family estates were sold away for arrears of revenue and it is a notorious fact that he offered pujas and sacrifices in the temple of Rajrajeswari, with increasing devotion, every time a property was knocked down.

AZIMGANJ.

Azimganj is the home of the Jainas, whose ancestors emigrated from Bikanir in the latter half of the eighteenth century. One of the first to settle was Kharga Singh, who was living at Agra and came to Murshidabad at the invitation of Jagat Sett in 1765. Another imigrant was Horjimul who came in 1774.

The lucrative trade of the Jainas and their money-lending transactions changed their fortunes and some of their descendants, though exacting in their business, became noted for their charities. Several members, by their genorosity and public spirit, attracted the notice of Government and had honors conferred upon them.

One of these, the late Rai Dhanput Singh Bahadur, was the proposer and then a co-proprietor of the first line of railway in Murshidabad.

There is not a single place in India which, within a short compass, has contributed so many names to the list of Rai Bahadurs as Azimganj.

The Rose villa of Babu Dhanput Singh Nowlakha, near the railway terminus, is one of the loveliest spots in Murshidabad.

LALKOTHI.

About a mile to the south of Azimganj is Lalkothi, the site of a palace of the Nawab, adjacent to the

Moradbagh palace. There are two old mosques but the palaces have disappeared.

KRITESWARI.

About four miles from Dahapara is Kritkona, the "Tiruthkona" of the Reaz-us-Salatin and Rennell's map. It is also known as Kriteswari and is a place of great antiquity. When the body of Sati, borne on the shoulders of Mahadeva, was mutilated by the discus of Vishnu, her crown fell here. The Devi is named Bimola and is known as Kriteswari or the Crown goddess. Mention of this is to be found in the Purans.

The Bangadhicaris or Canongoes of Dahapara made extensive provisions for the maintenance of the sheva. One of their ancestors, namely, Bhagwan Rai, received jaigires from Delhi, one of which was Kriteswari, mentioned in his Sanad as Bhowanithan, or the place of goddess Bhowani, by which Kriteswari is also known.

The temple was overgrown with jungle and became delapidated. It was repaired by Bangadhicari Darpanaraen. He erected several new temples and excavated a tank close by, called the Kali Sagar. The annual fair held at Bhowanithan was instituted by Darpanaraen. His son Sivanaraen constructed a large culvert on the road to the temple. Rajah

Rajballav caused three images or symbols of Siva to be placed at Kriteswari. The temple of Kriteswari was a favorite resort of Rajah Ram Krishna, the husband of Rani Bhowani, who effected extensive repairs. One of the recently constructed temples bears date 1765, the year of the acquisition of the Dewani.

The temple of Kriteswari has had all along a great sanctity attached to it. The Seir-ul-Mutaqhuerin says that Meer Jaffer, when afflicted with the serious malady from which he died, took, under the advice of Maharajah Nanda Kumar, the *Charanamrita* of Kriteswari.

The old temple which is now a complete ruin was on the site which is north of the court-yard. The present temple, said to have been built by Darpanaraen, contains no image. A piece of black stone engraved with floral designs as the sacred symbol of the Crown is the object of worship and veneration. The original, which may be either a crown or the frontal bone, kept in a pot covered over with a red silk cloth, is known as the *Gooptapeet* and is seldom exposed or exhibited.

The two temples at the back of the main temple, towards the east, were built by Rajah Rajballav. The stone *linga* or symbol of Siva rent into two when Rajah Rajballav was flung into the river by Meer Kasem, with a heavy weight of stone tied round his neck.

The Temple of Kriteswari. The Image of Bhoirab at Kriteswari.

Gouranga. Stone Image at Rangamati.

MAJUMDAR'S MURSHIDABAD

FANCY PRESS

Old Kriteswari did not escape the influence of Buddhism, for one finds the image of Buddha, in the usual sitting posture of meditation, located in one of the temples close by and now worshipped as an image of Bhoirab.

The whole place is overgrown with jungle and the temples are in need of urgent repairs. Those last done were by Babu Ganga Das Rai of Nashipore, the late Naib Dewan of the Nizamut. There is no good water in the vicinity. A large concuorse of people assemble every Tuesday and Saturday during the month of Pous, when Khinchri, Baigan ka bhoorta and toddy play an important part in the pleasures and enjoyments of the masses. The tank at Kriteswari requires immediate reclamation. The neglected condition of Kriteswari is inconsistent with the religious professions of the Hindu millionaires of Bengal.

A tradition of the mysteries of Kriteswari has been handed down to posterity. A shell anklet seller, fatigued with his morning errand, had stepped down to drink of the water of the tank. On the step next to water, he found a very young girl who seemed to be about eight years old, performing her ablutions. She prevailed upon him to sell her a pair of his anklets. The man slided the rings into the tiny hands of the young purchaser and when he demanded the price, she referred him to her father, the Shebait of the temple of Kriteswari, living in the vicinity of the temple, mentioning that the money was in a certain place in the house. The man went to the Shevait and asked for the price of the anklets which his daughter had purchased. The Shevait thought the man was a cheat for he had no daughter. The man indicated the place where money was kept, and money there was where money never used to be kept. The Shebait still suspicious asked the man to shew him where his daughter was. They came to the steps of the tank but there was no body there. The man began to weep, being reprimanded by the Shebait as a cheat, when two beautiful hands, radient with the light of divinity, and bedecked with the pair of new anklets, jutted forth from water in the middle of the deep tank and soon disappeared. Both the Shebait and the seller, stupefied as they were at this miraculous appearance, knew what all this meant and the man could not be pursuaded to accept the price for which he had before been so importunate, for, thought he, he had purchased his salvation at a low price. The Shebait too considered himself the happiest mortal.

THE MORCHA.

Traces of what is called the Morcha or rampart are still visible in the remnants of the high and broad mud wall and embankment thrown up in 1742 on the western bank of the river, through Dahapara, as a defence against the attacks of the Mahrattas.

SOME BOATS OF THE NOWARA.

MAJUMDAR'S MURSHIDABAD. FANCY PRESS.

The semi-circular wall stands in mouldering heaps, overgrown with jungle, and is midway between Kriteswari and the western bank of the Bhagirathee.

THE NEOARA HOUSE.

On the bank of the river at Roshniganj, stands a small building which accommodated the office of the boat establishment of the Nazims. It is known as the Neoara house. A large number of boats, of all descriptions, used to float in the river or rest at anchor near this house. Of these the Ramsundar and Shamsundar, believed to possess mysterious powers, are still remembered. They would move without help but when unwilling, they would not budge an inch, the use of any amount of force notwithstanding.

These, as well as other large and commodious boats, some cumbrous and sluggish, while others light and fast, took on board small guns, many of which may still be seen in the Palace armoury. These boats were used for offensive and defensive purposes, for pleasure trips and for conveyance of goods.

The big and fast going barges of the Neoara department were used in sending down to Calcutta coin to the value of £800,000 out of the enormous wealth found in the treasuries of Serajuddowla.

Of most of these boats, the prow was usually the representation of some bird or other animal. The mourpankhi, the ghordour, the makar and hati-chehera &c. were some of the beautiful varieties. The chhip and the parenda were the two varieties of swift cutters. These two were propelled by hand oars, each being manned by two lines of numerous rowers. Each rower wore a silver armlet, filled with bullets, which made a peculiar jingling sound as the oars rose or fell.

It was the day of Bera which was the gala day of these boats, which were decked out in their gayest. Nautches were held on board and at night they were illuminated and to the strain of music they floated down with the Bera, which is still an interesting and unique festivity in Murshidabad.

Many days before the actual ceremony, which takes place on the night of the last Thursday of the month of Bhadro, a huge structure of bamboos and plantain trees is in course of preparation. Upon this platform are placed representations of mosques, domes, castles and minarets, done in talc and colored paper. Brilliantly lighted up, the moving city is floated down the river to the accompaniment of music and myriads of boats follow it. On the banks of the river at Roshniganj (or the store-house of light), a little to the north of the Neoara house and opposite to the Palace, is raised a high structure of bamboos, studded with millions of lights, which looks like the facade of

FANCY PRESS.

THE KILLAH FROM FARRABAGH.

a mosque or castle covered over with a sheet of light. The river being full, the effect is marvellous.

This ceremony was instituted by Serajuddowla in honor of Khajeh Khizir, the green lord, supposed to be the patron of the watery element. Its happy conception, apart from its religious aspect, accounts for its unbroken observance during the last century and a half. The influx of people to see the Bera is large.

CONCLUSION.

As the visitor, fatigued with the troubles of his travels, sits to rest on the terrace of the Neoara house, astonished at the majestic scenery and admiring the glorious sight that are presented to his vision by the Nizamut Killah on the bank opposite, bathed in the soft but effulgent rays of the setting sun, its towers and turrets reflected on the silvery stream that flows by, his eyes rivetted on the picture before him and his mind absorbed with an eventful past, his ears catch the sound of sweet music from the bandstand of the Killah, from which emanate, as are destined to emanate for all time to come, the majestic strains of *Rule Brittania* and

GOD SAVE THE KING.

APPENDIX.

1.

Mr. HOLWELL'S ACCOUNT OF HIS LIBERATION BY SERAJUDDOWLA.

"I was ordered prisoner under Mir Madan, general of the household troops and, with three gentlemen selected to be my companions, sent the same day (21st of June, 1756) to the camp, and soon loaded with fetters; and after enduring much pain and ill treatment, we arrived at Murshidabad, the capital of Bengal, on the 7th of July, and were deposited in an open stable, not far from the Suba's palace, under a guard of Moors and gentoos, where we were to remain till the Suba returned to the city...Our provisions were regularly sent us from the Dutch Tanksal in Corimabad..The 11th of July the Suba arrived, and with him Bundoo Sing, to whose house we were removed that afternoon, in a hackery, for I was not able to put my foot to the ground. Here we were confirmed in a report, which had before reached us, that the Suba, on his return to Hooghly, made enquiry for us when he released Messrs Watts and Collet, &c., with intention to release us also, and that he had expressed some resentment at Mir Madan, for having so hastily sent us up to Murshidabad.. Though we were here lodged in an open Bungalow only, yet we found ourselves relieved from the crowd of people which had stifled us at the stable....We were treated with much kindness and respect by Bundoo Sing....The 15th we were conducted in a hackery to the Kella, in order to have an audience of the Suba and know our fate. We were kept above an hour in the sun, opposite the gate: whilst here, we saw several of his ministers brought out disgraced, in the custody of sontabardars and dismissed from their employs, who, but a few minutes before, we had seen enter the Kella in the utmost pomp and magnificence. We received notice we could have no admittance to the Suba's presence that day. We were returned to our former place of confinement and spent another night in our miserable lodging. Near five the next morning, I was waked with the notice, that the Suba would presently pass by to his palace at Moti Jheel. We roused, and desired the guard would keep the view clear for us. When the Suba came in sight, we made him the usual salaam; and when he came abreast of us, he ordered his litter to stop, and us to be called to him. We advanced; and I addressed him in a short speech, setting forth our sufferings, and petitioned for our liberty. The wretched spectacle we made must, I think, have made an impression on a breast the most brutal; and, if he was capable of pity or contrition, his heart felt it then. I think it appeared, in spite of him, in his countenance. He gave me no reply, but ordered a Sontabardar and a chobdar immediately to see our irons cut off, and to conduct us wherever we chose to go, and to take care we received no trouble nor insult; and having repeated this order distinctly, directed his retinue to go on. As soon as our legs were free, we took boat, and proceeded to the Tanksal, where we were received and entertained with real joy and humanity."

2.

WHY THERE WAS SO LITTLE BLOODSHED AT PLASSAY.

Clive's reasons were that the English army was sheltered by so high a bank that the heavy artillery of the Nawab could not possibly do them much mischief, and that Serajuddowla had no confidence in his army, nor his army any confidence in him, and therefore they did not do their duty.

3.

CLIVE'S ENTRY INTO MURSHIDABAD.

Clive entered the city with but two hundred Europeans and five hundred Sepoys. The inhabitants, who were spectators upon that occasion, amounted to some hundred thousands and if they had had an inclination to have destroyed the Europeans, they might have done it with sticks and stones. "On that day"—said Clive—"being under no kind of restraint, but that of my own conscience, I might have become too rich for a subject."

4

CLIVE ENTERTAINS MEER JAFFER WITH A REVIEW.

The Colonel entertained the Suba with a review of his little army, to which he came in great state, in a car drawn by two elephants, accompanied by two of his children and several of his courtiers. The troops went through all their firings and evolutions with great briskness and regularity; and the Suba seemed lost in amazement at the quickness and uniformity of their motions; but nothing struck him so much as the quick firing of the field pieces, which, he said, exceeded every thing he could possibly have imagined; and he was altogether so well pleased with this entertainment, that he ordered ten thousand rupees to be distributed among them, for which the soldiers returned him their thanks, by three English huzzas.

5.

THE DEPOSITION OF MEER JAFFER.

Many extravagant charges were brought against Meer Jaffer in justification of his deposition. Among these were his tyranical, avaricious and indolent temper; his retention of abject surroundings, the instruments of his vices, the removal of which was necessary for good government; the banishment and slaughter of Khaja Hadi, Commander-in-chief; the assassination of Mir Kazem, general, at the gates of the palace; the slaughter of Yar Mahammed, Superintendent of buildings the massacre of the survivors of the family of Ali Verdi Khan, Nowazesh Mahamed Khan and Serajuddowla, namely Ghasita Begum, the widow of Nowazesh Mahomed Khan, Amna Begum, the mother of Serajuddowla, Muraduddowla, who had been adopted by Nawazesh Mahamed Khan, Surfennissa Begum, widow of Serajuddowla and her infant daughter by Serajuddowla, together with seventy women of inferior note, who all were said to have perished in one night at Dacca, where they had been detained prisoners since the accession of Meer Jaffer; the imposition of heavy taxes, to which was ascribed the unusual scarcity and dearness of provisions at Murshidabad; and the non-payment of salaries to the army.

It was, however, found out that most of these assertions had no foundation in truth and that the several persons, alleged to have been murdered by him, were then all living, with the exception of two, who had been put to death by Miran. Neither had Meer affer broken any of his engagements with the English.

The revolution, which ended in Meer Jaffer's deposition, was brougt about by Governor Vansittart, who had been but three months in Bengal, a time too short to enable one to have acquired a perfect knowledge of matters, so as to be able to determine that it was absolutely necessary to annul a treaty, ratified in the most solemn manner, by Colonel Clive and Admiral Watson, guaranteed by the credit of the Company and the honor of the British Nation. Before he ventured upon so bold a step as the subversion of a government, he ought certainly to have consulted every member of his council.

Colonel Coote and Major Carnac and other members of council, whose names commanded the highest veneration from every Englishman, wrote a letter, under date the 11th March, 1762, to the Secret Committee at London, giving their reasons against the revolution in favour of Meer Kasem.

The following extracts from that letter signed by Eyre Coote, P. Amyatt, John Carnac, W. Ellis, S. Batson and H. Verelst, men eminently competent to judge of the situation, will shew how unjustifiable was the deposition of Meer Jaffer :—

" At a time, when there was not the least appearance of a rupture or disgust between us and the Nabob Jaffier Aly Chan*; on the contrary, a friendship and harmony subsisted; Mir Cossim Chan, his son-in-law, came down to Calcutta, on some pretence or other, to visit Mr. Vansittart; and having stayed a short time, he returned to Morshedabad. A few days after Mir Cossim's departure, Mr. Vansittart went up to Morshedabad, on the pretence of a visit to the Nabob. Colonel Cailland, with a party of two hundred Europeans and some Seapoys, attended him; who to remove the suspicion which such a force would have necessarily occasioned, it was pretended were going up to Patna, to reinforce the army there. When Mr. Vansittart arrived at Moradbaug, the Nabob paid him two visits, at the last of which Mr. Vansittart, without any previous notice of his intentions, gave him the three letters — — —. The abruptness with which these letters were presented him, one close upon the other, and the unexpected proposals contained in them, terrified the Nabob; and he was entirely at a loss how to act, but desired time to consider on what was to be done. Mr. Vansittart, seeing his perplexity, strongly insisted on his immediately naming some person, from among his relations, to take charge of the Subaship; and very particularly recommended Cossim Aly Chan, who was sent for, and the Nabob was desired to stay till he came; but Cossim Aly Chan delayed so long and the Nabob was in such anxiety of mind, and so desirous to be released from the visit, being greatly fatigued, that Mr. Vansittart was obliged, in order to save appearances, to suffer

* The spelling as in the original letter has been retained throughout.

his departure to the palace, after having detained him much longer than his inclination. That night and the day following passed in concerting measures with Cossim Aly Chan, how to put in execution the plan before agreed on in Calcutta; a treaty having been signed for this purpose, in September, 1760, while Cossim Aly Khan was down here. In cosequence of these deliberations, our troops clandistinely crossed the river, the next night, under olonel Cailland, and being joined by Cossim Aly Khan and his party, surrounded the Nabob's palace. A letter from Mr. Vansittart was sent to the Nabob, demanding his immediate compliance with what had been proposed to him; to which the Nabob returned answer, 'that such usage was what he never expected from the English; that while a force was at his gates, he would enter into no terms; and that it was his desire our troops might be returned to Moradbaug.' A message was then sent, informing the Nabob, that if he did not directly comply, they should be obliged to storm the palace. Astonished and terrified by this menace, he opened the gates, exclaiming, that he was betrayed, that he perceived the designs against his government; that he had friends enough to hazard at least one battle in his defence; but as he had sworn to be their faithful friend, he would never swerve from his engagement, and rather suffer death than draw his sword against them. So suspicious was he of being sold, that 'he desired to know what sum of money Cossim Aly Chan was to give for the Subaship, and he would give half as much more to be continued; he hoped, however, if they intended to dethrone him, they would not leave him to the mercy of his son-in-law, from whom he feared the worst, but rather wished they would carry him from the city and give him a place of safety in Calcutta.' This last request of the Nabob's, the effect of his fear and despair, was immediately laid hold of, and construed in the light of a voluntary resignation. Accordingly our troops took possession of the palace; Mir Cossim was raised to the Musnud; and the old Nabob was hurried into a boat, with a few of his women and necessaries, and sent away to Calcutta, in a manner wholly unworthy of the high rank he so lately held; as is also the scanty subsistence allowed him here by his successor.

"Thus was Jaffier Aly Chan deposed, in breach of a treaty founded upon the most solemn oaths, and in violation of the national faith. A prince of whose friendship and attachment you have had many signal proofs; in whose cause our arms have, with much honour, been employed; and by a firm adherence to whom, the English had acquired, throughout the whole country, so universal a character of fidelity and constancy, that the most perfect confidence was placed by the natives in them." ....Want of money was the great difficulty the Nabob laboured under, but this did not proceed from any fault of his, but from the distracted state in which the country had been ever since Colonel Clive's departure; so that a very small part of the revenues came to his treasury. ....And here lay the Nabob's distress, that with one fourth part, if so much, of the accustomed revenues, he was obliged to maintain an army greater than any Nabob did before him; and the English army was not the least considerable part of his burthen. ......The people in general, very far from being pleased with the revolution, were extremely dissatisfied thereat.... The little disturbance at Murshidabad upon the occasion, proceeded from the apprehensions all degrees of people were under from so large a force being brought into the city in the dead of night; and Mir Jaffer, ... had taken no precautions for his own security.

"So bad an impression of us did the revolution create in the minds of the country people that the Burdwan Rajah..... concluding no reliance was to be placed in our engagements, he immediately flew off from his former declarations, and instead of acquesing under our government, he began to act in open rebellion; he stopped our trade; raised a large force, invited the Mahrattas into his country, withheld the payment of revenues, and acting in conjunction with the Beerboom Rajah, he espoused the cause of the Shahzadah, with whom he entered into correspondence."

"Several other zemindars who had remained quiet whilst Jaffier Aly Chan was Nabob, now finding the government overset, thought themselves at liberty. to withdraw their allegiance...."

"The Nabob's troops were rendered mutinous by the news of the revolution. They declared they knew nothing of Cossim Aly Chan, and that now they had lost their old master, they were without hopes...."

".... And as all the old Nabob's difficulties proceeded from his dominions being the seat of war, and the default of his revenues on that account, there is not the least doubt, had our arms met with the same success during his government, but that he would have extricated himself with equal ease."

"After what has been set forth, we believe few will imagine that Mir Jaffier was deposed by reason either of a want of ability to rule, or of his bad principles. We would willingly indeed suppose that it proceeded rather from the want of a true knowledge of the country policy, and from an error of judgment, than from lucrative views, had not Mr. Vansittart, and others of the projectors, made no secret that there was a present promised them by Cossim Aly Chan of twenty lack...."

"....It is replied 'the Nabob is master of his country, and being independent of us, is at liberty to rule and act as he pleases'.... and if it be true that the Nabob of Bengal is independent of the English, and master of his own actions, how can the gentlemen justify their proceedings against Mir Jaffier, whom they called to so severe an account for the administration of his own government, as to depose him, tho' he had not been guilty of any offence to our nation nor ever deviated from his treaty ?"

".... You will now, Hon'ble Sirs, be able to compare the present with the preceding government. So momentous a step, as sub-verting the former one, wc conceive, ought not to have been undertaken till after the most mature deliberation, and from a thorough knowledge of the country, its connections and interests. But this was far from being the case."

This letter was published in London and the wrong that was done to Mir Jaffer was sought to be remedied by his reinstatement in 1763, after the defeat and flight of Meer Kasem, who had so readily entered into the scheme of deposing his father-in-law, patron and lawful master.

6.
WHY THE MUSNUD DID NOT GO TO MIRAN'S FAMILY.

„Meer Jaffer's eldest son (Miran) left a prince only six years old when Meer Jaffer died. The Governor and Council did not choose to take that line of succession, contrary to the appointment of Jaffer in favour of his second son, though some of the gentlemen thought it would be better to have a long minority ; but the late Nawab having associated his son in the Government, they feared it might have the appearance of another revolution."

7.
MEER JAFFER'S PRESENTS TO ADMIRAL WATSON.

On the 26th July, 1757, Meer Jaffer sent to Admiral Watson, Commander of the British fleet, presents consisting of an elephant, two fine horses, a rich Moorish dress of gold, with turban and sashes, and a rose and plume composed of diamonds, rubies, saphires and emeralds. The Admiral received the Nawab's Ambassadars with marks of great respect and he made presents of fine cloth and velvet to each in return; dressed his ships, displayed his flags, saluted them with his cannon and wrote the following letter to the Nawab:—

"Mirza Jaffir Beg, whom you have done me the honor to depute to me, has delivered me your letter and other marks of friendship with which you have been pleased to favour me. He has also satisfied my desire, in giving me an ample account of your health and prosperity. But what pleases me beyond expression is to hear that all men rejoice in them; and, while they acknowledge you are worthy of them, pray for their continuance. This is a satisfaction your predecessor never knew; and which. while it gives the most sublime pleasure to a mind generous like yours, promises happiness to yourself and a quiet succession to your son.

"How much I and all my countrymen with it, can only be known by the benefits you have conferred on us; the extent of which can alone be measured by your generosity and our gratitude. May day by day make known the latter, to your content and our honor."

8.

LORD CLIVE'S JUSTIFICATION OF THE ACCEPTANCE OF PRESENTS FROM MEER JAFFER.

His Lordship contended that at that time there were no covenants existing; the Company's servants were at liberty to receive presents, from a Suba, when he was in a state of independence and could do with his money what he pleased. Clive added:—"I was one amongst the many who benefited by his favour. I never sought to conceal it ; but declared publicly in my letters to the secret committee of the India Directors, that the Nawab's generosity had made my fortune easy, and that the Company's welfare was now my only motive for staying in India. The Company had acquired a million and a half sterling and a revenue of near an hundred thousand pounds per annum from the success of their forces under my command, when ample restoration had been made to those whose fortunes suffered by the calamity of Calcutta......The city of Murshidabad is as extensive, populous and rich, as the city of London with this difference, that there are individuals in the first, possessing infinitely greater property than any in the last city ; these, as well as other men of property, made me the greatest offers (which nevertheless are usual upon such occasions, and what they expected would have been required) and had I accepted these offers I might have been in possession of millions, which the present Court of Directors could not have dispossessed me of."

His Lordship being asked, said he received about sixteen lacs of rupees clear, that he received no jewels but all in money ; that he believed Mr. Watts might have received altogether about eight lacs ; Mr. Walsh about five, Mr. Scrafton two lacs and others received sums which he could not recollect.

These donations were given exclusive of the sums stipulated for the gentlemen of the Committee, Council, Army and Navy.

9.

SUMS DISTRIBUTED FROM 1757 TO 1766.

REVOLUTION IN FAVOUR OF MEER JAFFER, 1757.

Mr. Drake, Governor . . .	£ 31,500
Colonel Clive	,, 234,000
Mr. Watts	,, 117,000
Major Kilpatrick	,, 27,000
Do as a private donation . .	,, 33,750
Mr. Manningham	,, 27,000
Mr. Beecher	,, 27,000
Six members of Council, one lac each .	,, 68,200
Mr Walsh	,, 56,250
Mr. Scrafton . .	,, 22,500
Mr. Lushington	,, 5,625
Captain Grant	,, 11,250
Stipulation to the Army and Navy . .	,, 600,000
	£ 1,261,075

Paid as restitution for losses and expenses to the Company, their servants and other Europeans £ 1,800,000

REVOLUTION IN FAVOUR OF MEER KASEM, 1760.

Mr. Sumner	£ 28,000
Mr. Holwell	,, 30,937
Mr. McGuire	,, 20,625
Mr. Smith	,, 15,354
Major York	,, 15,354
General Cailland	,, 22,916
M. Vansittart	,, 58,333
Mr. McGuire, 5000 gold Mohers . .	,, 8,750
	£ 200,269
As restitution money . . .	,, 62,500

REVOLUTION IN FAVOUR OF MEER JAFFER, 1763.

Stipulation to the Army . . .	£ 291,666
Do to the Navy . . .	,, 145,833
	£ 437,499
Restitution money . . .	,, 975,000
Major Munro	,, 3,000
Major Munro's Officers . . .	,, 3,000

ACCESSION OF NAJMUDDOWLA, 1765.

Mr. Spencer	£ 23,333
Messrs Playdell, Burdett and Grey .	,, 35,000
Mr. Johnstone	,, 27,650
Mr. Leycester	,, 13,125
Mr. Senior	,, 20,125
Mr. Middleton	,, 14,291
Mr. G. Johnstone	,, 5,833
	£ 139,357
Lord Clive from the "Begum Queen" *i. e.*, Mani Begum	,, 58,333

From 1757 to 1771, the total sums proved or acknowledged to have been received were :—

As Present	£ 2,169,365
As Restitution	,, 3,420,833
For Military charges . . .	,, 5,402,333
Revenue clear of charges . .	,, 18,490,382
	£ 29,482,913

10.

ABWABS ON KHALSA AND JAIGIRE LANDS IN BENGAL, 1722—1763.

No.	Names of Abwabs.	Imposed by.	Amount per year.
			Rs.
1	Wajehsat Khasnovisi .	Murshed Kuli Khan	2,58,857
2	Nazarana Mokerary ...	Shuja Khan ...	6,48,040
3	Serf Mathout	Do. ...	1,52,786
4	Mathout Pheelkhana ...	Do. ...	3,22,631
5	Fouzdari	Do. ...	7,90,638
6	Chout Mahratta	Ali Verdi Khan ...	15,31,817
7	Ahuk (Lime) and Kist Gour	Do. ...	1,92,140
8	Nazarana Mansurganj ...	Do. ...	5,01,597
9	Kefait Hustabood ...	Meer Kasem ...	14,72,599
10	Serf Sicca 1½ anna ...	Do. ...	4,53,488
11	Kefait Foujdaran ...	Do. ...	36,74,239
12	Towfir Jaigirdaran ...	Do. ...	8,81,014
		Total ...	1,17,91,853

11.

THE TUMAR OR STANDARD ASSESSMENT OF BENGAL AT THE CLOSE OF MEER KASEM'S RULE, 1763.

Items.	Amount.
	Rs.
Tumar or standard assessment	1,41,16,116
Abwab in eight items upto the death of Ali Verdi Khan, in 1756, with the Serf Sicca of Meer Kasem	42,23,467
Kefait of Meer Kasem, in three items, with Abwab Subadari of Murshed Kuli Khan in part	45,23,563
Towfir of Meer Kasem, including increase in the Jaigire Nowara of Dacca	3 ,62,358
Total imposts ...	1,19,09,388
Deduct—Establishment charges ...	4,01,276
Net Assessment of Bengal ...	2,56,24,223

12.

THE GRANT OF THE DEWANI.

The struggles for supremacy, between the Nawab's and the Company's agents, rendered the members of the Calcutta Council of opinion that the only means of attaining their object was to obtain the Dewani of Bengal, Behar and Orissa for the Company. The Emperor of Delhi, whose tottering power had been established by British arms, acquiesced in the bestowal of that important office upon the Company, the work of collecting all the revenues, and after defraying the expenses of the army and allowing a sufficient fund for the support of the Nizamut, of remitting the remainder to Delhi. This office the Directors were not willing to execute and so they wrote to the Calcutta Council, under date the 17th May, 1766,—"The experience we have already had in the province of Burdwan convinces us how unfit an Englishman is to conduct the collection of the revenues and follow the subtle Native through all his arts to conceal the real value of his Country, to perplex and elude the payments. We therefore entirely approve of your preserving the ancient form of Government in the upholding the dignity of the Suba. We conceive the office of Dewan should be exercised only in superintending the collection and disposal of the revenues, which office, though vested in the Company, should officially be executed by our Resident at the Durbar, under the control of the Governor and Select Committee, the ordinary bounds of which control should extend to nothing beyond the superintending the collection of the revenues and the receiving the money from the Nawab's treasury to that of the Dewannah or the Company. * * This we conceive to be the whole office of the Dewani. The administration of justice, the appointment of officers, zemindars, in short, whatever comes under the denomination of civil administration, we understand, is to remain in the hands of the Nawab or his Ministers."

The Imperial grant was obtained at Allahabad, where Sha Alum had come from Delhi, and Clive and Carnac, dubbed with authority by Najmuddowla, had gone from Murshidabad. Says Golam Hossien Khan, the celebrated contemporary Chronicler—"Thus a business of such magnitude, as left neither pretence nor subterfuge, and which at any other time would have required the sending wise Ambassadors and able negotiators, as well as a deal of parley and conference with the Company and the King of England, and much negotiation and contention with the ministers, was done and finished in less time than would have been taken up for the sale of a Jackass, or of a beast of burden, or of a head of cattle."

13.

LORD CLIVE'S BILL FOR AN ENTERTAINMENT IN HONOR OF THE GRANT OF THE DEWÁNI.

Items.	Amount.
	Rs.
Charges for building and fitting up an Assembly House with furniture for celebrating the late Peace concluded with Shujauddowla, &c.	4,853
Expense of feeding wild beasts and making a place for them to fight in	384
Charges paid for Fire works on the occasion ...	12, 79
Sundry presents to the keepers of the wild beasts	2,426
Expense of three public entertainments ...	3,927
Paid for Liquors	5,451
Total ...	29,220

14.

STATEMENT OF THE COLLECTIONS AND BALANCES OF THE LAND ASSESSMENT OF BENGAL COVERED BY THE GRANT OF THE DEWANI.

Year.	Period.	Gross Settlement.	Collections.	Balance.
		Rs.	Rs.	Rs.
1762-3	Meer Kasem . .	2,41,18,912	64,56,198	1,76,62,713
1763-4	Nanda Kumar . .	1,77,04,766	76,18,407	1,00,86,358
1764-5	Do. . .	1,76,97,678	81,75,533	95,22,144
1765-6	Mahamed Reza Khan	1,60,29,011	1,47,04,875	13,24,135

15.

THE FOUR DEWANS OR MINISTERS.

(1) Dewan Suba. (2) Dewan Khalsa.
(3) Dewan Nizamut. (4) Dewan Ton.

Before the advent of Murshed Kuli Khan, the defence and protection of the province of Bengal and the control of the administration of Justice were in the hands of an officer appointed by the Emperor, who was styled the Nazim : while the collection and disbursement of the revenues were entrusted to the Dewan similarly appointed When Murshed Kuli Khan arrived in Bengal as Dewan, the office of Nazim was held by Prince Azemoshan, upon whose departure, the functions of the two posts became united in the same person and Murshed Kuli Khan became the first Nazim and Dewan. Later on, a near relation of the Nazim or his heir-apparent used to be nominated as Dewan, the *Dewan Suba*, the Dewan

Kul or Prime Minister as he was called. As this appointment was nominal, a deputy sometimes used to be appointed for the transaction of business. This state of things continued up to 1765, when the Dewani passed over to the East India Company. The Nazimship remained in the house of Meer Jaffer; the first Nazim, stripped of his authority as Dewan, being Najmuddowla.

The duty of the *Dewan Khalsa*, under the Dewan Suba, was to collect the revenues. To this office only Hindus were appointed, with the title of Roy Royan.

The *Dewan Nizamut* had the control of the Criminal and Police administration and used to transact the duties appertaining to the Nawab's office as Nazim. To this, only Mahomedans were appointed.

The office of *Dewan Ton*, or Dewan of the household of the Nawab Nazim, used to be held by both Hindus and Mahomedans.

During the administration of Nawab Mobarakuddowla, when all powers passed into the hands of the East India Company, the offices of Dewan Suba, Dewan Khalsa and Dewan Nizamut being already abolished, the Dewan Ton managed the household and state affairs of the Nawab Nazim, under the denomination of Dewan Nizamut, and the Chief officer in charge of the affairs of the Nawab Nazim has since been known as the Dewan (or sometimes as Madarul Maham.)

16.

LIST OF DEWANS SUBA BANGALA AND NAIB DEWANS.

No.	Dewans Suba.	Naib Dewans.	Period.
1	Nawab Syud Ekram Khan.	... ...	Murshed Kuli Khan.
2	Nawab Syud Rezi Khan.	... ...	Do.
3	Nawab Serferaz Khan	Roy Royan Alum Chand.	Do. and Shuja Khan.
4	Nawab Hafezulla Khan.	Haji Ahmed .	Serferaz Khan.
5	Nawab Nawazesh Mahomed Khan.	Maharaja Jankiram.	Ali Verdi Khan.
6	... ...	Maharaja Mahindra Dullavram Bahadur.	Serajuddowla.
7	Nawab Syud Sadeqali Khan alias Nawab Miran.	Do. .	Meer Jaffer.
8	Nawab Meer Mahamed Kasem Khan.	Do. .	Do.
9	Nawab Najmuddowla	Maharaja Nanda Kumar.	Do.
10	Nawab Syud Mahomed Reza Khan, Mozaffer Jang.	... ...	Najmuddowla.
11	The East India Company.	... ...	1765—1858.

17.

LIST OF DEWANS KHALSA OR COLLECTORS OF REVENUE.

No.	Dewans Khalsa.	Period.
1	Bhoopat Rai	Murshed Kuli Khan.
2	Golap Rai (son of do.)	Diito.
3	Roy Royan Alum Chand, the first Roy Royan.	Shuja Khan.
4	Roy Royan Chain Roy	Ali Verdi Khan.
5	Roy Royan Raja Keerut Chand ..	Ditto.
6	Roy Royan Raja Umed Ram ..	Ditto and Serajuddowla.
7	Roy Royan Maharaja Nanda Kumar ..	Najmuddowla & Syefuddowla.
8	Maharaja Mahindra Dullavram ..	Syefuddowla.
9	Raja Gooroo Das (son of Nanda Kumar)	Mobarukuddowla
10	Raja Rajballav (son of Dullavram) ..	Ditto.

18.

LIST OF DEWANS NIZAMUT.

Serial No.	Names of Dewans Nizamut.	Year of appointment.	Nazims.
1	Moinuddowla Mobazeral Mulk Khan, Khanan Nawab Syud Mahomed Reza Khan Bahadur, Mozaffer Jang.*	1765	Najmuddowla.
2	Nawab Ali Ibraheem Khan Bahadur.	1772	Mobarukuddowla.
3	Raja Gooroodas Bahadur (son of Nanda Kumar).	1773	Ditto.
4	Nawab Mahamed Reza Khan (again).	1776	Ditto.
5	Nawab Sadr-ul-Huq Khan Bahadur, Nosrut Jang.	1778	Ditto.
6	Nawab Mahamed Reza Khan (again).	1781	Ditto.
7	Madar-ul-Mulk Brijendra Maharaja Sundar Singh Bahadur.	1784	Ditto.
8	Nawab Shamsuddowla Khalilulla Khan Bahadur.	1793	Baber Jang.
9	Raja Mahanand (son of Gooroodas).	1794	Ditto.
10	Raja Udwant Sing Bahadur .	1810	Ali Jah.
11	Raja Ganga Dhar Rai . . .	1821	Humayun Jah.
12	Rai Udoy Chand Mojumdar, (acting), Roy Royan.	1831	Ditto.
13	Raja Poresh Nath Bose . .	1839	Feredun Jah.
14	Raja Sita Nath Bose . . .	1841	Ditto.
15	Syud Sadeq Ali Khan, Madar-ul-Maham.	1848	Ditto.
16	Aman Ali Khan (not recognized by Government).	—	Ditto.

* In 1768, the Court of Directors of the East India Company approved of paying Dewan Mahomed Reza Khan a salary of nine lacs of rupees annually; while they allowed two lacs to Dullavram and one lac to Shetab Roy.

LIST OF DEWANS NIZAMUT—(*contd.*)

Serial No.	Names of Dewans Nizamut.	Year of appointment.	Nazims.
17	Raja Dakshmina Ranjan Mukerjee, Madar-ul-Maham.	1851	Feredun Jah.
18	Raja Prosanno Naraen Deb .	1854	Ditto.
19	Raja Rajendra Naraen Deb, Madar-ul-Maham.	1862	Ditto.
20	Babu Ganga Das Rai, Naib Dewan (Dewanship vacant).	1864	Ditto.
21	Babu Bangshi Dhar Rai, do. do.	1874	Ditto.
22	Khondkar Fazl Rubbee Khan Bahadur.	1882	Ali Kadr.

19.

WHAT A GUBERNOTORIAL TOUR TO MURSHIDABAD COST IN 1763.

	Rs.
Nawab's servants	2,442
Munshi and Palankeens for 3 months	658
Beldars	855
Watermen	421
Shoemakers	119
Carpenters	165
Ironsmiths	170
Sailmakers	162
Tailors	81
Coolis	6,480
Serangs	34
Tindals	108
Lascars	1,120
3 Budgerows (hire)	680
Hurcaras	1,004
37 Woolacks	5,041
The Governor's usual pay for 4 months	8,000
Batta for servants and other travelling expenses	6,000

20.

FROM MURSHIDABAD TO CALCUTTA IN TWO DAYS, IN 1764.

Meer Jaffer wrote in 1764 to the Governor and Council at Calcutta—" as soon as I receive intelligence of Lord Clive's arrival at Ingelee, I, who long to have the pleasure of seeing him, will set out from Murshidabad and make it but *two day's* Journey to Calcutta. I have fixed my departure on the 22nd of Jemady-ul-aula (the 17th November,) there being no luckier day in the month.

The Nawab returned to Murshidabad with Nanda Cumar on the 20th December, 1764, and the latter wrote to Calcutta—" I despatched today..on boats from the city the sum of two lacs balance remaining of the twenty lacs on account of the damages sustained by the merchants, please God they will arrive in *five or six* days ; a list of the several sorts of supees is sent to Nobokissen Munshi, he will deliver the same to you."

21.

THE INSTALLATION OF REZA KHAN.

On the 6th March, 1765, Mahamed Reza Khan wrote to the Governor at Calcutta—" Today, Sunday, the 10th of Ramzan, His Highness the Nawab Najmuddowla Bahadur sat on the Masnad in a fortunate hour and to the gentlemen of Council and the Nawabs Syefuddowla Bahadur and Mobarukuddowla Bahadur and the friends of the deceased Nawab, His Highness presented khilluts and he was pleased to honor me by conferring on me the Neabut of the Suba of Bengal &c., and by presenting me with a rich khillut and Serpainch and Jega set with jewels and an elephant and sword together with the title of Moinuddowla Mozaffer Jang Bahadur. As under God you, Sir, are the author of my fortune; if my whole body were composed of tongues, I should be unable to express the smallest degree of my gratitude."

22.

THE EAST INDIA COMPANY'S PRESENTS AND ENTERTAINMENTS TO THE NAWABS.

The President of the Calcutta Council proceeded to Hughly to make certain presents to Serajuddowla in September, 1752, which cost the Company as follows :—

	Rs.
35 Gold Mohers	557
Ready money	5500
Wax candles	1100
A Clock	800
Two pairs Looking glasses . . .	550
Two marble slabs	220
One pair Pistols	110
A diamond ring	1,436
26 Gold Mohers for Ali Verdi Khan's wife and women	429
Faqirs	184
Dutch Military Servants	756
Fouzdar of Hughly	770

The President in return for the above received an elephant and a Sirpainch, and Serajuddowla on his return to Murshidabad, wrote to Mr. Drake, (the President) "you are a great man, and that greatness becomes you, the head of all merchants and the standard of merchants."

Nawab Ali Verdi Khan himself, pleased with his grandson's reception and the presents, wrote to Mr. Drake—"By the favour of the Almighty the bright eyes and soul of Nawab Mansur-ul-Mulk, Bahadur, arrived at Murshidabad, on the 24th *Secandur Sun punch*; your friendship, praises, presents and going to meet him, he has told me a great deal about, so much that I cannot express it. I am extremely delighted and pleased with you and a thousand thousand times remain sensible of it, and in return, by the grace of God, the Company's business I will be very favorable to."

The Council, perceiving how presents were acceptable and efficacious in keeping up mutual good understanding, decided in December, 1754, to present, to the Nawab, "Persia Horses" and some fine wax work and as both the Company's "Persia Horses" were dead, to purchase two, offered for Rs. 2,500.

In June, 1758, the President of the Calcutta Council purchased a fine organ Clock, worth Rs. 5,000, for presentation to Meer Jaffer.

At the invitation of the President, Meer Jaffer visited Calcutta towards the close of 1758, and the Company made a present to him of the beautiful house in which he was accommodated and with which he was pleased. This house, which was near Jagannathghat and Maidaputty, still the property of His Highness the Nawab Bahadur of Murshidabad, was subsequently used as the residence of the Nawab's Ambassador at Calcutta. The Fouzedari Balakhana or Golkothee, which is in the possession of His Highness, is supposed to be a present made by the Company to Meer Jaffer.

In October, 1759, Clive charged the Company nearly eighty thousand rupees for entertaining Meer Jaffer at Calcutta. The presents to the Nawab included :—

	Rs.
Two pairs Lustres	2,100
Three hanging Lustres	3,500
One pair square Lanterns . . .	200
One pair round Lanterns. . . .	70
Nine large Looking glasses . . .	517
Three middling Do.	112
Ten Looking glasses	625
Four pairs Brass Candle sticks . . .	5

	Rs.
One hundred and one Gold Mohers presented to the Nawab at Rs, 15 each . . .	1,515
Three water bottles, one betel box, and one Rose water bottle, silver ornamented with Lazuli	2,186
One water bottle	1,404
One Rose water bottle and stand . .	164
Wax work, Turkish Lady . . .	222
,, Boy and Girl. . . .	108
,, Vergin Mary. . . .	33
,, 12 Standing Venuses . .	840
,, 1 Lying Venus . . .	84
,, 6 Kissing figures . . .	72
,, 8 Ladies under glass . .	160
,, Joseph and Mary . . .	33
,, Roman Charity . . .	56
One pair Curious cut Lustres, containing 32 snake arms and fans, each, . .	9,219
One pair plate glasses	1,479
Two pairs plate glasses	994
One double barrel gun	180
One silver mounted gun with gold lock hole .	124
One pair double pair pistols . . .	210
Figures of two ladies dressed in silver, playing two tunes	2,080
One pair stand round looking glasses . .	300

SOME ITEMS OF EXPENDITURE WERE :—

The Nawab's Diet	657
Omed Roy's do.	300
Souket Jang's do.	300
Kanai Ram's do.	250
Moni Ram's do.	250

	Rs.
Golam Hossein's Diet	250
Urzbegi's do. . . .	100
Bukshish to Nawab's Servants . . .	2,000
Do. Omed Roy's do. . . .	200
Do. Kanai Ram . . .	5,000
Do. Kanai Ram's Servants . .	50
Do. Moni Ram . . .	5,000
Do. Moni Ram's Servants . .	50
Do. Golam Hossein's do. . .	100
Do. Souket Jang's do. . .	200
Do. Urzbegi	2,000
Do. Urzbegi's Servants . .	300
Musicians for attending Court House Ball .	50
Hire for 61 boats for the Nawab going up the river	1,406
Charges for Sounding Trumpets, Horns and Kettle Drums at the entertainments .	54
Purchasing a Kafri boy	500
70 maunds of wax candles sent to the Nawab.	3,430
60 lbs. of Masulipatam cheroots . .	500

The Company presented to Meer Kasem the following articles in 1762 :—

	Rs.
4 pairs glass flowered cups and saucers .	100
1 glass fountain	1,000
3 boxes with wax figures . . .	1,200
1 Sea cocoanut	300
1 piece brocade silk	683
2 rolls of Madras Chintz with gold flowers .	200
25 pieces Europe Broad Cloth . . .	2,264
10 pieces Europe velvet	3,200
Saffron, 1 md. 10 srs.	900
Amber Grease (Perfumery) . . .	2,555

In December, 1763, Vansittart purchased the following articles for presents to the Children of Meer Jaffer :—

	Rs.
One silver toothpick	9
One do., large . . .	25
One gilt silver case with smelling bottle .	11
Do. do. large	26
One Chelsea China smelling bottle . .	18
One Lady's pocket stand with pens and pencil	32
One Snuff box painted with figures . .	6
Two Fuzees	240
Three pairs pistols	360

On Meer Jaffer's arrival at Calcutta on the 3rd September, 1764, his reception cost the Company Rs. 3,498, the principal items of expenditure being :—

	Rs.
Hire of 49 boats	1,504
30 Dandies belonging to the Mourpankhi, Bhowlia and Budgrow . . .	95
3 Manjhis	14
Sidha sent to the Nawab—	
40 mds. of rice	75
8 ,, dall	20
5 ,, ghee	77
6 ,, oil	51
3½ ,, salt	4
8 ,, wheat flour . . .	27
5 ,, sugar	36
6 ,, sweetmeat . . .	60
1 md. of morobba	19
1 ,, almond and kishmish . .	31
8 mds. of Tyre (curdled milk) . .	21
50 goats	50
Greens	16

	Rs.
Limes	7
Spices	40
Betel-nut and tobacco	11
Earthenware and firewood . . .	26
Baskets, gunny bags etc. . . .	24

On this occasion, the presents were 51 gold mohers given by the Company's Servants, civil and military and 40 given by the Aldermen, that is 91 gold mohers, at Rs. 12-11 per moher, costing Rs. 1,154. The whole Board went to Meer Jaffer's house and opened a representation of their demands.

Many of the presents may still be seen in the Palace.

23.

TREATY AND AGREEMENT BETWEEN THE GOVERNOR AND COUNCIL OF FORT WILLIAM, ON THE PART OF THE EAST INDIA COMPANY AND NAWAB MOBARUK-UD-DOWLA, DATED 21st MARCH, 1770.

ON THE PART OF THE COMPANY.

We the Governor and Council, do engage to secure to the Nawab Mobaruk-ud-Dowla the Subahdary of the Provinces of Bengal, Behar and Orissa, and to support him therein with the Company's forces against all his enemies.

ON THE PART OF THE NAWAB.

ARTICLE 1.

The Treaty, which my father formerly concluded with the Company upon his first accession to the Nizamut, engaging to regard the honour and reputation of the Company, and of the Governor and Council as his own, that entered into by my brothers, the Nawabs Nudjum-ud-Dowla and Syef-ud-Dowla the same Treaties as far as is consistent with the true spirit, intent and meaning there of, I do hereby ratify and confirm.

ARTICLE 2.

The King has been graciously pleased to grant unto the English East India Company, the Dewanship of Bengal, Behar and Orissa as a free gift for ever; and I having an entire confidence in them and in their servants, settled in this country, that nothing whatever be proposed or carried into execution by them derogating from my honour, interest and the good of my country, do therefore for the better conducting the affairs of the Subahdary and promoting my honor and interest and that of the Company, in the best manner, agree that the protecting the Provinces or Bengal, Behar and Orissa and the force sufficient for that purpose, be entirely left to their direction and good management, in consideration of their paying the King Shah Aalum, by monthly payments, as by Treaty agreed on, the sum of Rupees two lakhs, sixteen thousand, six hundred and sixty-six, ten annas and nine pie (Rupees 2,16,666-10-9) : and to me, Mobaruk-ud-Dowla, the annual stipend of Rupees thirty-one lakhs, eighty-one thousand, nine hundred and ninety-one and nine annas (Rupees 31,81,991-9) *viz*:, the sum of Rupees fifteen lakhs, eighty-one thousand, nine hundred and ninety-one and nine annas (Rupees 15,81,991-9) for my house, servants and other expenses indispensably necessary, and the remaining sum of Rupees sixteen lakhs (Rupees 16,00,000) for the support of such sepoys, peons and burkundauzes, as may be thought proper for my Suwarry only, but on no account ever to exceed that amount.

ARTICLE 3.

The Nawab Maeen-ud-Dowla, who was at the instance of the Governor and gentleman of the Council, appointed Naib of the Provinces, and invested with the management of

affairs, in conjunction with Maharajah Doolubram and Juggat Set, shall continue in the same post and with the same authority, and having a perfect confidence in him, I moreover agree to let him have the disbursing of the above sum of Rupees sixteen lakhs for the purposes above mentioned.

This Agreement (by the blessings of God) shall be inviolably observed for ever.

Dated the 21st day of March in the year of our Lord, 1770.

JOHN CARTIER.	**JOHN REED.**
RICHARD BECHER.	**FRANCIS HARE.**
WILLIAM ALDERSEY.	**JOSEPH JEKYELL.**
CLAUD RUSSELL.	**THOMAS LANE.**
CHARLES FLOYER.	**RICHARD BARWELL.**

24.

THE NAWAB NAZIM AS THE FOUNTAIN OF HONOR.

Upon the recommendation of Warren Hastings, the Governor General, Nawab Nazim Mobarakuddowla conferred titles to a number of personages. Warren Hasting's letters of recommendation dated 1780, 1781 and 1783, which were in the records of the Palace, have of late been sent to Calcutta for the Victoria Memorial.

In 1773, the title of Maharaja was conferred upon Kallyan Singh, the son of Maharaja Shitab Ray, of Behar.

In 1779, the title of Raja was conferred upon Dewan Ram Kanto (Kanto Babu), of Cossimbazar.

In 1780, the title of Maharaja was conferred upon Shib Chandra, the son of Raja Keerti Chandra, of Krishnagore.

In 1781, the title of Maharaja was conferred upon Radha Nath, the Zemindar of Dinajepore.

In 1783, the title of Jagat Sett was conferred upon Sett Hareck Chand.

In 1783, the title of Malukushshora (Poet Laureate), was conferred upon Meer Kamruddeen.

25.

NIZAMUT DEPOSIT FUND.

Previous to the year 1834, what subsequently came to be known as the Nizamut Deposit Fund, and formed the bone of contention for so many years, existed under three different heads, namely.

(1) Nizamut Agency Fund.

(2) Mani Begum's Deposit Fund, and

(3) Pension or Lapsed stipend Fund.

The first of these was established in 1816, for the payment of the Salaries of the Governor General's agent at Murshidabad and his establishment. The control over Nizamut affairs had hitherto been but ineffectually exercised by a British officer, under the denominations of Resident at the Nazim's Durbar, Pay master of Nizamut Stipends and Superintendent of Nizamut affairs.

Latterly the senior Judge of the Provincial Court of appeals and circuit at Murshidabad held *ex officio*, the situation of Superintendent of Nizamut affairs, performing his onerous duties gratuitously. The arrangements were considered inadequate and it was proposed that a distinct officer of high rank should be appointed, invested with dignity of a representative character and enabled to devote his time and attention exclusively to his duties. The salary, which was not to be charageble to the East India Company, was to be high, to enable the officer to keep up a certain appearance. The Nawab Nazim was consulted, at Furrabag, and in consultation with his father-in-law, Nawab Shumshere Jang, and the officers of his establishment, after some hesitation, gave his assent. The sum of Rs. 2,67,703, being the arrears of pension of Mani Begum, which was in the hands of the Collector of Murshidabad, formed part of the funds. To complete it, part of Mani Begums treasures, consisting mostly of old coin of sorts, was paid into the Collectorate. Government securities to the extend of Rs. 7,10,000 were purchased, the interest payable on which was assigned for the following purposes, namely,

	Principal.	Interest.
For paying the salary of the office establishment of the Agent to the Governor General at Murshidabad .	Rs. 7,10,000	Rs. 42,000
For the charges of an establishment at the tomb of Mani Begum . . .	,, 9,600	,, 576

The Mani Begum Deposit Fund was formed for the more distant exigencies of the Nizamut and of the Nizamut family. Mani Begum died on the 10th January, 1813, and in 1817, the arrears of her pension were invested in Government securities for the Agency Deposit Fund, while the arrears, which accummulated from 1817 to 1822, were in 1823, invested for the Mani Begum Deposit Fund, to which was to be added Rs. 1,81,368 per annum, and these resources were to be utilized for the construction of a Palace for the Nazim, the erection of proper offices and store rooms, the rebuilding of the public gate ways, the completion of the Imambara, the construction of pucca drains within the Killah, the removal of the decayed buildings, and the application of the materials for the purpose of strengthening the river bank, in front of the Palace yard, and other places, appertaining to the Killah. Rupees six lacs were accordingly invested for these purposes.

In 1790 Lord Cornwallis approved Mr. Ive's plan of 1787, for raising a Fund for providing for the future increasing family of the Nawab Nazim and for the discharge of the Nizamut incumbrances, staled to be forty-two lacs. The proposal was that the pensions, then paid to the Nawab's relations or to the descendants of former Subadars, should be declared heriditary and that the pensions of servants and dependents should be optional and that, of the unappropriated amounts, half should go to the Nawab Nazim and half for the formation of a fund, to be called the Lapsed Stipends Fund.

On the 30th April, 1837, the Government securities in deposit were Rs. 11,92,745, besides a cash balance of Rs. 9,519. The interest acurcing on this was considered sufficient and too large for ordinary requirements and the Governor General, therefore, directed that if there was a surplus, it might, with propriety, be laid out for municipal purposes at Murshidabad, by making roads, excavating tanks and otherwise adding to the comfort and salubrity of the neighbourhood of the Palace and of the city generally.

On the 5th July, 1837, the Agent to the Governor General at Murshidabad suggested that all the three funds namely the Agency Fund of seven lacs, the Mani Begum's Fund of six lacs and the Pension Fund of two lacs should be thrown into one Fund. They were consolidated and contributions for its support used to be made from the Nizamut stipend, which was payable upon the personal receipt of the Nawab Nazim.

Frequent complaints were made by the Nawab Nazim regarding his right to these Funds and the accummulations and interest thereon but by the Indenture of the 1st November, 1880, he relinquished, in favour of the Secretary of State for India in council all his claims and rights. By this agreement, the Nawab Nazim, who was incompetent to part with a square inch of land, retired, for the consideration of ten lacs of rupees, from the Subadary of Bengal, Behar and Orissa.

26.

CHHATTIS KARKHANAS.

Of the Chattis Karkhanas or thirty six department of the Nizamut, over which the Ekjai Sheristadar presided, a few still survive in the Abdarkhana, Ambakhana, Ashoorkhana, Battakhana, Bhindakhana, Chowkikhana, Langerkhana, Mewakhana, Shishakhana, Silehkhana etc. The story of the confused clerk of the Shutarkhana or Camel house, will bear repitition. The Nawab Nazim appeared at the Shutarkhana to inspect his camels and, happening to meet the mushref or clerk asked him who he was. Upset by the august presence, he replied, *Fitbwi Musbref Kbanaki Sbutar bai,*—I am the camel of the clerk house; of course what he meant to say was that he was the musherf of the Shutarkhana, that is the clerk of the Camel house.

THE END.

INDEX.

	Page.
Abul Kasem . . .	47
Abwabs	300
Aishbagh Jail . . .	183
Alam Chand . . .	3
Ali Jah	4
Ali Kadr	55
Ali Verdi Khan . . .	25
,, ,, ,, 's Tomb .	198
Almas Ali Khan . .	177
Amaniganj . . .	195
Amena Khanum .	26, 28
Amirannessa Begum. .	50
Antony Feringee . .	24
Armenian Church . .	233
Armoury	92
Ashutosh Nath Rai . .	224
Asif Ali Meerza. . .	68
Ata Ulla Khan . . .	24
Award of Nizamut Commissioners . . .	54
Azimannessa Begum.	22, 140
Azimganj	276
Azimnagar Mosque . .	140
Babar Jang . . .	45
Bachawali Tope. . .	119
Bagdanga	254
Bahadur Ali Khan Mosque	162
Baharamganj . . .	215
Baharam Jang . . .	215
Baikunt	22
Baikunt Nath Sen . .	233
Banamalipore Mosque .	197
Bangadhicaris . . .	202
Barafkhana . . .	180
Barnagar	274
Basant Ali Khan . .	176
Bashir Ali Khan . .	178
Begum Musjed . . .	161
Berhampore Cantonments	236
Berhampore Cemetry .	234
Bhagirathee . . .	4
Bhatlamati . . .	199
Bhogwangola . . .	271
Bhupendra Naraen . .	151
Bistupur Temple . .	228
Black Hole . . .	23
Bloodshed at Plassey .	288
Bohu Begum . . .	133
British Factory at Cossimbazar	222
Bukhtiar Khiliji . .	1
Byaspur Temple . .	228
Canongoe's Records . .	203
Chain Rai	215
Champapukur . . .	213
Chehel Satoon . . .	25

Page.

Chhattis Karkhanas . . 322
Choa 238
Chowk Musjed . . . 130
Chout 26
Chunakhali . . . 213
Clive 30
Clive's acceptance of Presents 296
Clive's Entertainment to Meer Jaffer . . . 289
Clive's Entry into Murshidabad . . . 288
Clock Tower . . . 127
Cossimbazar . . . 215
Cossimbazar Rajbari . 216
Court Houses . . . 183
Dacca 2
Dadpur 240
Dahapara 201
Darpanaraen . . . 201
Debts Act 185
Declaration of Nizamut Commissioners . . 54
Devi Singh . . . 146
Dewani 39
Dewans . 304, 306, 307, 308
Dhanput Singh . . . 276
Dilawar Jang . . . 215
Distribution of money at revolutions . . . 298
Dost Mahomed Khan . :97
Doyamoi Temple . . 233
Drake . . . 29

Page.

Dullavram 26
Dulhin Begum . . . 133
Dutch Cemetry . . . 226
East India Company's Presents . . . 117, 311
Ek Ana Chandpara . . 269
Emtazmahal . . . 206
Entertainments . . 303
Eraze Khan . . . 192
Eunuchs 177
Faizi . . . . . 3!
Farashdanga . . . 233
Faridpur . . . 240
Farrabogh . . . 200
Fateh Chand . . 24, 155
Fatteh Singh . . 252
Fazl Rubbee . . . 266
Feredun Jah . . . 52
Feroze Sha . . . 2
Findalbagh . . . 183
Fluk Kadr . . . 68
Fort William . . . 29
Fountain of Honor . . 3!8
Gadinasheen Begums . !32
Ganga Das Rai. . . 279
Ganga Dhar Rai . . 164
Ganga Govind Singh . 258
Gazanffar Hossein Khan 25
Genealogy of Bangadhicari Family . . . 204
Genealogy of Cossimbazar aj Family . . . 22

	Page.
Genealogy of Jagat Sett's Family	156
Genealogy of Jamo and Bagdanga Family	257
Genealogy of Kandi Family	261
Genealogy of Kunjaghata Family	232
Genealogy of Mozaffer Jang's Family	212
Genealogy of Nashipur Raj Family	152
Genealogy of Nizamut Family	13
Giria	270
Gour	1
Gouranga	229
Grant Hall	235
Grant of the Dewani	301
Great Gun	173
Gubernotorial Tours	309
Gysabad	272
Haji Ahmed	23
Hastings	209
Harrington's Scheme	46
Heera Jheel	205
Heeranand Saho	154
Hotar Sanko	228
Holwell	29, 288
Hossein Ali Meerza	67
Hossein Kuli Khan	28
Hussain ahomed Khan	25
Hussan Ali Meerza	55
Humayun Jah	50
Humayun Monzel	178
Hybut Jang	28
Idul Fitr	1
Iduz Zoha	130
Imambarah	120
Installation of Reza Khan	310
Itwar Ali Khan	177
Jaffraganj Cemetry	141
Jaffraganj Deori	142
Jagat Setts' House	153
Jahan Kosha	174
Jail	183
Jainas	276
Jamo	254
Janabe Ali	52
Jang's Imambarah	136
Janoji Bhonsle	41
Jelaluddeen	2
Jinnatunnissa	22
Journey to Calcutta	310
Kadam Sharif	176
Kalkapur	227
Kalibari	164
Kandi	258
Kansa	2
Kantoo Babu	216
Karamutulla	267
Kasi Singh	233
Katra Musjed	171
Kazi Mahamed Sharaf	214
Keerti Chand	149
Kerbela	195

	Page.
Khakan Meerza	68
Khamra	24
Khoshbagh	198
Khurshed Dula's Deori	129
Killah Nizamut	73
Kishen Chand	!47
Korans	80
Kowarpara	185
Krishna Nath	218
Krishna Nath College	238
Kriteswari	277
Kritkona	277
Kulhoria	134
Kunjaghata Rajbari	229
Kurtulub Khan	21
Kutubuddeen	1
Lalbagh	170
Lalgola	272
Lalkothi	276
Lamput Ghat	165
Land Assessment	304
Letters	`08
Lord Curzon's Visit	62
Lord Powi's	63
Lutfunnissa Begum	28, 206
Madapur	234
Madina	118
Mahomed Hadi	2
Mahomed Reza Khan	2:0
Mahomed Taki	23
,, ,, 's Tomb	159
Maharajah of Nattore	63
Mohipal	269
Makoo Jang	262
Mankar	240
Mani Begum	42, `32
Manindra Chandra Nandi	220
Mansur Ali Khan	52
Mansurganj	205
Mastaram Aulia	273
Meer Jaffer	32
,, ,, 's Deposition	289
,, ,, 's Presents to Watson	295
,, ,, 's Reinstatement	36
Meer Kasem	33
Mehter's Mosque	163
Mint	205
,, Duties	8
Miran	31
Mobarak Manzil	178
Mobarakuddowla	42
Mohan Lal	29
Moharram	124
Mohsan Ali Meerza	68
Moradbagh	208
Morcha	280
Mother-e-Company	134
Moti Jheel	186
Murshidabad	6-9
Murshidabad Act	185
Musnud Aulia	214
Musnud did not go to Miran's Family, why,	295
Mustapha Khan	192

	Page.
Secular Books . . .	83
Serajuddowla . . .	28
" 's Tomb .	198
Serferaz Khan . . .	24
Sha Alum	32
Shahamat Jang's Mosque.	190
Sha Khanum . . .	32
Shamsuddeen . . .	2
Sha Rostum . . .	65
Sheik Dighi . . .	268
Sherpur Atai . . .	268
Sheta Khan's Bazar . .	234
Shubeberat . .	132
Shubi Kerbela . . .	196
Shuja Khan . . .	22
" " 's Tomb. .	
Sonarundi	262
Souket Jang . .	29
Sris Chandra Sarbadhicari	239
State Buildings. . .	117
Stone Throne . . .	179
Sun Dial	128
Sunnyasicanga . . .	215
Surnomoi	219
Syefuddowla . . .	40
Syud Ahmed . . .	23
Syud Rezi Khan . .	22
Tara	31, 275

	Page.
Takt Mobarak . . .	170
Talibpur	263
Teliagarhi	24
Tiruthkona . . .	277
Toshakhana . . .	98
Treaties . . .	5, 319
Tripaulia Gate . . .	129
Tumar	301
Udai Chand . . .	167
Udai Naraen . .	274
Uduanala	271
Udwant Sing . . .	147
Vahed Ali Meerza . . .	68
Vansittart	208
Victoria Memorial Hall .	3
Viscount Valentine . .	6
Wala Jah . . .	49
Wala Kadr. . . .	67
Walsh	31
Warren Hastings . .	42
Wasif Ali Meerza, Prince	64
Yeasin Khan . . .	257
Zainuddeen	23
Zainuddeen Ali Khan .	47
Zainul Abideen . .	129
Zillar Rahaman . .	254
Zurbe Murshidabad . .	21
Zurd Musjed . . .	128

	Page.
Nabakissen	207
Nabaratna	86
Nafisa Begum	22
Naginabagh	160
Naib Dewans	306
Najibannessa Begum	133
Najmuddowla	37
Nakkatitola	185
Naktakhali	160
Nanda Kumar	230
Nashipur Rajbari	144
Nasir Ali Meerza	68
Navadwip	1
Nawabs, List of,	13
,, Titles of,	13
Nawab's High School	139
Nawab's Madrassa	138
Nawazesh Mahomed	23, 192
Nazarana Monsurganj	206
Nazir Ali Khan	178
Neshadbagh	210
Neminath	222
Neoara	281
Nizamut Adalat	44
Nizamut Stables	169
Noseri Banoo Begum	134
Nowroze	131
Old English Cemetry	223
Omichand	30, 153
Paikpara Rajbari	260
Palace	74
Panchu Feringee	24
Phuti musjed	158
Picture books	88
Picture Galleries	112
Plassey	30, 240
Poonneah	40, 187
Presents to Nawabs	311
Queen Anne	2
Raesunnissa Begum	133
Raghuji Bhonsle	25
Rai Saheb's House	165
Rai Udai Chand	165
Rajabazar Deori	156
Rajah Meah	264
Rajballav	43
Rajmehal Deori	137
Ram Chand	208
Ram Krishna	275
Rana Chhattar Singh	44
Ranajit Sinha	149
Rangamati	215
Rani Bhowani	274
Regulations	183
Roshnibagh	199
Sadeq Ali Khan	136
Sadeqbagh	27
Sagardighi	268
Saidabad	233
Sakrigali	24
Saktipur	251
Salar	265
Sangidalan	190
Sannyasidanga	215
Sargachhi	213
Scrafton	30